Costa Brava

DIRECTIONS

WRITTEN AND RESEARCHED BY

Chris Lloyd

ROUGH GUIDES

NEW YORK • LONDON • DELHI

www.roughguides.com

Contents

Introduction   **4**

Ideas   **9**

The big six 10
Girona 12
The Dalí Triangle 14
Ancient Costa Brava 16
Medieval Costa Brava 18
Bars 20
Music festivals 22
High days and holidays 24
Museums 26
Beaches 28
Parks and gardens 30
Mountain and coastal walks 32
The Camí de Ronda 34
Volcanoes 36
Shopping 38
Restaurants 40
Kids' Costa Brava 42
Activities 44
Luxury hotels and restaurants 46

Places   **49**

Places 49
Girona 51
Banyoles and Besalú 64
Parc Natural de la Garrotxa 69
Blanes 76
Lloret de Mar 80
Tossa de Mar 84

Sant Feliu de Guíxols and Platja
    d'Aro 88
Palamós and Sant Antoní de
    Calonge 98
Palafrugell and its beaches 105
Begur and its beaches 113
Pals, Peratallada and Ullastret 120
Central Baix Empordà 126
L'Estartit and Torroella de Montgrí ... 132
L'Escala and Empúries 139
The Golf de Roses 147
Figueres and around 155
Cadaqués and Cap de Creus 162
Port de la Selva 170
Serra de l'Albera and the north
    coast 176

Essentials   **185**

Arrival 187
Information 187
Transport 188
Accommodation 189
Activities 190
Public holidays and festivals 192
Directory 194

Language   **195**

Pronunciation 197
Words and phrases 199
Glossary 200

Index   **201**

Introduction to

Costa Brava

The most unfairly maligned stretch of coast in Europe, the Costa Brava has long been derided as a package-holiday, chips-and-sangria destination, an image based solely on two or three towns at its southernmost tip. The truth is that this diverse region matches extraordinary natural beauty with a rich cultural heritage, an accumulated legacy of centuries of invading armies that shows itself in a tapestry of walled towns, fortified farmhouses and ancient hilltop villages.

▲ Platja de Pals

The coastline is enchantingly serpentine – Costa Brava means "Rugged Coast". Spurs of the Pyrenees form wild sea-cliffs hiding secluded coves punctuated by extensive stretches of sandy beach. Away from the coast, the land rises dramatically through dolmen-scattered hills to brooding volcanic mountains. Holding sway over it all is the beautiful medieval city of Girona, boasting one of Spain's finest old quarters.

Favoured by artists and writers – especially after Salvador Dalí returned to his childhood home here – and vying with France's Côte

When to visit

Peak season is July and August. Weather at this time is rarely uncomfortably hot, although the influence of the Pyrenees means that conditions can change suddenly. The main towns are busy, but, if you choose your spot carefully, you can still find yourself alone in a tiny cove or enjoying the views from a tranquil mountain-top.

The coast is at its best between Easter and the end of June and then again during September, when temperatures aren't quite so high, the swimming is idyllic and the crowds either haven't arrived or have just left. Girona is perfect to visit any time of the year. Note that from October until Easter many hotels and services – especially in the more tourist-oriented coastal areas – close altogether.

▼ Belfry, Torroella de Montgrí

d'Azur as a playground for the rich and famous in the 1930s, the region saw its fortunes change under Franco, who pushed the area as a tourist destination, with scant regard for regional sensibilities or the environment. However, with the return of democracy in the 1970s, the region began to restate and strengthen native values with the aim of attracting a more discerning breed of visitor, and the Costa Brava has begun to overturn its largely undeserved foreign reputation as the repository of all that's worst in mass tourism.

▶ Blanes

▲ Beach huts, S'Agaró

The Costa Brava is roughly divided into three very different areas. The La Selva region in the south is the one most closely associated with mass tourism, sporting the popular resorts of Blanes, Lloret de Mar and Tossa de Mar. Further north lies the more refined Baix Empordà, with its Barcelona chic, while the Alt Empordà in the far north has a laid-back, bohemian air.

▼ Sa Riera cove

Costa Brava
AT A GLANCE

GIRONA

A walled medieval enclave, the compact and vibrant regional capital of Girona possesses a captivating old quarter, filled with fascinating museums, and a thriving cultural and nightlife scene.

THE DALÍ TRIANGLE

Birthplace and home for many years of Surrealist genius Salvador Dalí, the Costa Brava boasts three extraordinary museums devoted to his life and art.

ALT EMPORDÀ

The Alt Empordà, in the far north, has a relaxed, bohemian air. Its chief attractions are the sweeping sands and fertile orchards of the Golf de Roses and the enchanting, desolate landscape of the wild Cap de Creus headland.

▼ Teatre-Museu Dalí

▲ Pharmacy in the Barri Vell, Girona

▲ Kite, Aiguamolls National Park

LA SELVA

The southernmost part of the coast – Blanes, Lloret de Mar and Tossa de Mar – was most affected by the tourist boom, although the natural beauty of the area, marked by small coves interspersed with long sandy beaches, is still largely intact.

BAIX EMPORDÀ

Extending from Sant Feliu de Guíxols in the south to Pals in the north, Baix Empordà region never succumbed to the mass tourist boom and its crystalline, turquoise coves and stunning coastal paths are perfectly complemented by some chic restaurants and nightlife.

▼ Dona Marinera Statue, Lloret de Mar

▲ Cove at Sant Feliu

LA GARROTXA

The hinterland is dominated by the volcanic region of La Garrotxa, in the foothills of the Pyrenees; its ancient beech woods, lush hills and grassy calderas are perfect for gentle rambles or longer walks.

▼ Lake at Banyoles

Ideas

The big six

The Costa Brava is justly famed for its superb beaches and coves, but the region also boasts a wealth of other sights – guaranteed to tempt even the most dedicated sun-worshipper. Attractions range from picturesque medieval villages to the captivating city of Girona, and from the stunning natural beauty of the shoreline to the majestic mountain ranges inland, not to mention the rich artistic legacy left behind by painters such as Salvador Dalí.

▲ Girona

The region's capital, medieval Girona possesses a rich history and one of the most beautiful old quarters of any Spanish city.

P.51 ▸ GIRONA

▲ Dalí Triangle

The trio of outstanding museums honouring Surrealist artist Salvador Dalí affords an intriguing insight into the genius of one of Catalonia's most famous figures.

P.155 ▸ FIGUERES AND AROUND,
P.126 ▸ CENTRAL BAIX EMPORDÀ
& P.162 ▸ CADAQUÉS AND CAP
DE CREUS

▼ Coves and bays

Originally developed for tourism because of its beaches, the Costa Brava also harbours some extraordinary coves and tiny bays, where it's still possible to find tranquillity and solitude.

P.113 ▸BEGUR AND ITS BEACHES, P.162 ▸CADAQUÉS AND CAP DE CREUS, P.147 ▸THE GOLF DE ROSES, P.105 ▸ PALAFRUGELL AND ITS BEACHES AND P.84 ▸ TOSSA DE MAR.

▲ Camí de Ronda

Reclaiming the route of old coastguards' and shepherds' tracks, the stunning Camí de Ronda footpath wends its way along almost the entire length of the Costa Brava, hugging the shoreline and reaching otherwise inaccessible coves.

P.190 ▸ ESSENTIALS

▼ Empúries

One of the most important archeological sites in Spain, Empúries was founded by the Greeks in the sixth century BC and subsequently colonized by the Romans; both civilizations left an indelible mark on the region.

P.141 ▸ L'ESCALA AND EMPÚRIES

▲ Cadaqués

Sheltering in a bay below the desolate, windblown Cap de Creus headland, the beautiful, whitewashed village of Cadaqués, Dalí's former haunt, still attracts an arty, bohemian crowd.

P.162 ▸ CADAQUÉS AND CAP DE CREUS

Girona

Local writer Josep Pla called Girona a "small and delicate city" – a fitting epithet for this compact provincial capital, consistently rated in national polls as the most desirable place to live in Spain. It's undergone a huge transformation in recent years, from a rather provincial, conservative bastion to a dynamic and prosperous university city, modernizing itself while keeping its historical and cultural heritage intact. Boasting a delightful old quarter, a venerable culinary tradition and lively nightlife, Girona is the perfect place to get a feel for all that the Costa Brava has to offer.

▲ The Barri Vell

You could easily spend a day exploring the tiny alleys and busy squares of the enchanting Barri Vell, or old quarter.

P.51 ▶ GIRONA

▼ The cathedral

Girona's imposing cathedral has the largest Gothic nave in the world and a fascinating museum.

P.55 ▶ GIRONA

▲ El Call

At the heart of El Call, Western Europe's best-preserved Jewish quarter, the Centre Bonastruc ça Porta offers an intriguing insight into the history of Girona's medieval Jewish community.

P.53 ▶ GIRONA

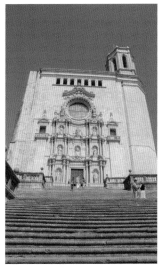

▶ The city walls

Parts of the medieval city walls are walkable; don't miss the Torre Gironella, its history as colourful as its setting.

P.56 ▶ GIRONA

◀ The Rambla Llibertat

The shaded, bustling Rambla is the ideal place for people-watching over an unhurried drink at any time of the day or night.

P.51 ▶ GIRONA

The Dalí Triangle

The famously eccentric Surrealist artist Salvador Dalí spent most of his life in the Costa Brava, and left behind him a trio of extraordinary museums, locally known as the Dalí Triangle and offering an insight into his highly individual life and art. The Teatre-Museu Dalí in Figueres, the second most-visited museum in Spain, houses an extensive selection of the artist's works. Púbol hosts the Castell Gala-Dalí, bought for his wife, while the fabulous Casa-Museu Dalí in Portlligat, near Cadaqués, is where Dalí lived and worked for some fifty years.

▲ Casa-Museu Dalí

The swimming pool in the Casa-Museu Dalí is a fine example of the artist's interest in pop art – using everyday objects to create his own surrealist art.

P.165 ▶ CADAQUÉS AND CAP DE CREUS

▼ Cadaqués

The childhood haunt of Dalí, the bohemian-chic enclave of Cadaqués is still very much the artist's fiefdom.

P.162 ▶ CADAQUÉS AND CAP DE CREUS

▼ Teatre-Museu Dalí

Dalí designed the fantastical Dalí Teatre-Museu himself, declaring it not just a museum but a monument to the senses.

P.156 ▶ FIGUERES AND AROUND

▲ Castell Gala-Dalí

Bought and designed by Dalí for his wife as her retreat, the Castell Gala-Dalí shows off the painter's supreme artistic skill, as well as his sense of mischief.

P.129 ▶ CENTRAL BAIX EMPORDÀ

Ancient Costa Brava

The Costa Brava has a rich ancient history. Prehistoric sites abound, especially in the mountainous regions of the Serra de l'Albera and the Cap de Creus, while isolated dolmens and standing stones are found throughout the entire area. In later ages, the indigenous Iberian tribes traded with Greek colonists, who in turn saw their settlements usurped by the Romans. Extensive finds from all three civilizations have been unearthed in sites such as Empúries and Ullastret, and in individual towns and villages.

▲ Ullastret

Extensively excavated, the large hilltop Iberian settlement of Ullastret provides a fascinating insight into the life and culture of Spain's earliest indigenous population.

P.123 ▶ PALS, PERATALLADA AND ULLASTRET

▲ Coves de Serinyà

The ongoing excavations at the Paleolithic Coves de Serinyà have turned up the oldest human remains in Catalonia and traces of wild animals no longer on the Iberian peninsula.

P.65 ▶ BANYOLES AND BESALÚ

▼ Cova d'en Daina dolmen

The wonderfully atmospheric Cova d'en Daina dolmen stands peacefully in an olive and holm-oak grove in the hills overlooking Palamós.

P.102 ▶ PALAMÓS AND SANT ANTONI DE CALONGE

▲ Empúries

The substantial Greek and Roman ruins at Empúries enjoy a fabulous location on the seashore and make for an absorbing few hours' exploration.

P.141 ▶ L'ESCALA AND EMPÚRIES

▶ Cabana Arqueta

Much more desolate than Cova d'en Daina, the 4500-year-old Cabana Arqueta dolmen lies at the end of a dusty footpath in the Serra de l'Albera, a region littered with dolmens and standing stones.

P.176 ▶ THE SERRA DE L'ALBERA AND NORTH COAST

◀ Poblat Ibèric de Castell

The ancient Iberian settlement of Castell occupies a tranquil setting overlooking an unspoilt beach; only a fraction of the site has been excavated so far, but initial work has unearthed some significant finds.

P.100 ▶ PALAMÓS AND SANT ANTONI DE CALONGE

Medieval Costa Brava

Catalonia and the Costa Brava enjoyed a golden age between the twelfth and the fifteenth centuries, when Catalan kings Jaume I and his son Pere II expanded into the Balearics, Sicily, Malta, Corsica, Sardinia and Naples, and Catalan became the main trading language used throughout the Mediterranean. A legacy of this period of growth is the wealth of Romanesque and Gothic architecture that survives to this day.

▲ Peratallada

The moated medieval hamlet of Peratallada retains a cobbled-alley charm, its attractive buildings harbouring fine restaurants and boutique hotels.

P.122 ▸ PALS, PERATALLADA AND ULLASTRET

▲ Besalú

The majestic toll bridge at the entrance to Besalú hints at the prestige that the town once enjoyed as capital of its own principality between the tenth and twelfth centuries.

P.66 ▸ BANYOLES AND BESALÚ

▼ Castelló d'Empúries

Castelló d'Empúries preserves some handsome Gothic buildings, the best of which is its huge church, intended as a cathedral until medieval rivalry between bishoprics dashed the idea.

P.151 ▸ THE GOLF DE ROSES

▲ Sant Pere de Rodes and Castell Sant Salvador

Set high on a mountain, the imposing Benedictine monastery at Sant Pere de Rodes, and the even more impressive Castell Sant Salvador towering over it, offer breathtaking views of the Golf de Roses and Cap Norfeu.

P.172 ▸ PORT DE LA SELVA

▸ Medieval festivals

Many towns stage medieval festivals to celebrate the rich history of the region, including Castelló d'Empúries, where the tiny streets come alive with troubadours and colourful market stalls.

P.176 ▸ SERRA DE L'ALBERA, **P.88** ▸ SANT FELIU DE GUÍXOLS AND PLATJA D'ARO, **P.120** ▸ PALS, PERATALLADA AND ULLASTRET

▼ Sant Quirze de Colera

Hidden in an enclosed valley at the end of a tortuous dirt track, the ruins of the thousand-year-old monastery of Sant Quirze de Colera are one of the most tranquil and atmospheric spots in the region.

P.177 ▸ SERRA DE L'ALBERA

Bars

From the cheery bar on the corner dishing out tapas over its stainless steel counter to the stylish waterside terrace, there's a terrific range of establishments in the Costa Brava in which to get a bite to eat, chill out or dance the night away. Distinctions between bars and clubs are often blurred; many places have an area for dancing and hobnobbing, as well as a tranquil terrace for stargazing and conversation.

▲ La Plata

Located in an atmospheric ruined building, La Plata in Palamós features an upstairs garden terrace and a stylish dance floor on the ground floor.

P.104 ▸ PALAMÓS AND SANT ANTONI DE CALONGE

◀ Cap de Creus

The tranquil terrace of the *Cap de Creus*, located on the easternmost point in Spain, is perfect for soaking up the stunning views out to sea.

P.166 ▶ CADAQUÉS AND CAP DE CREUS

▼ L'Hostal

One of Salvador Dalí's favourite spots, the hundred-year-old *L'Hostal*'s brush with Surrealism is more than apparent in its bizarre decor and esoteric crowd.

P.169 ▶ CADAQUÉS AND CAP DE CREUS

▲ Sala del Cel

One of the most famous clubs in the region, Girona's *Sala del Cel* attracts DJs from the hottest spots in Europe to this snazzily converted mansion on the outskirts of town.

P.63 ▶ GIRONA

▼ Bar Gelpi

Calella's beachfront *Bar Gelpi* is the best place on the coast to savour a late-night *cremat*, a traditional sailor's drink made from rum, cinnamon and coffee.

P.112 ▶ PALAFRUGELL AND ITS BEACHES

Music festivals

Since the return of democracy in 1975 and greater cultural freedom, an increasing number of music festivals have been inaugurated by towns and associations across the region, many of them held in beautiful settings outdoors. Festivals can run for a week to two months and embrace anything from traditional Catalan music and dance, through symphonic concerts and recitals to jazz and world music.

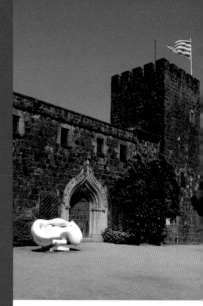

▲ Jardí Botànic Cap Roig

A long tradition of jazz in Catalunya, both imported and home-grown, finds its best expression in the enchanting setting of Calella's Jardí Botànic Cap Roig.

P.107 ▸ PALAFRUGELL AND ITS BEACHES

▲ Festival Internacional de Músiques de Torroella de Montgrí

Among the most prestigious in the region, the Torroella festival is staged at various venues throughout the town and features a fun parallel programme of street concerts and a world craft fair.

P.133 ▸ TORROELLA DE MONTGRÍ AND L'ESTARTIT

▶ Classical music festivals

Many churches play host to classical music recitals throughout the summer, most notably in Cadaqués.

P.162 ▸ CADAQUÉS AND CAP DE CREUS

▲ Peralada Festival

One of the oldest music festivals on the Costa Brava, the Peralada Festival is staged in the castle grounds and specializes in classical and cabaret-style artists.

P.159 ▸ FIGUERES AND AROUND

▼ Havaneres

A highlight of traditional Catalan music is the *havaneres*, sea shanties brought back from Cuba by sailors; the best place to enjoy them is on the beach at Calella's annual festival.

P.107 ▸ PALAFRUGELL AND ITS BEACHES

There's very little that can compare with a Catalan town in full swing as it celebrates Easter, carnival or its Festa Major, the local patron saint's day. Combining religious ceremony with surprisingly large doses of pagan ritual, each one is different, but they all involve generations of families dancing in the street, live music and boisterous revelry; there's a huge sense of enjoyment and everyone is made to feel welcome.

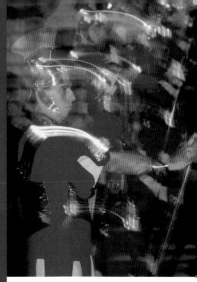

▲ Easter

More sedate than other celebrations, Easter is nonetheless a hugely entertaining spectacle, especially the colour and drama of Girona's Manaies, where Roman soldiers parade through the streets before the procession of the Virgin.

P.193 ▶ ESSENTIALS

▼ Dance of the dead

A macabre note is struck at the Dance of the Dead on Good Friday in the village of Verges, where people dressed as skeletons dance eerily through torchlit streets.

P.137 ▶ TORROELLA DE MONTGRÍ AND L'ESTARTIT

▲ Sailing boat festival

Many festivals recall Catalunya's seafaring tradition, one of the most stirring being the lateen sailing boat festival in Cadaqués.

P.193 ▸ ESSENTIALS

▼ Blanes fireworks competition

Fire plays a part in many holiday festivities, most notably at Sant Joan (June 24) and at the thrilling international fireworks competition during Blanes' Santa Anna celebrations (July 26).

P.193 ▸ ESSENTIALS AND P.78 ▸ BLANES

▼ Flower festivals

Springtime, and later, Corpus Christi see many festivals based around flowers, including Girona's enchanting flower festival in May, where the old quarter is decked in living colour.

P.193 ▸ ESSENTIALS

Museums

The region boasts some fascinating museums, often undeservedly neglected by many visitors in favour of the big three Dalí draws. There are some highly specialized collections dealing with such diverse subjects as medieval prisons, nineteenth-century émigrés and Modernista ceramics. Even in relatively small museums, you can see some fascinating artefacts, including huge Roman mosaics and Chagall originals in Tossa de Mar, medieval stencils used for the stained-glass windows in Girona cathedral, and Chinese shadow theatres in the Museu del Cinema.

▲ Museu Municipal, Tossa de Mar

Originally the art museum of a town once renowned for its artistic community, Tossa de Mar's Museu Municipal has expanded to include local history exhibits; highlights include stunning Roman mosaics and a painting donated by Marc Chagall during one of his stays in town.

P.85 ▸ TOSSA DE MAR

▼ Museu Terracota

The traditional pottery town of La Bisbal, home to a plethora of ceramics shops, tells the history of its unique industry through the engaging Museu Terracota.

P.126 ▸ CENTRAL BAIX EMPORDÀ

▶ Centre Cultural Verdaguer

Among the more captivating local museums is Lloret de Mar's Centre Cultural Verdaguer, an appealingly eclectic collection recalling the town's illustrious past and latter-day transformation.

P.80 ▶ LLORET DE MAR

▲ Museu del Cinema

Once a film-maker's private collection, Girona's Museu del Cinema is a fun find, filled with hands-on exhibits and cinema memorabilia.

P.59 ▶ GIRONA

▼ Museu d'Art

This stunning fourteenth-century palace houses a priceless collection of Catalan art, from the religious imagery of the Romanesque age to the lilting lyricism of Impressionist and Modernista artists.

P.56 ▶ GIRONA

▼ Medieval prison museum

One of the most curious museums in the Costa Brava is to be found in the tiny medieval prison in Castelló d'Empúries, where five-hundred-year-old graffiti still adorn the walls.

P.151 ▶ THE GOLF DE ROSES

Beaches

The Costa Brava's popularity as a tourist destination is largely due to its impressive collection of fine beaches. The region has one of the highest concentrations of Blue Flag sites in Europe, as well as a terrific variety of beaches. The dramatically scored and indented coast features sweeping bays and minuscule coves, long crescent-shaped tracts of sand and boulder-strewn clefts in the cliffs, any of which are superb for swimming, diving or soaking up the rays. What's more, it's still possible to find virtually empty, untouched beaches.

▼ Cala Rostella

One of a string of idyllic coves to the east of Roses, the unspoilt Cala Rostella, with its turquoise waters, is the reward for a dusty clamber down a hillside clad with holm oaks.

P.149 ▶ THE GOLF DE ROSES

▼ Cap Ras

Windswept Cap Ras headland, north of Llançà, is dotted with hidden inlets and handkerchiefs of beaches.

P.179 ▶ SERRA DE L'ALBERA

▲ Cala Boadella

Even the busiest of towns can spring a surprise with tranquil, uncrowded coves and beaches, such as Lloret de Mar's Cala Boadella.

P.81 ▸ LLORET DE MAR

▼ Llafranc beach

Town beaches inevitably get quite crowded, but many, such as Llafranc, are still hugely enticing and good for a dip.

P.107 ▸ PALAFRUGELL AND ITS BEACHES

▶ El Golfet

At the foot of steep stone steps at the end of a stretch of the Camí de Ronda, Calella's El Golfet is typical of the larger coves in the central Costa Brava, with high pine-covered slopes and a sandy beach.

P.107 ▸ PALAFRUGELL AND ITS BEACHES

▲ Platja de Pals

The fine, sandy Platja de Pals lies at the southern tip of the long, curved swathe of the Golf de Roses, creating an almost unbroken stretch of flat beach as far as Roses.

P.123 ▸ PALS, PERATALLADA AND ULLASTRET

Parks and gardens

The Costa Brava's rich volcanic soil and fertile stretches of shoreline are ideal for cultivation, as seen in a number of fine parks and gardens in the region. Popular with locals and visitors alike as peaceful, shaded havens from the heat, they range from formal Renaissance-style gardens to wilder and more natural parks.

▲ Jardins de Santa Clotilde

The Italianate Jardins de Santa Clotilde provide a relaxing break from the hubbub of neighbouring Lloret de Mar.

P.80 ▶ LLORET DE MAR

▲ Parc Nou

The pretty ornamental gardens of Olot's Parc Nou are laid out in Italian style around a small palace, now home to the Casal dels Volcans information centre.

P.71 ▸ PARC NATURAL DE LA GARROTXA

▲ Ermita de Santa Cristina

A semi-natural wilderness, the gardens around Lloret de Mar's Ermita de Santa Cristina wind down gentle slopes to a brace of fabulous beaches.

P.81 ▸ LLORET DE MAR

▼ Jardí Botànic Mar i Murtra

The best-known *jardí botànic* on the Costa Brava, Blanes' clifftop Mar i Murtra consists of a series of beautiful themed gardens.

P.78 ▸ BLANES

▲ Jardí Botànic Cap Roig

From its vantage point on the cliffs near Calella, the splendidly tranquil Jardí Botànic Cap Roig offers fantastic views of the rocky shoreline.

P.107 ▸ PALAFRUGELL AND ITS BEACHES

Mountain and coastal walks

The Costa Brava is where the Pyrenees meet the Mediterranean and the region features some stunning natural scenery. It has a rich variety of flora and fauna, including species such as the charming Albera cow which is unique to the region. Many of the wilder areas, both on the coast and in the mountainous hinterland, now enjoy protected status as Natural Parks and are ideal either for a day's gentle exploring or for longer activity breaks.

▼ Parc Natural dels Aigüamolls de l'Empordà

Formerly rice fields saved from the clutches of developers, the Aigüamolls bird reserve is a nesting ground for almost a hundred migratory and indigenous bird species.

P.149 ▸ THE GOLF DE ROSES

▼ Serra de l'Albera

The rugged terrain of the Serra de l'Albera mountain range, for centuries a major route through the Pyrenees, is home to dozens of prehistoric sites.

P.176 ▸ THE SERRA DE L'ALBERA AND NORTH COAST

▲ Illes Medes

The most important marine reserve in the western Mediterranean, the Illes Medes are home to many rare animal and plant species.

P.135 ▸ TORROELLA DE MONTGRÍ AND L'ESTARTIT

▲ Castell de Montgrí

Atop a hill overlooking a medieval town, the imposing Castell de Montgrí rewards walkers with marvellous views of the Illes Medes and surrounding countryside.

P.134 ▸ TORROELLA DE MONTGRÍ AND L'ESTARTIT

▲ The GR92 and GR11

One of the best ways to experience the diversity of the landscape is to walk parts of the two long-distance trails that run through it, indicated by red and white markings.

P.190 ▸ ESSENTIALS

▶ Cap de Creus

The easternmost point on the Iberian peninsula, the dramatic Cap de Creus head-land, a desolate, wind-bat-tered spot with breathtaking coves, is perfect for hiking.

P.166 ▸ CADAQUÉS AND CAP DE CREUS

The Camí de Ronda

The Camí de Ronda is a network of footpaths along the coast, much restored in recent years thanks to some imaginative investment. Sections of the footpath range from the gentlest of paved promenades running along the shore to arduous paths that wind along craggy clifftops and swoop down through pine groves to hidden coves. For more on the Camí de Ronda see p.143.

▲ Secluded coves

The best – and often the only – way to reach the more secluded coves is along the Camí de Ronda, such as this section here near Llançà.

P.179 ▸ THE SERRA DE L'ALBERA AND NORTH COAST

▲ Camí de les Dunes

The Camí de Ronda incorporates the Camí de les Dunes, built over a hundred years ago and linking the ruins at Empúries with some superb sandy beaches.

P.143 ▸ L'ESCALA AND EMPÚRIES

▶ La Gavina to Cala Sa Conca

An enjoyable section of the footpath starting from the sumptuous *La Gavina* hotel and winding past Modernista mansions to the stylish Cala Sa Conca.

P.91 ▶ SANT FELIU DE GUÍXOLS AND PLATJA D'ARO

▼ Tamariu to Llafranc

A rugged and very rewarding part of the trail leads along cliffs to some stunning coves between Tamariu and Llafranc.

P.110 ▶ PALAFRUGELL AND ITS BEACHES

▲ Sa Riera to Platja de Pals

The high clifftop walk north from Sa Riera gives access to some enticing little beaches before emerging onto the sands of the Platja de Pals.

P.116 ▶ BEGUR AND ITS BEACHES

▼ Cap de Creus

Some of the most rugged sections of the Camí de Ronda are to be found on the wild Cap de Creus headland, dropping down to some wave-sculpted coves.

P.166 ▶ CADAQUÉS AND CAP DE CREUS

Volcanoes

The stunning landscape of the Parc Natural de la Garrotxa is the domain of dormant volcanoes and thick forests of towering beeches. Forged by volcanic activity and earthquakes, the lush, undulating countryside is ideal for rambling and horse-riding, and you can even go ballooning. The county town of the park is Olot, carved out of the grey volcanic rock and an attractive blend of avant-garde and tradition.

▲ Montsacopa volcano

Overlooking Olot, the Montsacopa volcano offers superb views over the town and countryside.

P.70 ▶ PARC NATURAL DE LA GARROTXA

▼ Santa Pau

Starting point for a number of walks, the medieval village of Santa Pau harbours an atmospheric main square and a crumbling castle.

P.71 ▶ PARC NATURAL DE LA GARROTXA

▲ La Fageda d'en Jordà beech woods

One of the best ways to see the ancient and atmospheric beech woods of La Fageda d'en Jordà is by horse-drawn carriage.

P.69 ▸ PARC NATURAL DE LA GARROTXA

▼ A balloon trip over the Parc Natural de la Garrotxa

One of the rarest treats you can give yourself is gazing down into the calderas of the dormant volcanoes from a hot-air balloon.

P.69 ▸ PARC NATURAL DE LA GARROTXA

▲ The Casal dels Volcans

Olot's Casal dels Volcans houses a fascinating exhibition on the region's volcanoes.

P.71 ▸ PARC NATURAL DE LA GARROTXA

▶ Santa Margarida volcano

In the hollow of the grassy caldera of the Santa Margarida volcano nestles a tiny chapel, idyllically set among woods.

P.74 ▸ PARC NATURAL DE LA GARROTXA

Shopping

If you allow yourself to be tempted by all the shopping on offer in the Costa Brava, your finances are going to take a battering. The area's artistic tradition translates into a thriving trade in modern arts and crafts; La Bisbal, for example, draws visitors from far and wide to buy its celebrated ceramics. During the summer, some towns stage open-air medieval craft fairs, the best being in Peratallada and Castell d'Aro, while Torroella de Montgrí hosts an enjoyable world market to coincide with its music festival, featuring handmade and fair-trade products.

▲ Ambrosia, Girona

Girona boasts a fair number of specialist shops, none more enticing than Ambrosia, selling sweets and products made by convent nuns.

P.61 ▸ GIRONA

▼ Faure, Girona

With a long tradition of cakes and pastries rivalling that of neighbouring France, the Costa Brava is teeming with enticing pastisseries, such as Faure in Girona.

P.61 ▸ GIRONA

▲ La Bisbal pottery

In La Bisbal, ceramics capital of the region, every other shop sells the traditional, locally produced earthenware pottery.

P.127 ▶ LA BISBAL AND PÚBOL

▼ Markets

Nearly all the major towns have an open-air weekly market, where you can pick up anything from aubergines to xylophones.

P.59 ▶ GIRONA

▲ Wine

Steadily improving in quality, the region's wine is best savoured at the vineyards in the area around Peralada, where you can buy from the producers.

P.159 ▶ FIGUERES AND AROUND

Restaurants

There's a lot more to Costa Brava's food than the popular image of chicken-and-chips and sangria: traditional cooking closely wedded to regional products has created a very distinctive cuisine, while a small elite of top-flight chefs is forging an imaginative new slant on this tradition. Catalans are demanding diners, and it's not hard to find good restaurants serving regional cuisine amid the tourist fare: simply look out for cars with local number plates in the car park or listen for Catalan being spoken among the diners.

▲ Maria de Cadaqués

A local institution, Palamós's *Maria de Cadaqués* is famous for its superb fish and seafood.

P.103 ▶ PALAMÓS AND SANT ANTONI DE CALONGE

▲ Porto Cristo

Porto Cristo, occupying a luxury nineteenth-century merchant's mansion, serves up top-quality Catalan fare in an unhurried atmosphere.

P.174 ▸ PORT DE LA SELVA

▶ Casa Anita

The enticing aromas will lead you to *Casa Anita*, one-time Dalí favourite.

P.168 ▸ CADAQUÉS AND CAP DE CREUS

▼ El Bistrot

Formerly a café and revolutionary hotbed, Girona's bustling *El Bistrot* serves affordable modern cuisine amid potted plants and marble-top tables.

P.61 ▸ GIRONA

Kids' Costa Brava

The obvious attraction for most kids is endless days playing about in the sea and sand and all the fun activities on offer at most of the larger beaches, but should they ever get tired of this, there are plenty of choices away from the sea to keep them happy. These range from elaborate water parks to less obvious but equally enjoyable delights such as nature reserves and even a dreaded museum or two.

▲ Butterfly Park

The Butterfly Park is a delightful place, laid out to resemble a rainforest, where huge friendly butterflies flutter up close to inspect you.

BARTENDER

P.152 ▸ THE GOLF DE ROSES

▶ Aquadiver water park

The chutes and slides of the Aquadiver water park, outside Platja d'Aro, make for a fun day away from the beach.

P.94 ▶ SANT FELIU DE GUÍXOLS AND PLATJA D'ARO

▼ Beaches

Many beaches provide a plethora of fun activities for all ages, including banana boats, pedalos and ski-buses.

P.191 ▶ ESSENTIALS

▼ Museu del Joguet

The complex clockwork toys and simple wooden figures at Figueres' enjoyable Museu del Joguet are guaranteed to appeal to most children.

P.158 ▶ FIGUERES AND AROUND

▲ Centre de Reproducció de Tortugues de l'Albera

Set up to protect indigenous species of tortoise, the Centre de Reproducció de Tortugues de l'Albera is laid out as a small park to show the surprisingly endearing creatures' various habitats.

P.177 ▶ THE SERRA DE L'ALBERA AND NORTH COAST

Activities

You'll find countless opportunities for sporting and outdoor pursuits on the Costa Brava. Beside the obvious pleasures of messing about in some of the cleanest waters in the Mediterranean, there are all sorts of other activities to tempt you onto dry land. Walkers will love the gentle coastal rambles or arduous mountain treks. More sedate pastimes include golf at one of the region's excellent courses, while the more adventurous can thrill at skydiving or paragliding.

▼ Skydiving

One of the most famous airfields in Spain for skydiving, Empuriabrava offers courses for beginners and jumps for experienced skydivers.

P.152 ▶ THE GOLF DE ROSES

▼ Watersports

Many beaches offer a variety of watersports, from the thrill of windsurfing to the gentlest of kayak excursions pottering among otherwise inaccessible coves.

P.191 ▶ ESSENTIALS

▼ Diving off the Illes Medes

With its coral beds and numerous marine species, the protected Illes Medes reserve is a must for serious divers.

P.135 ▶ TORROELLA DE MONTGRÍ AND L'ESTARTIT

▼ Golf

Since the staging of the Spanish Open at the PGA Catalunya course in 2000, the region's superb golfing facilities have acquired a deserved prestige.

P.191 ▶ ESSENTIALS

▲ Flying

One of the most spectacular ways of viewing the coast is from the air on one of a number of pleasure flights.

P.191 ▶ ESSENTIALS

Luxury hotels and restaurants

Located in the wealthiest province in Spain, the Costa Brava has always catered for a well-heeled crowd. There are plenty of opportunities to treat yourself, whether it be splashing out in some of the best restaurants in Europe or living the high life in a sumptuous top-notch hotel. Latest in a long line of luxury establishments is the new breed of boutique hotels – often in historic buildings – boasting superb restaurants.

▲ Parador d'Aiguablava

The region's only *parador* (*paradors* being swish state-subsidized hotels) stands on a rocky promontory in the peaceful cove at Aiguablava.

P.116 ▸ BEGUR AND ITS BEACHES

▼ Palau Lo Mirador

Formerly a royal palace, the luxurious *Palau Lo Mirador*, set in its own gardens, boasts a superb restaurant and just a few rooms.

P.137 ▸ TORROELLA DE MONTGRÍ AND L'ESTARTIT

▲ La Gavina

The understated elegance of the Modernista *La Gavina* hotel, the first five-star establishment on the Costa Brava, is matched only by its fabulous clifftop setting.

P.95 ▸ SANT FELIU DE GUÍXOLS AND PLATJA D'ARO

▼ Castell d'Empordà

The marvellously tranquil *Castell d'Empordà* hotel, once the home of one of Columbus's captains, sits proud on a bluff overlooking La Bisbal.

P.130 ▸ CENTRAL BAIX EMPORDÀ

▲ El Bullí

You'll need to book anything up to a year in advance to get a terrace table at the world-famous *El Bullí* restaurant, renowned for its exquisite cuisine and idyllic setting on the coast.

P.154 ▸ THE GOLF DE ROSES

Places

Girona

Fought over virtually every century since the Romans established the fort of Gerunda in 75 AD, and nicknamed the "city of a thousand sieges", the city of Girona has a fascinating historical heritage – one in which Romans, Visigoths, Moors and the French have all played a part. Today it's a prosperous place with a thriving cultural scene, generating a sense of pride palpable in every corner of the city.

Girona has one of the most beautiful old quarters of any Spanish city: the compact Barri Vell climbs uphill from the bustling Rambla on the east bank of the Riu Onyar and extends through the atmospheric streets of El Call, the beautifully preserved medieval Jewish quarter, as far as the towering cathedral. Still partly protected by medieval walls, the Barri Vell boasts some outstanding museums and teems with shops, bars and restaurants. On the west bank of the river is the attractive nineteenth-century Mercadal district, home to lively shopping streets and squares, while the more modern Eixample, in the south, consists of leafy avenues of stylish shops and houses. Even though Girona's highlights can be explored easily in a day, you really want to stay a few days to make the most of all that the city has to offer.

Rambla Llibertat

Hub of the city is the Rambla Llibertat, a small pedestrianized avenue shaded by plane trees, and the perfect setting for idling at a café; the best time to see it is in the early evening when it throngs with people taking the *passeig*. From the Rambla emanates a warren of tiny

Visiting Girona

Girona airport (☎972 186 708) lies some 13km south; a taxi into town will cost around €20, while buses to the city run to coincide with scheduled flights (€1.75 single/€3.30 return).

The train station (☎972 207 093) is on Carretera Barcelona, about twenty minutes' walk southwest of the old town. Behind the train station on Plaça Espanya, the bus station (☎972 212 319) has frequent services to Barcelona, the coast and inland towns.

By road, Girona is easily accessed off the A7 *autopista* and the toll-free N-II.

The excellent main tourist office is at Rambla Llibertat 1 (Mon–Fri 8am–8pm, Sat 8am–2pm & 4–8pm, Sun 9am–2pm; ☎972 226 575, ⊛www.ajuntament.gi). There's also an information stand in the train station (Mon–Sat 10am–8pm, Sun 10am–2pm), and another in the arrivals hall of the airport (Mon, Tues & Thurs–Sun 9am–9pm, Wed 3–9pm).

The Punt de Benvinguda (Welcome Point) at c/Berenguer Carnicer 3 (Mon–Sat 10am–8pm, Sun 10am–2pm; Oct–Easter Mon–Sat closes 5pm, Sun 10am–2pm; ☎972 211 678), also run by the local tourist board, offers a free reservation service for hotels, restaurants, taxis and guided tours.

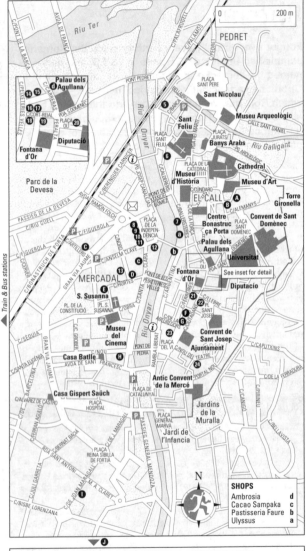

▲ **①, ②, ③ & ④**

0   200 m

PEDRET

PLAÇA SANT PERE

Sant Nicolau

Museu Arqueològic

Palau dels Aguilana

Diputació

Fontana d'Or

Sant Feliu

Banys Arabs

Cathedral

Museu d'Història

Museu d'Art

Torre Gironella

EL CALL

Parc de la Devesa

Centre Bonastruc ça Porta

Convent de Sant Domènec

Palau dels Aguilana

Universitat

Fontana d'Or

See inset for detail

Diputació

MERCADAL

S. Susanna

Convent de Sant Josep

Museu del Cinema

Ajuntament

Casa Batlle

Casa Gispert Saüch

Antic Convent de la Mercé

PLAÇA HOSPITAL

Jardins de la Muralla

Jardí de l'Infancia

PLAÇA REINA SIBILLA DE FORTIA

N

Train & Bus stations

SHOPS	
Ambrosia	d
Cacao Sampaka	c
Pastisseria Faure	b
Ulyssus	a

RESTAURANTS & CAFÉS				BARS & CLUBS		ACCOMMODATION			
L'Antiga	23	El Cul de		Aleshores	10	Alberg de		Coll	E
Le Bistrot	20	la Lleona	6	Café Royal	11	Joventut		Fornells Park	J
Boira	12	La Llibreria	21	Nummulit	13	Apts. Històric	A	Històric	H
Cal Ros	18	La Penyora	24	Particular	2	Bellmirall	B	Peninsular	C
Casa Marieta	9	La Polenta	17	Platea	8	Carlemany	I	Ultonia	G
El Cercle	22	Pol Nord	1	La Sala del Cel	3	Ciutat de Girona	D	Viladomat	G
Cipresaia	15	Tapa't	19	Sunset Jazz Club	5				
La Creperie		Zanpanzar	16	La Terra	7				
Bretonne	14			Via	4				

▲ LA RAMBLA WITH TERRACE CAFÉS

wall, is a tiny carving of an impish head – En Banyeta, supposedly a medieval usurer who was turned to stone and now watches over the citizens to make sure they pay their taxes. Legend has it that if you rub noses with him, all your debts will be cancelled.

From Plaça del Vi, Carrer Ciutadans leads to an impressive stone stairway, the Pujada de Sant Domènec; beside it, an archway joins the two parts of the plain facade of the Baroque mansion Palau dels Agullana; you'll see the unusual perspectives of this corner in dozens of paintings and arty shops all around town. Alongside the Palau dels Agullana is the Plaça de l'Oli, site of the old oil market and lined with bars and restaurants.

shopping streets, most notably Carrer Argenteria and Carrer Ballesteries.

A short walk from the south end of the Rambla lies the arcaded Plaça del Vi, once the site of the wine market and home to the austere fifteenth-century Ajuntament. On the northeastern corner of the Plaça del Vi, about 3m up the

El Call

The bars and antique shops of the slender Placeta del Correu Vell, site of one of the Roman city gates, now long gone, mark the entrance to El Call,

▲ EN BANYETA

the old Jewish quarter. North from here runs the canyon-like Carrer de la Força, originally part of the Via Augusta connecting Iberia with the rest of Europe. It formed the core of the Roman town and steadily increased in importance as the city grew, to become the heart of El Call, the Jewish Quarter. At its height, between the twelfth and fifteenth centuries, this short, steeply inclined street was home to a synagogue, ritual baths, school and Jewish butcher's, although no trace of them survives today. Now the street houses private apartments, interspersed with restaurants and galleries and two of Girona's best museums (see below).

At the top of Carrer de la Força stands the Portal de Sobreportes, built by the Romans in the third century and rebuilt regularly between the ninth and the fourteenth centuries; the small statue above the arch is the Verge de la Bona Mort (the Virgin of Good Death), who was believed to give a final blessing to condemned prisoners. Carrer del Rei Martí, the other side of the gate, suffered constant flooding until the medieval residents raised the street to balcony level. The original front doors are now underground.

Centre Bonastruc ça Porta

c/St Llorenç. May–Oct Mon–Sat 10am–8pm, Sun 10am–3pm; Nov–April Mon–Sat 10am–6pm. €2.

The Centre Bonastruc ça Porta combines a museum and cultural centre dedicated to the history of Girona's Jews with an associated research institute and library. The complex – about a dozen houses in the area where the synagogue is thought to have stood – is named after Nahmànides (known in Catalan as Bonastruc ça Porta), founder of the mystical Cabbalist school of Judaism and born in Girona in 1194. A doctor, philosopher and poet, Nahmànides became the rabbi of Girona and subsequently Grand Rabbi of Catalonia.

Alongside an array of artefacts, panels in the museum give a lively and informative insight into Girona's Jewish history and the daily life of the community; a detailed model shows how the quarter would have looked in the thirteenth century. Other exhibits include Hebrew tombstones, many used as building materials after 1492 and since recovered. The illustrated underlit floor depicts the present

Half-price museum tickets

At the first museum you visit, you'll be given a half-price voucher when you buy your ticket; this gives you a fifty-percent reduction at all of the city's other museums, with the exception of the Banys Arabs and Museu Capitular.

▲ CARRER DE LA FORÇA

in the world, where the bodies of the monks would have been preserved in a seated position.

Exhibits range from Roman and Visigoth artefacts found in the area, including a stunning mosaic depicting a chariot race, to models of the countless sieges by and battles with French and Spanish troops.

On the ground floor the city's modern development is charted through an assortment of exhibits, including old electric streetlights (Girona was the first city in Spain to have them, in 1886).

The Cathedral

Pl de la Catedral. March–June Tues–Sat 10am–2pm & 4–7pm, Sun 10am–2pm; July–Sept Tues–Sat 10am–8pm, Sun 10am–2pm; Oct–Feb Tues–Sat 10am–2pm & 4–6pm, Sun 10am–2pm. Cathedral free, Museu Capitular €3. The overriding impression of Girona's cathedral is one of sheer size. One of the largest Rococo staircases in Europe – an imposing flight of ninety steps, dating from 1690 – leads up to the ornate west facade, built between the fourteenth and eighteenth centuries, its sturdy Gothic bell tower and intricate Baroque high niches combining to create an oddly harmonious whole. A place of worship since Roman times,

site of the ancient "Bou d'Or" (Golden Calf) Jewish cemetery, which stood to the north of the city on the Montjuïc hill. The top floor is reserved for temporary exhibitions and houses a patio with a large marble Star of David set into the floor. These patios played an important part in the daily life of the quarter; since Jews weren't allowed to overlook Carrer de la Força they made up for this by creating their own interior courtyards and gardens.

Museu d'Història de la Ciutat

c/Força 27. Tues–Sat 10am–2pm & 5–7pm, Sun 10am–2pm. €2. Occupying the former eighteenth-century Capuchin Monèstir de Sant Antoni, itself built on a Gothic site dating from at least 1447, the Museu d'Història de la Ciutat (City History Museum) is an absorbing chronicle of Girona's history. The niches in the entrance are the remains of a Capuchin cemetery, one of only three of its kind

▲ CAPUCHIN CEMETERY IN MUSEU D'HISTÒRIA DE LA CIUTAT

the first cathedral replaced a Moorish mosque in 1038, and the building evolved over the centuries; most of the current limestone structure dates from the fourteenth and fifteenth centuries, but a few earlier parts survive, including the eleventh-century north tower and the Romanesque cloisters.

The scale of the interior is impressive: at just under 23m, this is the broadest Gothic nave in the world, and is second only to the Baroque nave of St Peter's in Rome (25m). Originally, the intention was to build three naves, but a controversial decision was taken in 1417 to follow the plans of Guillermo Bofill and build just one aisle. The most notable features are the fourteenth- to sixteenth-century stained-glass windows, some of the earliest examples in Catalonia, and the fourteenth-century embossed silver canopy over the high altar with its highly detailed gilded silver reredos.

Highlights of the Museu Capitular, inside the cathedral, are a beautiful tenth-century illuminated manuscript of the *Beatus* and the stunning eleventh-century *Tapis de la Creació* ("Tapestry of the Creation"), which originated in Italy; the earliest record of its being in Girona dates from 1538. The twelfth-century cloisters are reached through the museum.

Museu d'Art

Pujada de la Catedral 12. March–Sept Tues–Sat 10am–7pm, Sun 10am–2pm; Oct–Feb Tues–Sat 10am–6pm, Sun 10am–2pm. €2. In the lofty former Bishop's Palace, the Museu d'Art houses an impressive collection of Catalan art from the Romanesque and Gothic to the twentieth century. The most remarkable exhibits are a tenth-century portable altar from Sant Pere de Rodes, one of the very few preserved in Europe, and a minutely detailed twelfth-century crossbeam from the church at Cruïlles. An extensive collection of religious art includes the unique fourteenth-century stencils used to make the cathedral's stained-glass windows. The museum also boasts some wonderful works by nineteenth- and twentieth-century Catalan Impressionists, notably the landscapes of Joaquim Vayreda and the dreamy scenes of Girona by Santiago Rusiñol.

The city walls

Extending from the cathedral to the river, Girona's fourteenth- and fifteenth-century city walls take about

▲ PORTAL DE SOBREPORTES

an hour to walk, although climbing down at various points to explore could turn it into a half-day jaunt. The best place to start is the Jardins de la Francesa, reached through a passage between the cathedral and the Museu d'Art. On the buttresses to the right of the cathedral's apse is the only gargoyle with a human face; according to legend it depicts a witch who used to throw stones at passing religious processions and was turned to stone herself.

▲ INTERIOR OF BANYS ARABS

Studded with watchtowers, the walls offer fabulous views over the city. A couple of worthwhile detours are the Jardins dels Alemanys, a lovely, shaded garden amid the ruins of a seventeenth-century barracks for German mercenaries, and the crumbled ruins of the twelfth-century Torre Gironella, partly destroyed by Napoleon's troops in the 1809 siege.

Banys Arabs

c/Ferran el Catòlic. April–June & Sept Mon–Sat 10am–7pm, Sun 10am–2pm; July & Aug Mon–Sat 10am–8pm, Sun 10am–2pm; Oct–March Tues–Sun 10am–2pm. €1.50; audioguide €2.75. Not true Arab baths, but a twelfth-century building based on Moorish design, the Banys Arabs are one of the best-preserved medieval bathhouses in Spain. The scene, so it's said, of hot-blooded medieval frolics, the building was closed down in the fifteenth century, taken over in 1617 by a Capuchin convent,

and restored in 1929 by Modernista architects Rafael Masó and Emili Blanc.

An excellent free leaflet guides you through the various rooms; most impressive are the grand apodyterium (changing-room), with niches in the walls for clothes, and the plunge pool and caldarium, where parts of the underfloor heating system are visible. The green-tiled cupola can be reached via a spiral staircase and affords views of the cathedral.

Església de Sant Feliu

Pl Sant Feliu. July–Sept Tues–Sat 10am–8pm, Sun 10am–2pm; March–June Tues–Sat 10am–2pm & 4–7pm, Sun 10am–2pm; Oct–Feb Tues–Sat 10am–2pm & 4–6pm. A distinctive feature of Girona's skyline, the truncated tower of the gloomy fourteenth- to seventeenth-century Gothic Església de Sant Feliu struck by lightning in 1581 and never repaired. Inside, in the north

▲ MAIN DOOR OF THE ESGLÉSIA DE SANT FELIU

Museu Arqueològic

Pl Sta Llúcia. Tues–Sat 10.30am–1.30pm & 4–7pm, Sun 10am–2pm; Oct–May Tues–Sat 10am–2pm & 4–6pm, Sun 10am–2pm. €1.80. The Museu Arqueològic is sited in a twelfth-century Benedictine monastery. The facade incorporates an arched doorway thought to predate the rest of the building by up to a century. The collection of local finds dates from prehistory to medieval times; some of the most interesting are Iberian artefacts and objects from the Greek colonies at Empúries and Roses, and the Macau Collection, donated by the family of a local archeologist, which includes an elaborate fourth-century Roman sarcophagus entitled "The Seasons", discovered in 1847 in Empúries.

transept, lie the tombs of Sant Narcís, patron saint of Girona – a wooden thirteenth-century one, supposedly containing the saint's remains, and an elaborate Gothic one dated 1328, depicting scenes from his life. Either side of the high altar are eight second- to fourth-century sarcophagi – probably from the Roman necropolis that stood on this site – most of them Christian, although two older ones show lion-hunting and Pluto abducting Proserpine.

At the foot of the church's front steps is *El Cul de la Lleona* ("The Lioness's Rear"), a copy of a twelfth-century statue of a lioness climbing a pillar (the original is in the Museu d'Art). Myth has it that if a visitor kisses the animal's backside, they'll return to Girona.

Mercadal

Connected to the Barri Vell by footbridges – most notably the Pont de les Peixateries (Fishmongers' Bridge), built in iron and wood by the Gustave Eiffel company in 1877 – lies the nineteenth-century Mercadal quarter. The focal point here is the bar- and restaurant-lined Plaça Independència, with its heroic bronze statue cast in 1894 depicting the defenders of Girona. Running parallel to the river south of the square is the stylish nineteenth-century shopping street Carrer Santa Clara, with its waist-high streetlamps.

Towering plane trees northwest of Plaça Independència, across the busy Giratori del Rellotge roundabout, mark the Parc de la Devesa, scene of Girona's thronging Tuesday and Saturday markets and the *veles*, cool late-night summer bars.

Museu del Cinema

c/Sèquia 1. May–Sept Tues–Sat 10am–8pm, Sun 11am–3pm; Oct–April Tues–Fri 10am–6pm, Sat 10am–8pm, Sun 11am–3pm. €3. Built around the private collection of Tomás Mallol, an award-winning local film-maker, the Museu del Cinema offers just the right mix of hands-on exhibits and information. After a short introductory film – in Catalan only, but fairly self-explanatory – you take the lift to the third floor and work your way down through the themed levels, which feature imaginative displays of the origins of projected images in different cultures and the development of cinema.

Hotels

Hostal Bellmirall

c/Bellmirall 3 ☎972 204 009. Closed Jan & Feb. No credit cards. This beguiling *hostal*, with seven simple but cosy en-suite rooms, is housed in a fifteenth-century building on a fourteenth-century Barri Vell street. Their breakfasts are among the best in town. €58.

Hotel Carlemany

Pl Miquel Santaló ☎972 211 212, Ⓦwww.carlemany.es. A modern four-star hotel in the heart of the residential district about twenty minutes' walk south of the Barri Vell, with an exceptionally good restaurant. €110.

Hotel Ciutat de Girona

c/Nord 2 ☎972 483 038, Ⓦwww.hotel-ciutatdegirona.com. A comfortable, modern hotel near the shops of c/Sta Clara, with large, well-equipped and stylish rooms. €125.

Hostal Coll

c/Hortes 24 ☎972 203 086. A very simple *hostal* near c/Sta Clara, two minutes from the Rambla, with eight rooms, all en suite. €32.

Hotel Fornells Park

N-II km719, Fornells de la Selva ☎972 476 125, Ⓦwww.husa.es. A pleasant hotel with a pool and good restaurant, 3km south on the Barcelona road – a relaxing base for touring the area. €90.

▼ BRIDGE BUILT BY GUSTAVE EIFFEL

Hotel Històric

c/Bellmirall 4 ☎972 223 583, ⊛www.
hotelhistoric.com. In the same
building as the Apartaments
Històric Barri Vell (see p.61) and
under the same ownership, this
is a lovely four-star hotel with
six enchanting, stone-walled
rooms in the most atmospheric
part of town. €114.

Hotel Mas Ferran

Camí de la Bruguera s/n, 17150 Sant
Gregori ☎972 428 890, ⊛www
.masferran.com. A small, luxury
hotel, in an idyllic setting, this
stunning seventeenth-century
farmhouse 4km northwest of
Girona has great views of the
city and mountains, with a large
garden, gym and swimming
pool, and offers natural thera-
pies. €150.

Hotel Peninsular

c/Nou 1–3 ☎972 203 800, ⊛www
.novarahotels.com. A pleasant

place – far cheerier than it first
appears – on a pedestrianized
street. Rooms on upper floors
are brighter, but all are comfortable and have decent-sized
bathrooms and TV. €58.

Hotel Ultonia

Av Jaume I, 22 ☎972 203 850,
ⓔhotelultonia@husa.es. Attractive
hotel near Plaça Independència with attentive service, large
rooms with air conditioning,
and modern bathrooms. Some
on upper floors have spacious
balconies. €90.

Pensió Viladomat

c/Ciutadans 5 ☎ & ℻972 203 176.
An unpromising entrance leads
to a very friendly *pensió* with
lovely, airy rooms. Considering
its location in the Barri Vell, it's
a bargain, especially as the spacious rooms, mostly en suites,
have been refurbished to hotel
standard. €55.

Hostels

Alberg de Joventut

c/Ciutadans 9 ☎972 218
003, ℻972 212 023. In the
heart of the Barri Vell,
this very upmarket hostel
with TV and computer
rooms, and rooms sleep-
ing two to ten, is ideally
situated. €17 (€19.40 for
over-25s).

Turisme rural

Can Pinyarol

c/Mosca 3, Juià ☎972 490
258. Imposing yet appeal-
ing three-storey place
(rented whole) with four
bedrooms, sleeping eleven,
in a small village 8km
northeast. €760 per week.

▲ PLAÇA INDEPENDÈNCIA

Girona PLACES

Mas de la Roda

c/Creu 31, Bordils ☎ & ☏972 490 052, ⓦwww.masdelaroda.com. Four huge rooms offered individually on a B&B or half-board basis in an imposing stone house ten minutes' drive northeast, with organic meals cooked by the owner. €45 B&B, €58 half board.

Mas Saló

Sant Martí Vell ☎972 490 201. About 9km northeast of Girona, this a big old house sleeping up to eight, set in pleasant gardens with a pool. The doubles are large and airy with wooden furniture, and the house is rented whole. €600 per week.

Apartments

Apartaments Històric Barri Vell

c/Bellmirall 4 ☎972 223 583, ⓦwww.hotelhistoric.com. Large, atmospheric, well-equipped self-catering apartments for up to six people at knockdown prices in a twelfth-century building very near the cathedral. €90.

Shops

Ambrosia

c/Carreras Peralta 4. This fabulous shop lies behind a spacious courtyard in a fifteenth-century building and sells products made exclusively in monasteries and convents, ranging from herbal remedies to Gregorian chant CDs.

Cacao Sampaka

c/Sta Clara 45. This shop's designer, handmade chocolate will entice even the least sweet-toothed. More esoteric flavours

include curry, and anchovy and hazelnut.

Pastisseria Faure

c/Argenteria. The best cake shop in a city with a strong pedigree, this prestigious establishment is known for its tasty local *xuxos*, long, sugary doughnuts overflowing with confectioner's custard.

Llibreria Ulyssus

c/Ballesteries 29. Well-stocked and informative travel bookshop with good sections on Girona and the region's history, art and culture.

Cafés

L'Antiga

Pl del Vi 5. Winter closed Mon. In an old terraced building beneath the arches, this place is popular for coffee, cakes, great breakfasts and delicious, thick hot chocolate.

El Cercle

c/Ciutadans 8. Closed Mon. A bohemian-chic café that attracts a mixed arty and trendy crowd for the temporary exhibitions adorning its stone walls.

La Llibreria

c/Ciutadans 8. Tasty snacks are served in this small, friendly café inside a cavernous bookshop.

Tapa't

Cort Reial 1. Winter closed Mon. Small, cheerful tapas bar with a wide selection of dishes at any time of day. Equally pleasant for afternoon coffee.

Restaurants

EL Bistrot

Pujada de St Domènec 4. One of Girona's best eateries, with

1890s decor. At lunchtime you can get an extensive *menú del dia* for €12, while evenings are à la carte. Go for the imaginative *pà amb tomàquet* meals, crêpes – including plenty of vegetarian ones – or the grilled meat and *mar i muntanya* dishes.

Boira

Pl Independència 10. Traditional Catalan cooking with a modern slant in a lovely setting backing onto the river. The very reasonable *menú del dia* costs €10. Try the cod cannelloni in onion sauce or double-cooked duck with pears in red wine.

Cal Ros

Cort Reial 9. Closed Sun eve & Mon. This old-fashioned place under the arches serves some of the city's finest Catalan fare at reasonable prices. Known for its rice and cod dishes, it also offers some fabulous desserts, notably curd mousse with blackcurrant sorbet.

Casa Marieta

Pl Independència 5. Closed Sun eve & Mon. One of the oldest restaurants in Girona, with a high, vaulted ceiling, serving traditionally cooked local meat and fish plus filling stews at affordable prices. Try the very good *pica-pica* starter.

El Celler de Can Roca

Ctra Taialà 40, St Gregori. Closed Sun & Mon. Recently voted best restaurant in Spain, this two-Michelin star establishment, 4km northwest of town, serves truly amazing combinations, including superb *mar i muntanya* dishes at prices commensurate with its calibre.

Cipresaia

c/General Fournàs 2. Closed Thurs. Comfortable and classy old-world establishment at the foot of c/Força, serving fine Mediterranean cuisine, including good fresh fish and tasty *Entrecot de Girona* in anchovy sauce.

La Creperie Bretonne

Cort Reial 14. Closed Sun. An anarchic warren of small, extravagantly decorated rooms, with an excellent selection of crêpes and Breton cider and a wide choice for vegetarians.

El Cul de la Lleona

c/Calderers 8. Closed Mon. Small, welcoming joint serving up a cuisine combining subtle Moroccan influences with chunky Catalan flavours. Especially good are the salads with orange and rosewater dressing, while the Arab pastries and mint tea are delicious.

La Penyora

c/Nou del Teatre 3. Closed Tues. Very popular little place that is unusual in offering two *menús del dia*, one for carnivores and one for vegetarians.

La Polenta

Cort Reial 6. Closed Sun. Simple veggie joint serving a small range and a very good *menú del dia* for €8.

Pol Nord

c/Pedret 120 ☎972 200 927. Closed Sun. One of the most popular and prestigious restaurants on

▲ VIEW FROM THE CITY WALLS TO CATHEDRAL

c/Pedret, serving Catalan cuisine with a creative slant, including some delicious *mar i muntanya* dishes.

Zanpanzar

Cort Reial 10–12. Tues–Sun noon–11.30pm. Out front is an atmospheric bar with excellent Basque-style tapas (keep the toothpicks: they charge you by the number left on your plate). At the back the moderately priced restaurant serves succulent meat and fish dishes, top choices being sea perch with green pepper, and cider-roast lamb.

Bars

Aleshores

Pl Independència 4. House music in a long, narrow, packed bar with a dance floor at the end.

Café Royal

Pl Independència 1. Daily 9am–3am. Relaxing bar that's good for breakfasts and an afternoon tipple. Quieter than the nearby competition after dark.

Nummulit

c/Nord 7. A lively, fun bar popular with gays that plays mainly 1980s music to a mixed crowd and wide age range.

Particular

c/Pedret 76. A friendly little bar in a 600-year-old limekiln, with hip-hop, drum 'n' bass and *mestissatge* (a mix of ethnic and modern beats).

Sunset Jazz Club

c/Jaume Pons i Martí 12. Tues–Sat 8pm–3am, Sun 6pm–3am. An upmarket jazz club set in an atmospheric cavern on the northern edge of the old town,

▲ CARRER SANTA CLARA

playing live music most weekends except August – with the occasional midweek jam session – and serving great cocktails.

La Terra

c/Ballesteries 21. A pleasant, colourfully tiled bar overlooking the river, drawing a vaguely hip crowd.

Via

c/Pedret 72. Daily 11pm–5.30am. This lively joint has a stark house bar downstairs and vibrant salsa bar upstairs.

Clubs

Platea

c/Real de Fontclara 6. A large DJ bar behind Plaça Independència with a big dance floor, playing an eclectic selection from salsa to rock to a mainly studenty clientele.

La Sala del Cel

c/Pedret 118. Daily 11pm–6am. A huge multi-level club in an old *masia* – mainly house, with some chill-out rooms and terraces. Visiting and resident DJs put it on the club circuit for locals and the Barcelona crowd.

Banyoles and Besalú

At the centre of the triangle formed by Girona, Figueres and Olot lie the towns of Banyoles and Besalú. Chiefly noted for its distinctive figure-of-eight lake, Banyoles sits on a small, fertile plain and has a backwater simplicity. Nearby Besalú, which enjoyed a brief spell of independence and majesty a thousand years ago, is famous for its eleventh-century fortified bridge and has a knot of tiny streets with smart hotels and restaurants. Located between the two towns are the prehistoric Coves de Serinyà caverns, set among evergreen oaks.

Estany de Banyoles

Banyoles' charm lies in its lake, the Estany de Banyoles, circled by wooded hills and reached by a clearly signposted main road from the town centre. Fed by underground streams, the lake is up to 62m deep in parts and is surrounded by seven *estanyols*, or ponds, including the Estanyol Can Sisó, which inexplicably turns red in the winter, and the Estanyol Nou ("new"), which

appeared overnight in 1978. A mini-train runs hourly (daily 10am–7pm; 15min; €3.60) from Plaça Major to the east side of the lake. Half-hour boat trips (March–Dec Tues–Sun 10am–7pm; €3.60) leave every hour from the eastern shore, where you can also rent rowing boats (€3/hr). Swimming is allowed at designated areas.

Another pleasant way to take in the lake is to walk or cycle

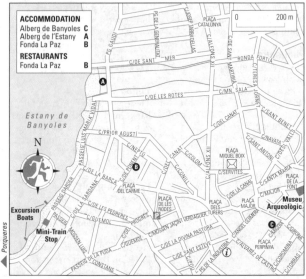

Visiting Banyoles

Girona–Olot buses stop on Passeig de l'Indústria near the main crossroads, at the entrance to the old town. The tourist office is on the same road at no. 25, but will be moving to Plaça Major at the end of 2005 (June–Aug Mon–Sat 9am–2pm & 4.30–7pm, Sun 10am–1pm; Sept–May Mon–Fri 9am–2pm & 4.30–7pm, Sat 10am–1pm; ☎972 575 573, ⊚www.plaestany.org). A new information office (July–Sept daily 10am–8pm) is scheduled to open soon on the eastern shore of the lake.

right round it (8km) along a clearly marked path; bikes can be rented from Las Vegas, Passeig Draga 2 (€3/hr), near the mini-train stop. A third of the way round, walking southwest, you come to the lovely twelfth-century Església de Santa Maria, a waterside church with low, sculpted capitals around the door. Some 3km further, before coming full circle, you'll see a detour signposted to the Mirador ("Belvedere"), a climb of roughly 500m rewarded by fabulous views over the lake.

Banyoles

A good fifteen-minute walk east of the lake, Banyoles itself is surprisingly dreary, although the medieval porticoed Plaça Major, home to the town's Wednesday market since the thirteenth century, is worth a detour. Of passable interest, the Museu Arqueològic (Tues–Sat 10.30am–1.30pm & 4–6.30pm, Sun 10.30am–2pm; €1.80), set in the fourteenth-century Pia Almoina, or almshouses, displays local finds, including medieval ceramics.

Coves de Serinyà

April to mid-July Tues–Fri 10am–4pm, Sat & Sun 11am–6pm; mid-July to mid-Sept daily 11am–7pm; mid-Sept to April Tues–Fri 10am–4pm, Sat 11am–5pm, Sun 10am–3pm. €3. The atmospheric Coves de Serinyà, Paleolithic limestone caves, have only been opened to the public in recent years and are still being excavated; to date, they've turned up over thirty thousand objects, including evidence of human habitation alongside remains of lions, panthers, hyenas and elephants.

Two caves are accessible at present. Finds at Cova d'Arbreda, overlooking the narrow valley, date from between 100,000 and 15,000 years ago, the most signifi-cant being flint from southern

▲ BANYOLES: LAKE WITH BOATHOUSES

▲ CENTRAL SQUARE IN BANYOLES

France; as local flint was too brittle for use as tools, the nomadic cave-dwellers would travel hundreds of kilometres north each year to find other sources of flint. A 200,000-year-old tooth, the oldest human remain in Catalonia (now on display in Barcelona), was found at the Cova de Mollet, at the foot of the slope. The numinous Cova de Reclau Viver at the end of the path has turned up finds, including Bronze Age funeral urns, dating back 40,000 years.

Besalú

The most stunning entrance to the medieval town of Besalú is across its fortified pedestrian toll bridge, dating from the eleventh century, but destroyed and rebuilt many times, most recently in the Spanish Civil War. Built in an L-shape, its foundations governed by the position of the rocks in the river, the stone bridge gives an idea of Besalú's erstwhile importance, for it is overwhelmingly large in comparison with the diminutive size of the town today. Occupied in turn by Romans, Visigoths, Franks, Moors and the French, the town was declared a site of national historical interest in 1966; most of what survives dates from a 200-year period of

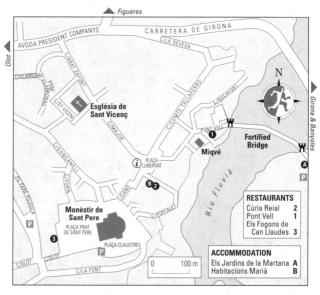

RESTAURANTS
Cúria Reial   2
Pont Vell   1
Els Fogons de
  Can Llaudes   3

ACCOMMODATION
Els Jardins de la Martana   A
Habitacions Marià   B

Visiting Besalú

Buses stop on the main C66 road, a short walk from Plaça Llibertat, where you'll find the tourist office at no. 21 (daily 10am–2pm & 4–7pm; ☎972 591 240, ⊛www.ajuntamentbesalu.org); they offer four very informative daily 75-minute guided tours of the town's monuments (€2.10). Parking is limited, with just a small car park at the start of the bridge, often clogged up with tour coaches.

---

independence between the tenth and the twelfth centuries.

At the centre of the town's warren of narrow streets is the enchanting sixteenth-century porticoed Plaça Llibertat, site of Besalú's Tuesday market since medieval times, and where you'll find a couple of cafés and some small shops selling local produce.

Southwest of the square, on fan-shaped Prat de Sant Pere, stands the Benedictine Monèstir de Sant Pere, founded in 977, of which only the eleventh-century church survives. The imposing facade is crowned by a simple Romanesque belfry, while the interior is notable for its fine colonnaded ambulatory.

Tiny Carrer Ganganell leads to the architectural mishmash of the twelfth-century Església de Sant Vicenç, extensively rebuilt. Its simple Romanesque facade and main door contrast with an ornate thirteenth-century rose window and intricately carved Gothic side door.

Down by the river is a twelfth-century Miqvé (mid-June to mid-Sept Mon–Fri 10.30am, noon, 1.30pm, 4.30pm & 6pm, Sat & Sun 1.30pm & 6pm; mid-Sept to mid-June Mon–Fri 10.30am, noon, 1.30pm & 4.30pm, Sat & Sun 1.30pm; visits set off from tourist office; €1.05), discovered by chance in 1964 and one of only three medieval Jewish ritual purification bathhouses left in the world. Little more than a high-ceilinged room with steps down to the pool, the building nonetheless exudes an atmosphere of calm and spirituality. Excavations nearby are unearthing parts of the synagogue.

Hotels

Els Jardins de la Martana

c/Pont 2, Besalú ☎972 590 009, ⊛www.lamartana.com. This lovely new hotel, in a renovated house at the foot of the bridge, with views of the town across the river, offers ten comfortable rooms, enchanting wood-panelled lounges and shaded gardens. €110.

Habitacions Marià

Pl Llibertat 7, Besalú ☎ & ☎972 590 106. The best budget option in town, with eight charming, old-fashioned rooms in an ancient building just off Plaça Llibertat. €42.

Fonda La Paz

c/Ponent, Banyoles 18 ☎972 570 432. A friendly and comfortable *pensió* in a side street near the lake. It's a far better option than the overpriced places on the

▼ BESALÚ: MONÈSTIR DE SANT PERE

▲ STREET SCENE, BESALÚ

waterfront and has a good restaurant. €45.

Sant Ferriol

Jardins de St Ferriol, Sant Ferriol ☎972 590 532, ⓦwww.santferriol.com. Boasting just twelve large rooms, this sumptuous hotel in a stone *masia* 2km west of Besalú has every creature comfort, with its combination of spa, gardens and excellent restaurant. €170.

Hostels

Alberg de l'Estany

Pg Lluís M Vidal, Banyoles ☎972 576 747, ☎972 582 535. A reasonable eighty-bed hostel that's good for exploring the lake and is popular with cyclists. Bikes can be rented. €19.

Turisme rural

Can Maholà

17850 Beuda ☎972 590 162, ⓦwww. beuda.com/mahola. These two fully equipped and spacious stone houses, for four and eight people respectively, stand high on a tree-lined hill atop the village of Beuda, 5km north of Besalú. Weekend rates €200 & €385 respectively.

Mas Salvanera

17850 Beuda ☎972 590 975, ⓦwww. salvanera.com. With four antique-furnished, en-suite doubles, this rambling seventeenth-century mansion in a hamlet above Besalú offers bucolic tranquillity. €115.

Restaurants

Cúria Reial

Pl Llibertat 15, Besalú. Down some steps across the square from the tourist office, this cheerful restaurant and bar serves uncomplicated, good-value meals and snacks and has pleasant views from the terrace.

La Masia

Porqueres, Estany de Banyoles. A rambling lakeside restaurant with terraces and gardens, popular with locals, though it can be expensive unless you go for the very good-value *menú del dia* at €9.

Els Fogons de Can Llaudes

Prat de Sant Pere 6, Besalú ☎972 590 858. Closed Tues. Enjoying an atmospheric setting in an eleventh-century chapel, this place serves up traditional and local dishes with a contemporary spin. You'll need to reserve 24 hours in advance and have a bit of room on your credit card.

Fonda La Paz

c/Ponent 18, Banyoles. A moderately priced restaurant near the lake, offering creative local cuisine and a great choice of *menús del dia* for €6–9.

Pont Vell

c/Pont Vell 28, Besalú. Offering great views of the river, this small restaurant will set you back some €36 for extremely good Catalan cuisine with a modern slant.

Parc Natural de la Garrotxa

In the foothills of the Pyrenees, the Parc Natural de la Garrotxa extends over 120 square kilometres, dipping and climbing through a landscape of dormant volcanoes moulded into lush, rolling hills by more than ten thousand years of erosion. One of the best bases for exploring the area is Olot, the park's engaging county town. It's flanked by two villages: Castellfollit de la Roca, to the northeast, perched precariously above a basalt precipice, and, to the southeast, the enchanting Santa Pau, dominated by an imposing semi-ruined castle and starting point for some spectacular walks. Marked footpaths set out on crisscrossing tracks through the ancient Fageda d'en Jordà beech wood to the wildest volcanoes, dormant for over eleven thousand years. The best place to find out more about the volcanoes is the fascinating Casal dels Volcans information centre, just outside Olot.

Olot

Don't be put off by Olot's rather unprepossessing outskirts – beyond these lies a very pretty old quarter. Often described as conservative with a radical undertone – or trendy with traditional roots – Olot's labyrinthine Barri Vell, huddled at the base of the

Exploring the park

The tourist offices in Olot (see p.71) and Santa Pau (see p.72), as well as the Casal dels Volcans in Olot (see p.71), have details of walking itineraries in the Garrotxa Park lasting from thirty minutes to six hours. We've also suggested our own walking route, on p.74. For a real treat consider taking a breathtaking early-morning balloon ride over the volcanoes (€140); the price includes cava and cake on board and a hearty breakfast after you land. Reserve through Vol de Coloms in Santa Pau (☏972 680 255, ⊛www.garrotxa.com/voldecoloms). Affording equally thrilling views, Parapent Passió offers parapenting for beginners (☏609 853 224, ⊛www.parapent-passio.com). For more earthbound exploration of the park, you could join a 4x4 trip to areas that are otherwise inaccessible by car (reserve at the Santa Pau office, c/Major 24, ☏972 680 078; €9–48). Horse riding (€16/hr) is organized by Hipica Les Forques, Ctra Olot–Sta Pau km7 (☏972 680 358), and Camping La Fageda, nearby at km3.8 (☏909 702 821). Hipica Les Forques also runs horse-drawn carriage excursions (€6) and mini-train rides around the woods and volcanoes (daily 10am–1pm & 3–6pm; €6). The Area Recreativa de Xenacs, 3km south of Olot in Les Preses (☏972 195 087), organizes walks, archery and mountain biking, and also has a good restaurant.

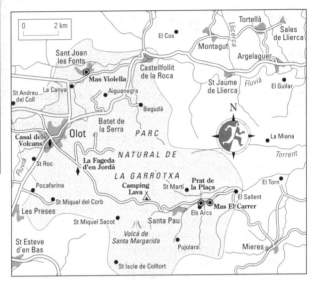

squat Montsacopa volcano, is a bustling area of avant-garde art galleries, cafés and shops. Most of the buildings date from the eighteenth and nineteenth centuries – the medieval town

was almost completely destroyed by devastating earthquakes in 1427 and 1428.

Southwest of the simple Plaça Major, eighteenth-century Església de Sant Esteve, built on the site of a tenth-century church, dominates the skyline from its perch at the top of a flight of sweeping steps. Rebuilt after the earthquakes, and successively renovated, it has an uncluttered facade marked by empty niches where statues of saints stood until their destruction in the Spanish Civil War. The highlight of its lofty interior is the Baroque Verge del Roser wooden altarpiece.

From Sant Esteve, a marked trail (no. 17) guides you along a pleasant path to the top of the Montsacopa volcano (15min). On the edge of the wooded summit crater, affording superb views over the surrounding countryside, stands the picturesque eighteenth-century Ermita de Sant Francesc chapel.

▲ CARRER MAJOR IN OLOT

Visiting Olot

Regular buses from Girona, Figueres, Barcelona, Lloret de Mar and outlying villages pull in at the bus station on c/Bisbe Lorenzana, and there are ample metered parking spaces and underground car parks around the old town. The helpful tourist office (July & Aug Mon–Sat 10am–2pm & 5–8pm, Sun 11am–2pm; Sept–June Mon–Fri 9am–2pm & 5–7pm, Sat 10am–2pm & 5–7pm, Sun 11am–2pm) is on the ground floor of the same building as the Museu Comarcal de la Garrotxa at c/Hospici 8.

Some 400m east of Sant Esteve is the rather sombre-looking Església Nostra Dona del Tura, first mentioned in 872 and reconstructed after the Civil War; inside is a small twelfth-century wooden sculpture of the Verge del Tura, patron saint of the town, reputedly unearthed by a bull.

On the fringes of the Barri Vell, the Museu Comarcal de la Garrotxa (c/Hospici 8; Mon & Wed–Sat 10am–2pm & 4–7pm, Sun 11am–2pm; €1.60) chronicles the town's history, especially its late nineteenth-century renaissance – thanks mainly to a burgeoning industry in religious images – which saw a flowering of the arts and the emergence of the Olot School of painters. These artists were influenced by the Impressionists and noted for their use of sombre, "volcanic" colours in contrast to the bright Mediterranean palette of other Catalan schools. Particularly representative are Joaquim Vayreda's lowering mountain landscapes. Other highlights include Josep Clarà's appealingly simple life sculptures.

Casal dels Volcans

July–Sept Mon & Wed–Sat 10am–2pm & 5–7pm, Sun 11am–2pm; rest of year Mon & Wed–Sat 10am–2pm & 4–6pm, Sun 11am–2pm; ⊛www.agtat.es. Exhibition €2. Set in a handsome Italianate mansion in the centre of landscaped Parc Nou is the Casal dels Volcans information

centre. Its fascinating exhibition consists of photos and models chronicling the region's turbulent geological history, including perfectly formed natural basalt columns, and even a floor-shaking simulation of an earthquake. The Casal also provides excellent free maps and walking itineraries of the Parc Natural de la Garrotxa.

Santa Pau

Santa Pau's defensive perimeter of windowless house walls hides a beautifully preserved medieval core. Despite wars, occupation and earthquakes, the village has remained largely unchanged since the thirteenth century, and any necessary restoration has been sensitively done.

Although popular with visitors, Santa Pau rarely gets overrun, except possibly on Sundays when the village's fine

▼ STATIONS OF THE CROSS UP TO VOLCANO MONTSACOPA

Parc Natural de la Garrotxa   PLACES

Casal dels Volcans, ⓑ ⓒ ⓓ ④ ⑤

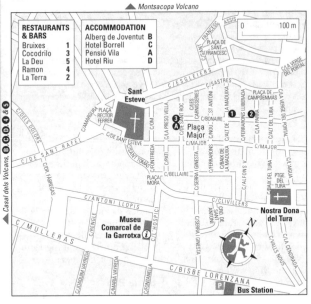

▲ Montsacopa Volcano

RESTAURANTS & BARS

Bruixes	1
Cocodrilo	3
La Deu	5
Ramon	4
La Terra	2

ACCOMMODATION

Alberg de Joventut	B
Hotel Borrell	C
Pensió Vila	A
Hotel Riu	D

0 _____ 100 m

hotel restaurants (see p.73) are
full of Catalans enjoying a long
lunch.

▼ SANTA PAU

At the heart of the cobbled
old quarter are two adjacent
squares, lined with houses
sporting low wooden balconies covered in flowers. The
porticoed thirteenth-century
Plaça Major is in the shape of
an irregular triangle and built
on sloping ground, which gives
it an enjoyably anarchic air.
Scene of the Monday market
since 1297, it's dominated by
the enormous Gothic Església
de Santa Maria, built in the
fifteenth century. The thir-
teenth- to eighteenth-century
castle (no access), an angular,
crumbling edifice, once the
baronial seat of the region, rises
over the small Placeta dels Balls,
formerly the castle moat.

The tourist office, pl Major 1
(Mon & Wed–Sat noon–6pm,
Sun noon–3pm; ☎972 680 349),
is a mine of information on
walking routes in the area and
local history.

▲ FOOTPATH SIGNPOST

Castellfollit de la Roca

Castellfollit de la Roca teeters on the edge of a sheer precipice 60m above the Fluvià River. Sadly, the rather drab town fails to live up to its dramatic location, but it's worth wandering through the narrow streets to the viewing platform above the chasm.

An enjoyable detour runs 3km west to the charming village of Sant Joan de les Fonts, from where signposts lead you across a medieval stone bridge to the Columnes basàltiques, a soaring cliff of perfectly symmetrical basalt columns doused by a waterfall.

Hotels

Hotel Borrell

c/Nònit Escubós 8, Olot ☎972 276 161, ☎972 270 408. Though set in an outwardly nondescript modern building, this hotel is very friendly and has the most comfortable, air-conditioned rooms near Olot's city centre. €60.

Cal Sastre

c/Cases Noves 1, Santa Pau ☎972 680 049, ☻www.calsastre.com. Relatively pricey, but worth the extra, this establishment has a good restaurant and seven old-fashioned guest rooms. €70.

Can Menció

Pl Major 17, Santa Pau ☎972 680 014, ☎972 262 622. An atmospheric café serving hearty snacks which doubles as village shop and rents out cheerful rooms. €40.

Hotel Riu

Ctra Sta Pau s/n, Olot ☎972 269 444, ☻www.riu.com. Plush, modern hotel at the edge of town with fabulous views of the volcanoes, a great restaurant and lovely, big rooms with terraces. €82.

Pensió Vila

c/St Roc 1, Olot ☎972 269 807, ☻www.pensiolavila.com. Small but very central *pensió* in an old building belying its modern en-suite rooms. It can get noisy at weekends from revellers in the streets. €47.

▼ APPROACH TO CASTELLFOLLIT DE LA ROCA FROM THE GORGE

PLACES Parc Natural de la Garrotxa

A volcano walk

The following circular walk, starting and finishing in Santa Pau, is a combination of two of the walking routes suggested by the Casal dels Volcans (nos. 1 & 4); the itinerary takes in the most interesting volcanoes, as well as the beech forest. It takes a good five hours to complete, but is relatively easy with no steep climbs, though the final few metres up to the Santa Margarida volcano are a bit of a scramble. You can get a free detailed map of the park from the Casal dels Volcans.

Trails are marked with a black number beside a symbol of two ramblers in a coloured square, which also shows the next stop and final destination.

From Santa Pau, set off from the car park by the bridge into the old town, and follow trail 4 signs to Santa Margarida along the river for about 30min, when you'll pass the Volcà de la Roca Negra on your left. After the Collellmir farmhouse, the route joins up with trail 1, which heads for 30min up to the crater of the Volcà de Santa Margarida. At the summit, in the hollow of the grassy caldera, a wooded landscape frames a tiny chapel (no access). Cross the caldera and head down the other side of the volcano, following trail 1 marked to Croscat, for about 45min as far as the Area de Santa Margarida; here you'll find the Lava campsite (see below) and, opposite, the Santa Margarida café, where you can get a drink or a filling meal.

From the café, it's about another 1hr 15min to Can Passavent, skirting the base of the Volcà de Croscat. A further 45min brings you to the Area de Can Serra (also accessible by car, signposted off the Olot–Santa Pau road). Here you can rent a horse-drawn carriage through the dense beech woods of La Fageda d'en Jordà, well worth the detour (1hr round trip; €5). Pushing on, follow the rugged, twisting trail 1 for 30min until it emerges into the open and passes the medieval chapel of Sant Miquel de Sa Cot and its grounds – a popular picnic spot. The path eventually brings you back to where you left trail 4 at the foot of the Santa Margarida volcano, for the easy river walk back to Santa Pau.

Hostels

Alberg de Joventut

Pg Barcelona 15, Olot ☎972 264 200. A lovely 1920s mansion in its own gardens is the setting for this youth hostel, with basic dorms and a midnight curfew. €19.

Turisme rural

Mas El Carrer

Veïnat dels Arcs, Santa Pau ☎ & ☎972 680 487. Roomy self-catering apartments in a rambling sixteenth-century *masia* on the outskirts of the village, with a large swimming pool and pleasant gardens. €530 per week.

Mas Violella

Ctra GI-522 km1, 17857 St Joan les Fonts ☎650 430 798, ⊛www .masviolella.com. Eighteenth-century farmhouse 5km north of Olot, with fully equipped individual apartments, a garden and small swimming pool. €350 per week.

Prat de la Plaça

Pla de la Cot 65, Santa Pau ☎972 680 509. Idyllic eighteenth-century mansion with stunning views, sleeping up to eleven people and rented whole. €1400 per week.

Campsites

Camping Lava

Ctra Olot–Sta Pau km7 ☎972 680 358,

▲ HORSE CARRIAGE IN FAGEDA D'EN JORDÀ

℗972 680 315. The best site in the area, *Camping Lava* is reasonably shaded, has log cabins and a swimming pool, as well as a good restaurant.

Restaurants

La Deu
Ctra La Deu, Olot. Closed Mon. Founded in 1885 and located in a *masia* 2km east of the centre, *La Deu* is a local institution and deservedly famous for its marvellous, moderately priced *cuina volcànica*.

Ramon
Pl Clarà 4, Olot. Open daily. On the edge of the old town, this reasonably priced traditional restaurant is among the best options in the Barri Vell for regional Catalan cooking.

La Terra
c/Bonaire 22, Olot. Mon–Fri 1–4pm. Down-to-earth veggie restaurant in the Barri Vell, serving a good, inexpensive lunchtime menu.

Bars

Bruixes
c/Bonaire 14, Olot. Daily 7pm–3am. Slightly hippyish, laid-back bar, with a witch theme (*bruixes* in Catalan), attracting esoteric types.

Cocodrilo
c/St Roc 3, Olot. Tues–Sat 8pm–3am. Cool cocktail bar with an eclectic crowd of late-evening sophisticates and a late-night chilled-out crowd.

▲ OLOT

Blanes

Marking the southernmost tip of the Costa Brava, the thriving fishing port of Blanes is neatly divided into two very different halves by the jagged Sa Palomera rock that juts out into the sea. To the north, fronted by the sedate Platja de Blanes, lies Blanes' old town, or Barri Vell, with its low buildings and medieval streets, while to the south stretches the long swath of sand and high-rise blocks of the modern S'Abanell resort. On the steep hillsides above Blanes is the tranquil Jardí Botànic Mar i Murtra, a short walk from the town's best beach, Cala Sant Francesc.

The Barri Vell

The sandy, gently shelving Platja de Blanes, the town's main beach, is much less crowded than the hotel-heavy S'Abanell. Site of the Monday market, the beachfront promenade, with its restaurant terraces and shady gardens, heads east to the workaday port, which comes alive for the late-afternoon fish auction.

Overlooking Blanes is the sixteenth-century Castell de Sant Joan (no access). The tiring climb up from the port (1.3km), on a turn-off from the Mar i Murtra road, rewards you with sea views, along with the sound of cicadas and the scent of eucalyptus.

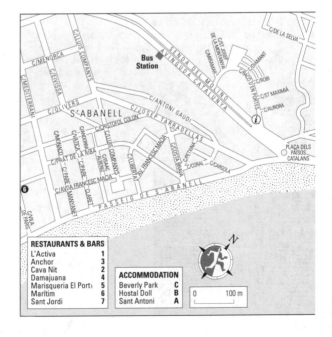

RESTAURANTS & BARS

L'Activa	1
Anchor	3
Cava Nit	2
Damajuana	4
Marisqueria El Port	5
Marítim	6
Sant Jordi	7

ACCOMMODATION

Beverly Park	C
Hostal Doll	B
Sant Antoni	A

0   100 m

Visiting Blanes

The bus station is on Avinguda Catalunya, very near the tourist office on Carrer Racó d'en Portes (Mon–Sat 9am–8pm; ☎972 330 348, ⊛www.blanes.net). There's also a small information stand in the port (Easter–Sept daily 10am–2pm & 4–7pm). The train station is 2km southwest of the port (☎972 331 827), with services to and from Barcelona (every 30min) and Girona (every 2hr); half-hourly shuttle buses (free with a train ticket) run to the bus station.

Several operators run regular boat services (Easter–Oct daily 9am–5.30pm) between Blanes and Tossa de Mar (and beyond), stopping at all main beaches.

One street in from the promenade, the sheltered Passeig de Dintre is home every morning to a lively fruit and veg market. From here follow the busy shopping street of Carrer Ample inland to see an impressive fifteenth-century Gothic fountain decorated with gargoyles, set into the wall halfway along on the right; sliced in two by the buildings, it was probably once the centrepiece of a long-gone square amidst a much grander Carrer Ample.

Northeast stands the fourteenth-century Església Parroquial i Palau dels Vecomtes de Cabrera (the Parish Church and Palace of the Viscounts of Cabrera). Largely destroyed by French troops in the seventeenth century, it was restored in the eighteenth century; all that remains of the original structure is the crenellated facade, with a high arched doorway and towering square belfry. The interior is very simple, with a plain vaulted ceiling.

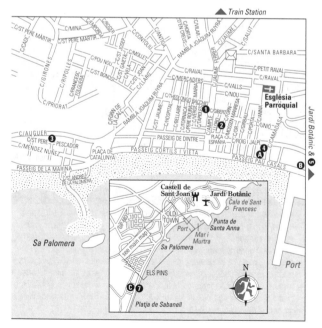

▲ BLANES: GOTHIC FOUNTAIN

Jardí Botànic Mar i Murtra

Pg Karl Faust 9. April–Oct daily 9am–6pm; Nov–March Mon–Fri 10am–5pm, Sat & Sun 10am–2pm. €3. Bus #3 from Plaça Catalunya every 15min; 15min. On a headland 1km northeast of the port lies the Jardí Botànic Mar i Murtra, founded in 1924 by German industrialist Karl Faust on the site of an eighteenth-century garden. You could spend a pleasurable afternoon here wandering on hilly paths amid the flora, looking out over the turquoise sea.

The gardens are arranged by theme: there's a Subtropical Garden, which includes a rambling cactus collection, and a Temperate Garden, featuring bamboo groves and towering Chilean palms. The loveliest is the Mediterranean Garden, full of olives and tamarisks tumbling down to the cliff edge, punctuated with belvederes. Steps from the largest of these climb through an avenue of cypresses to a small square surrounded by orange trees; at its centre is a tiled fountain decorated with Goethe's poem *Where the Oranges Blossom*.

S'Abanell

The modern S'Abanell suburb – a 1960s residential and tourist development – is a bit of a sprawl, but it's saved by the glittering sands of Platja S'Abanell, which, despite the hotel crowds, has some quieter areas a few hundred metres west of the centre. As you'd expect, there's a huge range of watersports on offer, from water-skiing to parasailing.

Cala Sant Francesc

Blanes' finest beach, the sheltered horseshoe-shaped bay of Cala Sant Francesc, attracts a select, local crowd. The tranquil, unspoilt cove shelves gently and its crystalline waters are great for swimming.

Hotels

Beverly Park

c/Mercé Rodoreda s/n, S'Abanell ☎972 352 426, ℱ972 330 110, ⓦwww.

Blanes, fireworks competition

In the last full week of July, during Blanes' Festa Major, Sa Palomera is the setting for one of the most spectacular free fireworks displays in Spain. First held in 1906, the awe-inspiring feast of noise and colour now attracts pyrotechnics teams from all over the world competing for the festival's prestigious trophy, and thousands of spectators pack the beach and promenade. Shows start nightly at 10.30pm, with most vantage points filling up long beforehand. The best views are from the sea, with the old town as a backdrop: boat operators offer excursions from S'Abanell beach or neighbouring Lloret de Mar to see the displays – tickets (€9) and information are available from the beach stands.

hotelbeverlypark.com. Closed Nov–March. Plush hotel in a quiet area of S'Abanell with modern en-suite rooms – good for relaxing around the pool or working out in the gym after a fine buffet breakfast. €72.

Hostal Doll

Pg Pau Casals 70–71 ☎972 330 008. Friendly budget *hostal* at the quieter, port end of the old town, with good, but slightly gloomy, en-suite rooms. €40.

Sant Antoni

Pg del Mar 63 ☎972 331 150, ☎972 330 226. Closed Nov–Feb. Pleasant, good-value two-star on the old-town seafront, with simple but comfortable en-suite rooms boasting good views of the sands and fishing port. €55.

Restaurants

L'Activa

c/Theolognio Bacchio 5. Closed Tues. Set in a brightly lit, renovated medieval building, this plush and expensive upstairs restaurant specializes in locally caught seafood and grilled meats and has a *pastisseria* downstairs serving mouthwatering cakes.

Cava Nit

c/Forn 5. 8pm–midnight. Closed Tues. A wide variety of tasty sweet and savoury crêpes, plus Catalan-style pizzas. The platters of cheeses, pâtés and *embotits* are very filling, and there's plenty of choice for vegetarians.

Damajuana

c/Roig i Jalpí 5. Tues–Sun 1–4pm & 8–10.30pm. Quiet and moderately priced Italian-Argentinian restaurant serving good fresh

▲ JARDÍ BOTÀNIC MAR I MURTRA: VIEW TO THE SEA

pasta and salads, as well as a filling *menú del dia*.

Marisqueria El Port

Port Pesquer. Closed Sun eve. Tucked away behind the fish market, this down-to-earth eatery with outside tables serves excellent fresh fish, seafood and tapas.

Bars and clubs

Anchor

c/S'Auguer 4. Closed Mon. Small, friendly bar, run by an Englishwoman and set in an old backstreet fisherman's cottage. Subtly lit and with a lively but intimate feel, it's usually packed with locals.

Marítim

c/Vila de Paris 2. A late-night magnet in S'Abanell, playing a wide range of music from Spanish pop to house. One or two other bars in the same short street are also worth checking out, but don't bother arriving before 1am.

Sant Jordi

Pg S'Abanell 33. Daily 9pm–3am. Imagine a public baths designed by Gaudí and then turned into a salsa dance hall and you've got the Sant Jordi, one of the oldest and most stylish clubs in Blanes. Its tiled pillars and garish mural only add to its undeniable charm.

Lloret de Mar

Lloret de Mar is like a dissolute uncle: you know you should be shocked, but you can't help feeling a sneaking affection. On the one hand there is the gaudy over-commercialization that has made Lloret a byword for all things cheap and nasty, while on the other – underneath the tack – beats a two-thousand-year-old heart. High-rise monstrosities stand side by side with characterful mansions, and one of Europe's highest concentrations of clubs crowds around a tiny fifteenth-century church. Fanning out from Lloret's charming old town are some of the prettiest – and most crowded – beaches on the Costa Brava.

The Barri Vell

The best way to appreciate Lloret is to take a walk through the Barri Vell's maze of narrow pedestrian streets: nowhere is the town's diversity more evident than around Carrer de la Vila and Plaça Església. A bakery, confectioner's and butcher jostle with tattoo parlours, tearooms and dance clubs; all-day English breakfasts are as common as *pà amb tomàquet*. Standing aloof from its surroundings, the late-Gothic Església Parroquial has a later addition of an ornate domed roof, capped by brightly coloured tiles. Inside, look out for the seven enormous, sombre paintings of the *Passion* by an unknown, late sixteenth-century artist.

Centre Cultural Verdaguer

Pg Camprodón i Arrieta 1. June–Sept daily 10am–8pm; Oct–May Tues–Sat 10am–2pm & 4–6pm, Sun 10am–2pm. Free. For some insight into Lloret's past you couldn't do better than visit this museum, set in the former home of the Garriga family, Indianos who grew wealthy in Cuba before returning home to Lloret. Exhibits include a display of model ships, crafted from South American hardwood rescued from local mansions that were torn down to make way for hotels, and photographs of old Lloret. The top floor is a recreation of how the house might have looked in its heyday, its sturdy Indiano furnishings marrying traditional Catalan styles with Modernista and colonial influences.

Jardins de Santa Clotilde

Ctra Blanes km9.3. Tues–Sun 10am–1pm & 3–7pm. €3. Laid out a hundred years ago in Modernista style, with terraces, fountains and statues, these gardens are

Visiting Lloret de Mar

The main tourist office is on the edge of town at Avgda Alegries 3 (Mon–Sat 9am–1pm & 4–7pm; ☎972 365 788, ⊛www.lloret.org), but there's a more central one in the town hall at Pl de la Vila 1 (June–Sept Mon–Sat 9am–9pm, Sun 10am–2pm; Oct–May Mon–Sat 9am–1pm & 4–8pm; ☎972 364 735), and a desk at the bus station (Easter–Sept Mon–Sat 9am–9pm, Sun 10am–2pm).

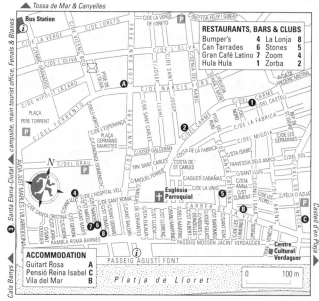

PLACES Lloret de Mar

RESTAURANTS, BARS & CLUBS

Bumper's	4	La Lonja	8
Can Tarrades	6	Stones	5
Gran Café Latino	7	Zoom	4
Hula Hula	1	Zorba	2

ACCOMMODATION

Guitart Rosa	A
Pensió Reina Isabel	C
Vila del Mar	B

Església Parroquial

Platja de Lloret

0   100 m

a cool retreat from the town
and offer some inspiring views
of the sea through avenues of
tall cypresses and pines. Visitor
numbers are limited to fifty at
a time; if you go in the early
afternoon when everyone's at
the beach, you're likely to have
the place to yourself.

Ermita de Santa Cristina

Standing on the site of a much
earlier church in a peaceful,
shaded clifftop garden overlooking the sea, this small chapel is
only occasionally open, but it's
worth visiting for its tranquil
gardens and the neighbouring
sandy beaches of Cala Santa
Cristina and Cala Treumal;
both coves can be accessed
by car from the Blanes road.
Laced with paths winding down
through groves of evergreen
oaks, pines and olives to the
two sheltered coves below, the
gardens are a welcome respite
from the clamour of the town.

Platja de Lloret and Fenals

Lloret's main beach, a sheltered
swath of fine sand, is as full of
basting bodies in summer as
you'd expect. It's bookended
by the 1930s folly, Castell d'en
Plaja, at one end, and the Dona
Marinera (Sailor's Wife) statue
at the other – legend has it that
if you stare at the same spot on
the horizon as the statue, and
touch her right foot, you'll be
granted a wish.

Neighbouring Fenals beach
gets equally crowded, although
the far southwestern corner,
framed by pines, is much less
frenetic than the hotel-lined
strip nearer Lloret.

Cala Boadella

South of town lies the rock-
strewn, tranquil Cala Boadella,
although the approach to it is
in danger of being spoilt by
galloping construction. Divided
in two by a rocky outcrop, the
south side, popular with fami-

▲ LLORET: DONA MARINERA STATUE

lies, is mixed nude and clothed, while the north side is entirely nude.

Cala Canyelles

Accessible by car or the tortuous Camí de Ronda, Cala Canyelles is a long, attractive beach north of Lloret, with a small fishing quay and reputable restaurant (see p.83); it's also great for snorkelling and boating.

Cala Morisca

Cala Morisca is reachable only by a fairly arduous hour-long walk from Cala Canyelles, following the signposted GR92 path through the pines and then down a gully. Though rarely empty, the beach is a just reward: its tiny rock-strewn shore is almost virgin and the waters are excellent for snorkelling.

Hotels

Guitart Rosa

c/St Pere 67 ☎972 365 100, ⓦwww. guitarthotels.com. This late nineteenth-century colonial mansion, set in its own shaded grounds around a pool, is sheer indulgence at a reasonable price. Some of the rooms are in the original

house, others in the similarly attractive modern annexe. €110.

Pensió Reina Isabel

c/Vall de Venecia 12 ☎972 364 121, ⓕ972 369 978. Closed Nov–Feb. Quirky place popular with backpackers, with a hundred-year-old magnolia growing in the middle of the reception area. All the bright, airy rooms are well maintained, and some are en suite. €42.

Hostal Santa Cristina

Ermita Sta Cristina 7 ☎972 364 934. Closed Nov–Feb. Charming *hostal* in the grounds of the Ermita Santa Cristina, 4km south of Lloret, with sparsely furnished en-suite rooms, gloriously faded sitting rooms and a good-value restaurant. €55.

Vila del Mar

c/de la Vila 55 ☎972 349 292, ⓦwww. hotelviladelmar.com. Closed Dec–Feb. Compact, welcoming four-star hotel just back from the seafront and smartly decorated in an eighteenth-century style. The comfortable, quiet en-suite rooms – with air conditioning – are a welcome haven from the noisy old-town streets. €150.

Campsites

Canyelles

Platja Canyelles ☎972 364 504, ⓕ972 368 506. Closed Nov–March. A quiet, shaded site with good amenities a short walk from the beach at Canyelles.

Santa Elena-Ciutat

Ctra Blanes ☎972 364 009, ⓕ972 367 954. Closed Nov–March. The best option nearest to the town (a fifteen-minute walk away), this campsite is well equipped and has mobile homes for rent.

Restaurants

Can Tarrades

Pl Espanya 7, Lloret. Nov–March closed Mon–Thurs. Bright, moderately priced place with superb Catalan cooking; try the seafood or grilled meat specialities. The tempting starters, especially the *escalivada*, are among the best in town.

La Lonja

c/St Cristòfol 2, Lloret. Oct–March closed Mon–Thurs. Down-to-earth restaurant serving solid Catalan fare, especially seafood, with an inexpensive *menú del dia*. Also worth trying is the excellent range of tapas.

El Trull

Cala Canyelles. A splendid restaurant with a large terrace overlooking Cala Canyelles. The varied menus includes seafood, meat, pizzas and *pà amb tomàquet*, and features a daily seafood special, costing up to €42.

Zorba

c/Carme 2, Lloret. Daily 1pm–midnight; closed Nov–March. An amiable little place, with a cool blue-and-white interior terrace, serving top-notch Greek food at inexpensive prices.

Bars

Gran Café Latino

Pl Espanya 3. Daily 9pm–6am; Nov–March closed Sun–Thurs. A sumptuous mansion converted into a stylish salsa bar, with a medium-sized dance floor downstairs and a quieter gallery bar upstairs.

Hula Hula

c/Carme 34. May–Oct daily 8pm–6am; Nov–April Fri & Sat 10pm–6am.

Done up as a Polynesian fishing village, complete with bamboo, papier-mâché gods and fishing nets, this engagingly kitsch bar serves extravagant cocktails, while Latino, salsa and Spanish pop pull in a wide range of ages and nationalities.

Stones

c/Sta Caterina 11. Daily 9pm–5am; Nov–March closed Sun–Thurs. Genial bar with a large dance floor, play-ing very loud 1960s and 1970s rock classics to a broad cross-section of locals and tourists.

Clubs

Bumper's

Pl del Carme 4. Daily 9.30pm–5.30am; Nov–March closed Sun–Thurs. Popular with a young crowd looking for Caribbean, salsa, swing and pop. The garden bar, featuring palms, glass dance floor and tropical fish, is great for chilling with a cocktail.

Zoom

c/Ponent s/n. Daily 10pm–3am; Nov–March closed Sun–Thurs. Lloret's best house-only bar, a stylish factory-chic underground warehouse with no seating. Chill-out rules until 1am, after which the DJ cranks things up.

▲ LLORET: PLAÇA ESGLÉSIA WITH CHURCH

Tossa de Mar

The only medieval walled town on Catalonia's coast, Tossa de Mar was one of the first towns in Spain to be adapted for tourism, though it saw development on a much more human scale than some of its neighbours on the southern Costa Brava owing to its setting – hemmed in by the sea on one side and the Cadiretes mountains on the other. The town has a mildly bohemian air about it, a hangover from its popularity as an artists' retreat in the 1930s; Marc Chagall visited, and dubbed it "The Blue Paradise" for the clarity of sea and sky.

What really sets the place apart is its unique Vila Vella (Old Town), protected by swooping defensive walls on the rugged Cap de Tossa headland at the southern tip of the town. Neighbouring is the pretty and compact eighteenth-century Vila Nova (New Town). Although there are some lovely beaches within easy reach of the town, more impressive still are the coves to the south and, especially, north.

Vila Vella

The walled Vila Vella was started in 1186 and rebuilt in 1387. The main entrance is through the Torre de les Hores, a fortified gateway with a plaque commemorating the town charter granted by Abbot Ramon de Berga. Staircases nearby give access to walkable sections of the ramparts. A network of tiny streets, lined with whitewashed houses, snakes uphill from the

Torre de les Hores to a squat nineteenth-century lighthouse on the pine-clad summit of the headland. A path leads down to Platja Gran (see opposite) past a statue of Ava Gardner, who visited Tossa on a film-shoot in 1950, and the remains of a medieval church. Views of the bay from the ruined walls of the church are spectacular.

A narrow path leads from the Vila Vella down to Platja Es Codolar, a tiny, sheltered cove with room for sunbathing between fishing boats pulled up onto the beach.

Vila Nova

Vila Nova centres on the pedestrianized Plaça d'Espanya, a favourite meeting point for the locals. Nearby, the Església Parroquial de Sant Vicenç was originally located in Vila Vella, but was rebuilt here in 1755 as Tossa developed out of its original core on the promontory. A relatively simple Gothic

---

Visiting Tossa de Mar

The tourist office is at Avgda del Pelegrí 25 (Easter–Sept Mon–Sat 9am–8pm, Sun 10am–2pm; Oct–March Mon–Sat 10am–1pm & 4–7pm, Sun 10am–2pm; ☎972 340 108, ⓦwww.tossademar.com) and there's also an information stand (June–Sept daily 10am–2pm & 4–8pm) on Platja Gran. Boats to and from Blanes, Lloret, St Feliu and Palamós stop off at Platja Gran.

St Feliu de Guíxols & Lloret de Mar ▲

0   100 m

Bus Station

N

AVDA FERRAN AGULLO
AVDA FERRAN AGULLO

Vila Vitalis

C/GIVEROLA
C/SANT VICENÇ
C/MIRAMAR
C/TOMAS BARBER
C/SANT SEBASTIA
C/GIVEROLA
C/POLA

AVINGUDA DEL PELEGRÍ
C/MARIA AUXILIADORA
C/BERNATS
C/MARIA AUXILIADORA

C/LA GUARDIA
PLAÇA DE
L'ANTIC HOSPITAL
DE SANT MIQUEL
C/CURT

C/AMETLLERS
C/PAU MOREU
C/LA GUARDIA
C/NOU
C/OR TRUETA
C/NOU
AVDA COSTA BRAVA

C/TORRENT D'EN BOU
C/TARULL
C/ROSA RISSECH
C/SANT ANTONI
C/FRANCESC MAS I ROS
C/DOCTOR TRUETA

C/DELS TAPERS
C/ROSA RISSECH
C/ESGLÉSIA
C/SANT MIQUEL
C/JOSEP PLA
C/POU DE LA VILA

Església de
Sant Vicenç ❶
C/P. LOLA BECH
C/P. FRANCESC SERRA

C/SANT JOSEP
C/DE LES FLORS
C/ESGLÉSIA
PLAÇA
ESGLÉSIA Ⓐ
C/SANT TELM
PLAÇA
D'ESPANYA
C/DEL MAR
PASSEIG DEL MAR

VILA
NOVA
C/SOCORS
Capella
de Socors
Ⓑ

C/ESTOLI ❷
PASSEIG DEL MAR
▶ Mar Menuda

C/CLOS
C/PORTAL
Platja Gran

C/PESCADORS
C/SET
AIGÜERS

C/RIQUETA
C/PONT VELL
C/DODLAR

Platja Es Codolar ◀

Torre de
les Hores
PLAÇA
D'ARMES ❸
C/PORTAL
C/DEL TINT

Museu
Municipal
❹
VILA VELLA

Ava Gardner Statue ●

▼ Lighthouse

ACCOMMODATION	
Pensió Cap d'Or	C
Diana	B
L'Hostalet de Tossa	A

RESTAURANTS & BARS	
Can Simon	3
La Lluna	4
Mar i Cel	2
Tahiti	1

structure with a very plain altarpiece, it stands out for its beautiful Romanesque font and the sombre painting by Xavier Espinola commemorating the arrival in the bay of Sant Ramon de Penyafort, Tossa's patron saint.

The new town backs the two main beaches: Platja Gran, the domain of the body beautiful, with clear, gently shelving waters, and Mar Menuda, popular with divers and cluttered with fishing boats. At the latter, look for a natural cross of pink feldspar visible in the granite rock: legend has it that this is where Sant Ramon de Penyafort gave a dying man his absolution in 1235, upon which a flash of lightning marked the stone with the sign of the cross.

Museu Municipal

Pl Roig i Soler 1. June–Sept Mon–Fri 10am–2pm & 4–7pm, Sat & Sun

▲ TOSSA: AVA GARDNER STATUE

10am–7pm. €2.25. A local history and modern art museum, the Museu Municipal was opened in 1935 in the eighteenth-century former governor's residence. Its collection owes much to the community of artists and writers who spent their summers in Tossa in the 1930s. Must-sees are the imaginatively displayed Roman mosaic from a nearby villa and donations from Marc Chagall, including his haunting *Celestial Violinist*.

The beaches

The winding road running south and north of Tossa leads to some of the prettiest coves on the southern Costa Brava. Few are easily accessible, and so most don't get too crowded. To the south lie popular Cala Llevador, a sandy little cove, and Platja Llorell, a larger affair with watersports and *xiringuitos*. A shore-hugging footpath that connects the two leads on to a couple of idyllic beaches: Cala d'en Carles, a sandy cove, and the tiny Cala Figuera, completely unspoilt and popular for nude bathing.

Winding for 22km around 365 curves through lush pine and cork woods, and providing sudden glimpses of thrusting headlands and tiny coves down below, the corniche road north from Tossa to Sant Feliu de Guíxols is one of the most spectacular drives in the western Mediterranean. Highlights here are the stunning cliffs and turquoise waters of the Cala Futadera, a wonderfully tranquil cove (park at the belvedere just after signs to Cala Giverola and walk down). Further on, at the end of a thirty-minute walk from an impromptu car park, unspoilt Platja Vallpresona is framed by pines and sheltered by rocks, and is entirely nudist, as is the long sweep of the sandy Platja del Senyor Ramon further along.

Hotels

Pensió Cap d'Or

Pg del Mar 1 ☎ & ☎ 972 340 081. Closed Nov–March. Excellent-value, family-run place nestling under the walls of the Vila Vella. Delicious breakfasts, included in the rates, are served overlooking the sea, and the airy rooms have tranquil views of the beach. €60.

Diana

Pl Espanya 6 ☎ 972 341 886, ⊛ www. Diana-hotel.com. Closed Nov–March.

Stunning two-star hotel on the promenade, occupying a Modernista mansion built by an Indiano in the nineteenth century and featuring some superb architectural features. €131.

L'Hostalet de Tossa

Pl Església 3 ☏ 972 341 853, ⓦ www. hostalettossa.com. Very friendly, family-run hotel occupying an old building with comfortable balconied rooms. Great buffet breakfast. €68.

Campsites

Pola

Cala Pola ☏ 972 341 050. Closed Nov–April. In a pretty cove off the corniche road to the north; pitches are more expensive the closer you get to the sea.

Restaurants

Can Simon

c/Portal 24. By far the best, and one of the most expensive, of the string of restaurants on the edge of the Vila Vella, serving great *mar i muntanya* dishes and fabulous home-made desserts.

La Lluna

c/Abat Oliva s/n. Closed Nov–March. An excellent restaurant, serving only tapas and set in an atmospheric old building in one of the Vila Vella's narrow climbing streets. You can cobble together an inexpensive meal from the selection chalked on the board and wash it all down with a local wine.

Bars and clubs

Mar i Cel

c/L'Estolt 4. Popular with all ages, this small bar has a lively atmosphere and serves a good range of cocktails in its cool interior garden.

Tahiti

c/St Josep 28. Popular with a local crowd, *Tahiti* plays live music most nights in the summer and has a decent selection of cocktails.

PLACES · Tossa de Mar

▼ TOSSA: PLATJA ES CODOLAR

Sant Feliu de Guíxols and Platja d'Aro

Linked by a busy stretch of road and steadily growing into each other, the towns of Platja d'Aro and Sant Feliu de Guíxols could hardly be more different. A working fishing port and one-time cork manufacturing town, Sant Feliu de Guíxols is the faded grande dame of the Costa Brava. There's a lot of old money here, plus a striking blend of Indiano and Moorish-style architecture and restaurants that are famous throughout Catalonia for their quality. Neighbouring Platja de Sant Pol boasts genteel hotels, while the wealthy residential enclave of S'Agaró was built in the 1920s as a Modernista utopia, attracting the rich and famous.

Platja d'Aro, on the other hand, consists of a neon strip of bars and shops separated from its beach by a mishmash of high-rise apartments and leafy Mediterranean suburbia: if you're looking for somewhere quiet or picturesque, then this isn't the place for you. What Platja d'Aro does offer is excellent nightlife, a beautiful three-kilometre beach and some great shopping. At either end of the main strip of sand is a string of delightful coves, which are much quieter, even in the height of summer. Inland, Platja d'Aro's parent town, Castell d'Aro, hides a tiny and charming medieval heart.

Sant Feliu de Guíxols

Nowhere is Sant Feliu's old-world style more apparent than in the mansions lining the broad seafront Passeig del Mar. The most striking is the *Casino dels Nois* café, built in 1899 in Moorish style with brightly coloured swooping arches and windows; it's now the favourite haunt of elderly domino players and office workers lingering over afternoon coffee. The promenade is transformed during the impressive Catifa de Flors ("Carpet of Flowers") on the feast of Corpus Christi in June, when it's decorated with thousands of flower petals, arranged in bright patterns. Along with

Visiting Sant Feliu de Guíxols

Buses from Girona stop on Plaça del Monèstir in front of the tourist office (same times as the City History Museum; ☎972 820 051, ⊕www.guixols.net). The spectacular GI682 corniche road north of Tossa de Mar enters town by the monastery, while the southbound C253 arrives at the northeast end of the beach. There's metered parking on the seafront and car parks near the tourist office. Boats arrive on the beach from all points south as far as Blanes and north as far as Palamós.

Festival Internacional de la Porta Ferrada

From July to September every year, Sant Feliu hosts the Festival Internacional de la Porta Ferrada, featuring world music, theatre and dance. Performances are staged in the Teatre Municipal or the Monastery Church, while a range of free open-air concerts takes place on the seafront and around town. The tourist office has full information and tickets (€10–36).

Plaça del Mercat, the promenade is also the venue for Sant Feliu's weekly fair, held every Sunday since the fifteenth century.

The town's history is reflected in the different ages and styles of its monastery. Much of it lies in ruins and is open to the elements, but the better preserved buildings house a museum, and you can also visit the church. The complex's most prominent exterior features are the Porta Ferrada, a horseshoe-shaped Romanesque facade which dates from the ninth and tenth centuries, and the ornate Baroque Arc de Sant Benet, built in 1747, standing alone in front of the monastery.

Built in the fourteenth and fifteenth centuries on the site of an earlier Romanesque construction, the church (daily 8–11am) has a broad Gothic nave and three polygonal apses, crowned by beautifully intricate keystones. Within the monastery, the Museu d'Història de la Ciutat (City History Museum; July & Aug daily 10am–2pm & 4–8pm; Sept–June Tues–Sat 10am–1pm & 4–7pm, Sun 10am–2pm; €3.60) houses an exhibition on Sant Feliu's cork industry and archeological finds discovered in the monastery.

Ideal for lazing after a spot of sightseeing, Platja de Sant Feliu is backed by genteel, shady gardens; it's not usually crowded and the gently shelving waters make it good for families.

Platja de Sant Pol

Separating Sant Feliu from the S'Agaró headland to the north of the town is the sweeping expanse of Platja de Sant Pol. As wide as it's deep, the crescent-shaped, sandy bay offers good swimming in its protected waters, while a string of smart hotels and restaurants along the uncluttered seafront makes it an ideal, relaxing base for exploring the area.

S'Agaró

The dreary main road of shops and restaurants linking Sant Feliu de Guíxols with Platja d'Aro gives little hint of the delight that lies in store at S'Agaró, an attractive village

▼ SANT FELIU: PORTA FERRADA

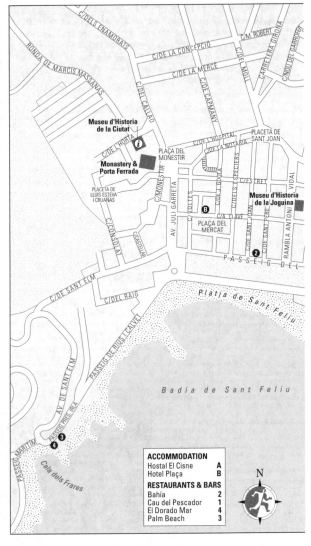

boasting many fine examples of Modernista architecture.

Tucked away on a headland 2km northeast of Sant Feliu, S'Agaró was created in the 1920s by Josep Ensesa Gubert as a community of seaside villas for the wealthy, and the design of all the mansions was entrusted to Rafael Masó, the architect responsible for many of Girona's most attractive buildings. An inn, *Hostal de La Gavina*, originally intended for guests of residents, quickly found itself playing host to the

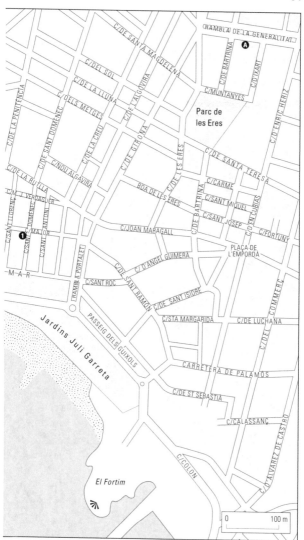

likes of Charlie Chaplin, Orson Welles, Bogart and Bacall and, later, Ava Gardner and Frank Sinatra, and became the Costa Brava's first five-star hotel.

Visitors' cars aren't allowed into S'Agaró (there's a free car park outside), making a wander through the quiet streets a pleasure. Don't miss the nearby stretch of the Camí de Ronda (see p.190), which gently snakes along the shoreline here and leads to the area's loveliest beach, Cala Sa Conca, also accessible by car from the Platja d'Aro road. The gently curving beach is cleft by a craggy outcrop: the northern side is less busy and better for snorkelling, the bigger southern side prime swimming territory.

Platja d'Aro town centre

Platja d'Aro's main drag, formed by Avinguda S'Agaró and Avinguda Cavall Bernat, offers some of the region's best shopping, with big-name designer clothes stores and some classy local establishments. Most are open all year and have extended summer hours (daily 10am–2pm & 5–10pm).

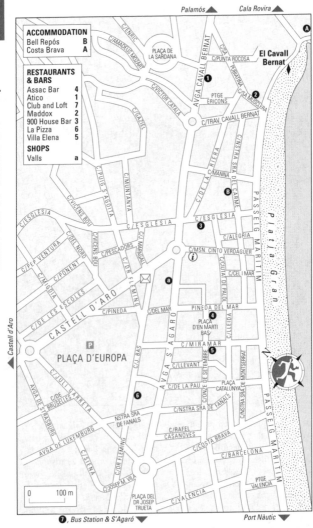

ACCOMMODATION
Bell Repós   B
Costa Brava   A

RESTAURANTS & BARS
Assac Bar   4
Atico   1
Club and Loft   7
Maddox   2
900 House Bar   3
La Pizza   6
Villa Elena   5

SHOPS
Valls   a

0   100 m

Palamós · Cala Rovira · El Cavall Bernat · Platja Gran · Castell d'Aro · Port Nàutic · Bus Station & S'Agaró

▲ SANT POL: MODERNISTA HOUSE ON SEAFRONT

properly excavated and saved, and what little remains has been laid out as a public area with seating.

Platja Gran

Almost the entire length of Platja d'Aro's beach is backed by an uneven toothy grin of high-rise blocks, interspersed with some older low-rise buildings, fronted by a pedestrianized promenade with terraces and restaurants. The sweep of coarse golden sand, shelving moderately steeply into clear water, sees families and firm-bodied clubbers working on their tans. The southern tip of Platja Gran, marked by the chic Port Nàutic and capped by the Punta de Pinell headland, gets slightly less crowded.

At the northern end of the Platja Gran, three incongruous-looking nineteenth-century villas are a reminder of how the town has changed, while 100m further on is the huge standing stone known as El Cavall Bernat, the backdrop to free summer jazz concerts. Its name came into use in the sixteenth century as a euphemism for the original Carall Bernat, thought to mean "revered phallus" ("carall" is Catalan for "phallus").

Platja d'Aro's northern beaches

North of Platja d'Aro, the Camí de Ronda footpath dips and

As evening suffuses into night, the pavement cafés become a popular spot for an aperitif and some prime people-watching. Later into the night a hedonistic crowd moves in, as the stylish, laid-back bars and thumping discos get going.

Every February, the same streets play host to one of the Costa Brava's best Carnival processions, with floats and extravagant fancy-dress parades accompanied by revelry all weekend long.

On the northern edge of town is Ciutat de Palol, a small square that was the site of a wine- and oil-producing Roman villa, in use between the first century BC and the seventh century AD. Badly neglected during the tourism boom, it has now been

Platja d'Aro activities

Thrill-seekers in Platja d'Aro will enjoy a helicopter flight along the spectacular shoreline with Turisvol, at Camping Riembau (☎972 817 123), while more leisurely excitement is to be had with a balloon ride over the Baix Empordà by L'Empordanet (☎972 641 550); both cost around €140. Several operators along the seafront and in the Port Nàutic offer a range of watersports, while the Escola Municipal de Vela (☎972 818 929), in the port, is the place for windsurfing and kayak rental. Divers have several options, including Amfos Sub d'Aro, Avgda Cavall Bernat 4 (☎972 828 212), which runs courses and offers equipment rental. Aquadiver, Ctra Circumval. lació (☎972 818 732), is a water park on the northwestern edge of town with slides and chutes. You can enjoy a leisurely round of golf at the eighteen-hole Golf d'Aro course (☎972 826 900), set on the Mas Nou hill overlooking the coast, or opt for Pitch & Putt Platja d'Aro, in Les Suredes (☎972 819 820), 1.5km west of town on the road to Castell d'Aro.

climbs for 4km, from the northern end of the Platja Gran along the water's edge as far as Sant Antoni de Calonge, offering paths down to some beautiful beaches. A number can also be reached by footpaths off the C253 road towards Palamós, which has roadside parking.

The first you come to is the attractive, busy Cala Rovira, originally the Roman port for the area. It's also known as Cala dels Escalencs after the fishing families from L'Escala, who – until the advent of tourism in the 1950s – used to spend their summers here camped on the beach, fishing the waters and selling their catch in Sant Feliu de Guíxols. A terrifically colourful and emotive *festa* to mark this history takes place on the first weekend after the Diada holiday (Sept 11), when dozens of traditional Vela Llatina boats make the journey from L'Escala and families camp on the beach in makeshift shelters for two days of traditional crafts, havaneres and cremat.

Neighbouring Cala Sa Cova offers a gently shelving beach and safe bathing up to a clearly defined line of underwater rocks, and its pretty setting amid pines helps you to overlook the number of people. Smaller and more inviting is Cala del Pi, 200m further north along the Camí de Ronda; its underwater rocks and craggy point make it perfect for snorkelling. A long tunnel separates this from Ses Rodones de Terra, where stone steps lead down through clumps of bamboo to a rugged mosaic of boulders and beach, a favourite with nude bathers.

Further along the footpath, Cala Belladona is less busy than its neighbours, and you'll find good snorkelling and swimming a long way out into the steeply shelving sea. Finally, Platja de Can Cristus, most easily reached from the road, has a good sandy beach, but can get crowded owing to the presence of two large campsites nearby.

Castell d'Aro

Charming narrow streets and ancient houses form the medieval core of Castell d'Aro, perched on a small hill above the main road. Set on a small square is the solid Gothic-style Església de Santa Maria, built in 1784 and sporting a facade as simple as its interior. Near the main door, an octagonal font from 1670 harks back to an earlier building on this site.

Most of the chapels are plain plaster or stone, except for two on the right of the door, which have highly intricate murals of the Ascension.

Next to the church, the restored Castell de Benedormiens looks as though it's grown out of the rock. Built in the eleventh century, it was burnt in 1462 and then destroyed by an explosion in 1879, after which it was left to moulder until restoration last century. Little of the original structure remains, although excavations in the old moat are turning up some finds, including many relating to an iron-working industry in the area. Its three floors house changing free art exhibitions.

During the last weekend of August, Castell d'Aro's church square and surrounding streets host a medieval market, with traditional crafts and food on sale and music played by troubadours.

Hotels

Bell Repós
c/Verge del Carme 18, Platja d'Aro ☏972 817 100, ☏972 816 933. Closed Oct–May. This family-run hotel is set on a quiet side road, very close to the centre and beach. Most of the airy rooms give onto an inviting garden and have balconies. Discount offers in June and September. €56.

Hostal El Cisne
Rambla Generalitat 11, Sant Feliu de Guíxols ☏972 324 810. Simple but modern and comfortable *hostal* in the centre of Sant Feliu and with a reasonable restaurant. €45.

Costa Brava
Punta d'en Ramis 17, Platja d'Aro ☏972 817 308, ⊛www.hotel costabrava.com. Closed Nov–Feb. Opened in the 1920s as a restaurant, this became the Baix Empordà's first beach hotel, perched on a low cliff. It's a charming place, with oak beams and marble balustrades. €116.

La Gavina
Pl de la Rosaleda s/n, S'Agaró ☏972 321 000, ⊛www.lagavina.com. A byword in Spain for opulence, this thoroughly sumptuous hotel, with oak beams and light stone, is also famous for the quality of its restaurant and the splendour of its headland setting and facilities, including the huge pool on the low cliff-edge. €295.

Mas Tapiolas
Veïnat de Solius, Santa Cristina d'Aro ☏972 837 017, ⊛www.euro-mar.com. A converted mansion in lush gardens outside Platja d'Aro, with forty exquisite rooms and an expensive, extremely good modern Catalan restaurant. €198.

▼ S'AGARÓ: CALA SA CONCA

Hotel Plaça

Pl Mercat 22 ☎972 325 155, ⓦwww. hotelplaza.org. Modern hotel in the lively market square with a relaxing rooftop terrace and air-conditioned rooms. The pleasant family who own it take pride in the smallest detail. €100.

Hotel Sant Pol

Platja de Sant Pol s/n ☎972 321 070, ⓦwww.hotelsantpol.com. Closed Nov. Friendly, family-run sea-front hotel, with an excellent restaurant and large, modern balconied rooms, some featuring Jacuzzis. €105.

Shops

Valls

Avgda S'Agaró 8, Platja d'Aro. A rambling and well-stocked Aladdin's cave of a department store, this classy one-stop shop has a very good selection of brand-name clothes, sports goods and toys.

▼ CASTELL D'ARO: CASTELL DE BENEDORMIENS

▲ PLATJA D'ARO: CAVALL BERNAT STANDING STONE

Restaurants

Bahía

Pg del Mar 17–18, Sant Feliu de Guíxols. One of the oldest and most famous seafood restaurants in the area, with a plush summer terrace. It does succulent traditional dishes and an especially good *pica-pica* menu for starters. Prices are moderate and the *menú del dia* at €12 is excellent value.

Cau del Pescador

c/St Domènec 11, Sant Feliu de Guíxols. Closed Tues & Jan. Atmospheric restaurant in an old fisherman's house serving terrific fish and seafood caught locally, all at very reasonable prices.

El Dorado Mar

Passeig Irla 15, Sant Feliu de Guíxols. Closed Wed & Nov. A legendary Art Deco restaurant founded in 1971 by a local man, who subsequently set up similar restaurants in Barcelona and New York. The food is superb and based around imaginative and succulent variations on local seafood and fresh fish dishes. Eating à la carte is expensive, but the *menú del dia* is very reasonable.

La Pizza

Pl Europa 21, Platja d'Aro. Daily noon–midnight; Nov–March closed Mon–Thurs. This smart but reasonably priced Italian restaurant is in an arcade connecting the main drag with Plaça Europa. Its pizzas and sweet and savoury crêpes are the best in town, served in an unhurried atmosphere.

La Taverna del Mar

Pg de Sant Pol 11, Sant Pol. Closed Tues & Dec. With a fabulous terrace overlooking the beach at Platja de Sant Pol, this expensive 1930s restaurant has a top-notch seafood platter and lobster stew.

Villa Elena

c/Onze de Setembre 3, Platja d'Aro. A popular, moderately priced restaurant in an old mansion with a pleasant terrace. It specializes in Catalan and international cuisine, and has superb fish, pasta and rice, as well as excellent *patates d'Olot* (baked potatoes stuffed with meat).

Bars

900 House Bar

c/Església 54, Platja d'Aro. 8pm–3am. This stylish, minimalist bar is the only all-out house bar in Platja d'Aro and draws a lively young crowd, who make this their last stop of the night.

Assac Bar

c/Pineda de Mar 22, Platja d'Aro. 8pm–3am. Catering mainly for twenty- and thirty-somethings, this lively terrace bar in a large house is a popular starting point for the night's entertainment or as a late-night cool-down, and serves good *chupitos* to thumping rhythms.

Clubs

Atico

Avgda Cavall Bernat 114, Platja d'Aro. 9pm–5am. This stylish club, located in a cellar despite its name, has a broad age appeal, reflected in the eclectic tastes in music and the even more eclectic crowds milling around the door from 2am onwards.

Club & Loft

Avgda S'Agaró 120, Platja d'Aro. 10pm–5am. Three-floored club, with the denizens of the more frenetic *Club* and the smoother *Loft* coming together for a breather on the open-air *Terrace*.

Maddox

c/Sa Musclera 1, Platja d'Aro. 11pm–5am. By day a swimming pool with a terrace bar serving snacks, this beachside venue becomes a six-bar club at night, spread over two floors – one for a younger house crowd and the other for an older salsa crowd. Overheated dancers can enjoy a midnight swim in the pool.

Palm Beach

c/President Irla 1, Sant Feliu de Guíxols. Haunt of the trendy and affluent, this club has a roster of DJs to keep the young crowd happy with ambient, jungle, techno house and trip-hop.

PLACES Sant Feliu de Guíxols and Platja d'Aro

▲ ERMITA DE SANT ELM OVERLOOKING THE BAY AT SANT FELIU

Palamós and Sant Antoni de Calonge

Palamós is a thriving and energetic town which, thanks to its flourishing fishing and cork industry, has a life of its own, independent of tourism. Its neighbour, Sant Antoni de Calonge, is an old fishing village steadily redefining itself as a holiday town. It's almost becoming an extension of Palamós, as new low-rise buildings spread inexorably along its coast; the development though is agreeably low-key and the town is endowed with a fine beach.

Northeast of Palamós lie the popular La Fosca beach and beautiful S'Alguer. Equally appealing is Platja Castell, a little further north, crowned by the atmospheric ruins of an ancient Iberian settlement.

Palamós

In its medieval heyday Palamós was a thriving royal port; its strong fortifications, however, were useless against the Turkish pirate Barbarossa, who ferociously sacked the town in 1543, an event vividly described by Cervantes in *La Galatea*.

A section of the old medieval sea wall survives today and marks the boundary of the old quarter, a bustling knot of pedestrianized streets centred on Plaça Major, full of upmarket clothes shops, organic food stores, pavement cafés and some extremely good restaurants.

Just south of here lies the small quarter of Sa Planassa, buzzing with stylish, laid-back terrace bars and restaurants, where you're fairly unlikely to hear any language other than Catalan. To the east is the marina, a busy leisure port by day and hot spot by night, to which the younger, smart set from Sa Planassa adjourn after midnight.

In the working port, the small Museu de la Pesca (mid-June to mid-Sept Tues–Sun 10am–9pm; mid-Sept to mid-June Tues–Sat 10am–1.30pm & 3–7pm, Sun 10am–2pm & 4–7pm; €3) presents a surprisingly fascinating history of fishing in the region, told from an environmental viewpoint. The museum manages to hold your interest through numerous artefacts, models of techniques still in use, and videos, such as those showing the daily lives of four fishermen. Pride of place goes to a precarious-looking long liner fishing boat built in 1920.

Visiting Palamós

The informative tourist office (Mon–Fri 9am–2pm & 5–8pm; ☎972 600 500, ⊛www.palamos.org) is at Passeig del Mar 22, and there's also an information kiosk (Easter–Oct Mon–Sat 10am–2pm & 4.30–7.30pm, Sun 10am–2pm) near the corner of Passeig de Mar and Avgda Onze de Setembre.

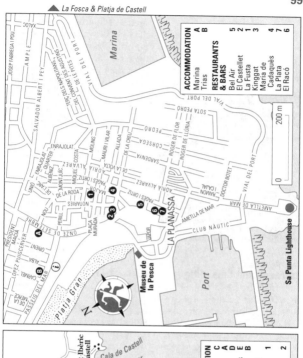

▲ *La Fosca & Platja de Castell*

ACCOMMODATION
Marina	A
Trias	B

RESTAURANTS & BARS
Bel Air	5
El Castellet	2
La Fusta	1
Kingqat	3
Maria de Cadaqués	4
La Plata	7
El Racó	6

0 — 200 m

Sa Punta Lighthouse

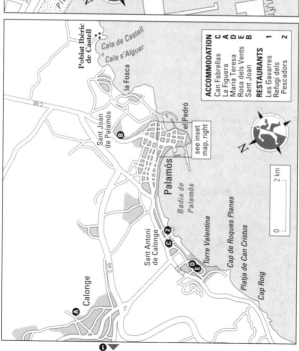

ACCOMMODATION
Can Fabrellas	C
La Figuera	A
Maria Teresa	D
Rosa dels Vents	E
Sant Joan	B

RESTAURANTS
Les Gavarres	1
Refugi dels Pescadors	2

0 — 2 km

▲ SANT ANTONI DE CALONGE: CALA MURTRA

La Fosca and Cala S'Alguer

Accessible by car (5min), or on foot (20min) via the Camí de Ronda, the lovely golden sand and gently shelving water of the bay in La Fosca have conspired to make it one of the most popular beaches in the area with upmarket second-homers, but it still doesn't ever feel too crowded. A ten-minute walk east follows the shore past the ruins of the Castell de Sant Esteve to the even prettier Cala S'Alguer, rarely crowded and backed by hundred-year-old fishermen's huts, now converted into beach cabins.

Platja de Castell and Cala Estreta

Platja de Castell became a local cause célèbre in the 1990s when a popular referendum saved it from development into a tourist resort. The clear waters of the sheltered half-moon cove and the broad expanse of glittering sand are no secret, so don't expect to have it to yourself.

Platja de Castell is separated from S'Alguer by a five-minute stretch of footpath running near the Mas Juny mansion, built by the artist Josep Maria Sert with the proceeds of a commission to paint the murals in New York's Waldorf Astoria hotel; Philip Leacock's *The Spanish Gardener* (1957), starring Dirk Bogarde, was filmed almost entirely at the house.

Perched on the headland bounding Platja de Castell to the north and visited by surprisingly few people are the atmospheric ruins of the Poblat Ibèric de Castell, an Iberian settlement dating from the sixth century BC. The site has been excavated in earnest only since 2000 and ninety percent of it is still to be discovered. Uncovered so far is a series of terraces guarded by the remains of two defence towers and crowned by an acropolis where a temple would have stood.

An arduous but beautiful stretch of the Camí de Ronda (1hr to Cala Estreta) – or a dirt track accessible to cars – leads from Platja de Castell to a string of secluded crystalline coves, popular with nude bathers, ending at Cala Estreta, a trio of pretty sandy coves with mixed clothed and nude bathing where you can normally find plenty of space for swimming in the steeply shelving water.

The best – and sometimes the only – way to visit some of the more secluded coves along the way is to rent a kayak at Platja de Castell and paddle there yourself.

Sant Antoni de Calonge

Sant Antoni de Calonge is not particularly picturesque, but it has good-value accommodation and benefits from a pretty beach on its doorstep and even more enticing coves a short walk

Visiting Sant Antoni and Calonge

The tourist office at Avgda Catalunya s/n, St Antoni (Mon–Fri 9am–2pm & 4.30–7pm, Sat & Sun 10am–2pm; ☎972 661 714, ✆www.ajcalonge.org), has information about Sant Antoni de Calonge and Calonge. There's also an information stand in the car park in Calonge (July–Sept Mon–Sat 10am–2pm & 4–8pm, Sun 10am–2pm).

away. Palamós is within walking distance, and the fleshpots of Platja d'Aro are a bus or taxi ride away if you fancy a break from the quiet family atmosphere of Sant Antoni.

The dusty approaches to Sant Antoni are indicative of the number of new constructions going up, and the stylish new promenade, with angled street lamps and decking, is a further sign of transition from fishing town to holiday haven. The fine beach can get a little crowded; its southern end, known as Torre Valentina after a watchtower that still stands in the gardens of nearby plush apartment blocks, is the preserve of sculpted sun-worshippers.

Sant Antoni's southern coves

The rugged Camí de Ronda leads from Sant Antoni past Torre Valentina to a string of delightful coves, most of which are reached by stone steps from the trail. All with iridescent turquoise waters, the first four are ideal for swimming and snorkelling among the rocks; the first, Cala Murtra, is protected by the Roca Grossa island, popular as a goal for swimmers. Rocky promontories and sandy inlets lead past these to the larger Cala del Forn and Platja de Can Cristus; both are very pretty and offer good swimming, but since they are the nearest

to a string of campsites on the main road and also have *xiringuitos*, they are correspondingly busier. An enjoyable way of exploring the coves is by kayak, which you can rent at Platja de Can Cristus.

The Camí de Ronda continues south from here, ending up in Platja d'Aro, although note that the route between Platja de Can Cristus and Platgeta de l'Ermita is a particularly treacherous clamber over slippery rocks and past thorns.

Calonge

Some 3km inland, Sant Antoni's medieval parent, Calonge, makes for an enjoyable morning's stroll. The best time to visit is Thursday morning, when the weekly market packs the narrow streets. The town

▲ CALONGE: PARADE GROUND OF CASTLE

is dominated by a Gothic castle, currently being restored and entered through a pair of imposing towers on Plaça Major. The courtyard boasts superb acoustics and makes the perfect setting for a fun jazz and classical music festival in July and August. The castle is rivalled in grandeur by the nearby Església de Sant Martí, a Baroque structure built on an earlier tenth-century site. Inside, remains of the original construction are visible in the north wall.

La Cova d'en Daina

Sitting on the brow of a hill, around 10km west of Sant Antoni de Calonge, the megalithic tomb of La Cova d'en Daina exudes an overwhelming calm. The only sounds you're likely to hear as you approach the four-thousand-year-old burial chamber along an avenue of cork oaks are birdsong and

the soughing of the wind in the trees.

Thought to have been built between 2200 and 1700 BC, the site was discovered in 1894 and excavated in the 1920s by local archeologist Lluís Esteva Cruañas, who unearthed human bones and teeth, flint arrowheads, knife and pottery fragments and necklace beads. Thanks partly to having been partially reconstructed in 1956, the cromlech and tumulus are still clearly defined, as are the access and burial chamber proper. The entrance to the tomb is oriented to the southeast, which allows sunlight to reach the interior on the summer and winter solstices, presumably in accordance with religious beliefs.

Hotels

Pensió Can Fabrellas

c/Vermell 25, St Antoni de Calonge ☎972 651 014. Closed Oct–April. An unprepossessing building on the road parallel to the seafront hides a very pleasant *pensió* with a decent restaurant and a quiet patio garden, run by an amiable family. Rooms are basic but comfortable and all have balconies. €42.

La Figuera

Urb Mas Pere, Calonge ☎972 660 523, ⓦwww.lafiguera.com. Sumptuous hotel and restaurant in the hills, with great views of the coast. Choose between rustic rooms in the fourteenth-century house or modern decor in the annexe. Rooftop pool and Jacuzzi. €170.

Maria Teresa

Pg Mundet 3, St Antoni de Calonge ☎972 651 064, ⓕ972 652 110. Closed Nov–March. A pleasant,

▼ CHURCH IN SANT ANTONI DE CALONGE

family-run seafront establishment. The large, en-suite, balconied rooms give onto the beach or the interior garden, while the restaurant serves fine traditional food. €81.

Marina

Avgda Onze de Setembre 48, Palamós ☎972 314 250, ⓦwww .hotelmarina-palamos.com. This friendly, central hotel set around a tiny courtyard is excellent value for money and is a two-minute walk from the beach as well as the shopping and nightlife areas. €65.

Rosa dels Vents

Pg Mundet s/n, St Antoni de Calonge ☎972 651 311, ⓕ972 650 697. Closed Oct–April. Comfortable place overlooking the beach near Torre Valentina, offering spacious bedrooms, most with balcony, and a relaxing bar and terrace. €125.

Sant Joan

Avgda Llibertat 79, Palamós ☎972 314 208, ⓦwww.hotelsantjoan.com. A twenty-minute walk from the centre, this lovely hotel in an eighteenth-century *masia*, with pool and garden, is great value for money. The rooms are old-fashioned but attractive and very spacious. €94.

Trias

Pg del Mar, Palamós ☎972 601 800, ⓦwww.hoteltrias.com. Closed Oct–March. Delightful hotel on a shaded part of the promenade offering genteel charm with service to match, plus an excellent fish restaurant, free parking for residents and a heated pool.

▲ ROMANYÀ DE LA SELVA, CHURCH DOORWAY

All the large, solidly furnished rooms have balcony and air conditioning. €162.

Restaurants

La Fusta

c/Mauri Vilar 11, Palamós. A cheerfully decorated interior and bustling terrace in a tiny old-town street provide the setting for appetizing, economical Catalan meals.

Les Gavarres

Romanyà de la Selva. A rambling restaurant with a tranquil terrace in a tiny hamlet, serving superb *mar i muntanya* food and offering a great wine list, making the trek out worthwhile.

Maria de Cadaquès

c/Tauler i Servià 6, Palamós ☎972 314 009. Closed Mon & Dec–Jan. Founded in 1936 as a fishermen's tavern, this is one of the most famous, and busiest, restaurants in Catalonia. Superb local fish and seafood at commensurate prices are served in a wood-beam interior hung with artworks.

El Racó

Pl St Pere 1, Palamós. Part of a chain that now extends to Barcelona and Madrid, this is the original *El Racó*, a stylish and friendly place serving an imaginative fusion of Italian and Catalan cuisine at moderate prices. Vegetarians are well catered for.

Refugi dels Pescadors

Pg Mar 55, St Antoni de Calonge. Friendly, traditional seafood restaurant serving good-quality Catalan dishes at reasonable prices.

Bars

Bel Air

c/Onze de Setembre s/n, Palamós. Favoured by a younger crowd, this lively, unassuming bar is reached by a flight of steps from Sa Planassa and has a spectacular view over the port and beach from an upper-floor picture window.

El Castellet

c/Onze de Setembre 81, Palamós. Signed photos of George Harrison and a small tribute to Brian Jones give some idea of the age and provenance of this, the oldest, bar in Palamós, which used to attract a hippy crowd from all over Europe. Much less esoteric these days, it's still a curiosity for the wonderfully kitsch decor and for its location in what was once the sea wall.

Kinggat

c/Notaries 32, Palamós. Atmospheric bar in an old fisherman's house between the church and Sa Planassa. Downstairs is dominated by the different types of music – from salsa to techno – filling the standing-only room, while upstairs is more for chatting leisurely under the wooden beams.

La Plata

Pl St Pere 11, Palamós. Dominated by a soaring, thirty-metre-high back wall, the ground floor of this superb bar at the end of Sa Planassa is given over to dancing, while the subtly lit, roofless upstairs floor is perfect for a mellow drink.

Palafrugell and its beaches

A busy market town, Palafrugell is the parent town of three of the most beautiful villages on the coast – Calella, Llafranc and Tamariu. All three have embraced tourism without being swamped by it. Each has its own distinct character: Calella, the largest of the three, has a more relaxed charm than refined Llafranc, while Tamariu is a haven of gentility.

Palafrugell

The bustling, commercial town of Palafrugell harbours a compact and delightful nineteenth-century quarter. The charming pedestrianized streets all lead to the central Plaça Nova, where you'll find congenial terrace bars to help you relax after the rigours of a morning's shopping and exploring. This same square and the adjacent streets overflow every Sunday morning with the Costa Brava's liveliest market.

Much of the town's history is linked to cork production, chronicled in the small but engaging Museu del Suro (Cork Museum; mid-June to mid-Sept daily 10am–2pm & 4–9pm; mid-Sept to mid-June Tues–Sat 5–8pm, Sun 10.30am–1.30pm; €1.50), at c/Tarongeta 31. Displays illustrate how cork is formed, while an exhibition of nineteenth-century machines and panels sheds light on how the raw material was worked. There's also an exhibition of cork sculptures, from altarpieces to abstract art.

Calella de Palafrugell

Low-key development in a perfect natural setting of rugged shoreline and clear waters has helped make Calella de Palafrugell one of the most enjoyable towns on the Costa Brava: it has succumbed neither to the mass tourism of the south nor to the near-snobbish exclusivity of some of its smaller neighbours to the north. Its necklace of tiny coves set against a backdrop of whitewashed arches and early twentieth-century houses attracts holiday-makers seeking peace and quiet with a hint of luxury.

Most of the action revolves around a number of thoroughly charming beaches. The first, Port-Bo, a Blue Flag, coarse-sand beach strewn with fishing

Festes de Primavera

Traditionally regarded as a strongly independent town, nowhere is Palafrugell's spirit better exemplified than in its Festes de Primavera (Spring Fair). This exuberant celebration, held on the last weekend in May, was invented in 1962 to get round Franco's prohibition of Carnival throughout Spain, and has survived him to become one of the liveliest events in the local calendar, featuring a procession, live music and *sardanes*.

Visiting Palafrugell and its beaches

Palafrugell's tourist office is beside the church on Plaça Església (May–Sept Mon–Sat 10am–1pm & 5–8pm, Sun 10am–1pm; Oct–April Mon–Sat 10am–1pm & 4–7pm, Sun 10am–1pm; ☎972 611 820, ⊛www.palafrugell.net). There's a smaller information office at c/Carrilet 2 (same hours except July & Aug Mon–Sat 9am–9pm, Sun 10am–1pm; ☎972 300 228).

In Calella, the office is in an old fishermen's hut at c/Voltes 6 (July & Aug daily 10am–1pm & 5–9pm; April–June, Sept & Oct Mon–Sat 10am–1pm & 5–8pm, Sun 10am–1pm; ☎972 614 475), while Llafranc's is on c/Roger de Llúria (same times as Calella; ☎972 305 008). Tamariu's tourist office is on c/Riera (June–Sept Mon–Sat 10am–1pm & 5–8pm, Sun 10am–1pm; ☎972 620 193).

In summer, buses run on a circuit from Palafrugell to Calella and Llafranc roughly every 30min in July & Aug, dropping to every 45min in early June & late Sept, when there's also a lunchtime gap (12.30–3.30pm). Four buses a day serve Tamariu (late June to mid-Sept only). Pick up timetable information at tourist offices or the Sarfa bus company (c/Torres Jonama 73–79, Palafrugell).

boats, is backed by a tiny square with terrace cafés. Neighbouring Calau, separated by a craggy rock, lies at the foot of white-washed arches and is protected by a flotilla of small pleasure boats moored in the crystalline waters. Also winner of a Blue Flag is Canadell, with its promenade of nineteenth-century villas. At the north end of the cove, stone steps lead up to the Camí de Ronda footpath, which rounds the point by the *Hotel La Torre* and meanders 1km along an undulating pine-clad path to Llafranc.

South of Calau and separated from it by a finger of rock, sheltered Port Pelegrí is favoured by divers and boaters, but also makes for some great

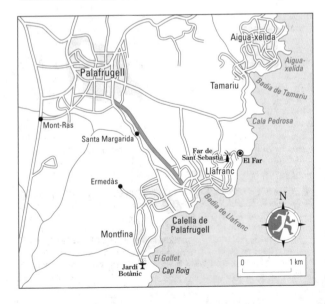

bathing. This is the last sandy cove before a one-kilometre stretch of indented coastline to El Golfet; most of it can be followed along the serpentine Camí de Ronda, which starts after the *Hotel Sant Roc* and swoops up and down along the water, revealing secluded rocks and handkerchiefs of sand. At the southern end, the sheltered El Golfet cove is half-hidden at the foot of a steep, winding flight of steps, its deep waters overlooked by pines clinging tenaciously to the cliff.

Jardí Botànic Cap Roig

Daily 9am–8pm; winter closes 6pm. €2.20. The enchanting Jardí Botànic Cap Roig, a series of themed gardens laid out on terraces around a modern castle, were begun in 1927 by Nicolai Woevodsky, an exiled colonel from the army of Nicholas II of Russia, and his aristocratic English wife, Dorothy Webster, and combine his interest in architecture with his wife's passion for archeology and gardening. The gardens consist of cypress-lined terraces, bougainvillea, yellow sage and oleander, and arches wreathed in scented flowers. Hidden away are small seating areas offering views of the crisp blue sea beyond. The best views are from the cactus garden, where the towering cacti watch over a small offshore archipelago, Les Illes Formigues (Ant Islands), and Mirador de la Lady (Lady's Belvedere), which looks out towards the white arches and coves of Calella.

▲ PALAFRUGELL: STREETS IN THE OLD QUARTER

At the gardens' centre stands the castle, a solid, twin-turreted building with an elaborate fifteenth-century doorway rescued from a ruin. It's not open to the public, but the square in front of it is the location every summer for a prestigious open-air jazz festival (information and tickets from the tourist office).

Llafranc

Set in a half-moon bay, Llafranc is more genteel than its neighbour and has an exclusive air, boasting more yachts and restaurants than shops or bars. It tends to be the domain of second-homers and discerning tourists seeking tranquillity and fine cuisine in splendid surroundings.

The focus of town is the stylish Passeig Cipsela, the ideal place for an aperitif and the setting for the evening *passeig*. The fine golden sands of the sheltered

PLACES Palafrugell and its beaches

Havaneres

Port-Bo beach manages to accommodate upwards of 40,000 spectators on the first weekend in July for the thronging Havaneres festival, when sea shanties are sung from boats in the bay.

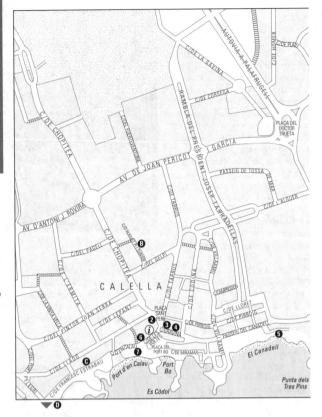

Blue Flag beach attract no short-age of sunbathers in the height of summer.

The southern end of the short seafront is marked by modern buildings and a narrow road; follow this northwards and, beyond the popular meeting place of Plaça Promontori, you'll see grand early twentieth-century villas, some adorned with Modernist decoration and balconies. Behind Plaça Prom-ontori, on calle Coral, are the remains of a Roman wine press.

At the northern end of the beach are the yachts and dinghies of the Port Nàutic. From the port, steps lead up to the Passeig

Carles Vilà for the calf-aching climb through winding residen-tial streets to the Far de Sant Sebastià lighthouse, where you'll be treated to some breathtaking views of the coastline and out to sea. Behind the *El Far* hotel is the tiny excavated area of an Iberian settlement, Sant Sebastià de la Guarda, and the enticing start of a section of the GR92 footpath, which becomes steadily more gruelling as it snakes inland through pine woods as far as the cliff edge near Tamariu (90min).

Tamariu

The smallest and quietest of Pala-frugell's satellite villages, Tamariu

ACCOMMODATION

Casamar	A
Mediterrani	C
Port-Bo	B
Sant Roc	D

RESTAURANTS & BARS

La Bella Lola	3
La Gavina	4
Gelpi	7
Habana Café	2
Llevant	1
Tango	6
El Tragamar	5

is rather modest in the way that only the very wealthy can be. It's more a spot in which to relax than to sightsee, and everything is focused on the small seafront. The promenade – lined with tamarinds, source of the town's name – has a subtle, unhurried charm, populated by Catalan children scampering around the feet of their well-to-do parents. The seafront is a jumble of small shops, pavement restaurants and houses, where elderly locals sit outside on wicker chairs chatting. The coarse sand of

Llafranc activities

To explore the stunning coves and caves either side of Llafranc, you can rent kayaks and motorboats from Tourist Service, c/Cipsela 1 (☎972 301 748), or take an excursion with Barracuda, based in the port (☎607 871 213), which uses boats and inflatable dinghies to explore the most inaccessible caves between Palamós and Begur. The area north of Llafranc is popular with divers, owing to the spectacular Els Ullastres underwater mountains and trench, but you should dive only when accompanied by a reputable instructor; in Llafranc, Snorkel, Avgda del Mar s/n (☎972 302 716), and Triton, Pl dels Pins (☎972 302 426), offer courses and excursions.

▲ CALELLA: ARCADED HOUSES ON SEAFRONT

the Blue Flag beach, sheltered by the high walls of the cove, is frequented by young Catalan families and only a few foreigners.

A short distance north past the restaurants, a paved footpath ends at the tranquil, rocky Cala d'Aigua Dolça, popular with evening strollers and anglers. The coves beyond here are inaccessible by foot or car, but the area around Foralló d'Aigua Xelida, a rock standing off the neighbouring Punta d'Esguard point, is very good for diving, as it's riddled with caves and features the submerged mountain of Llosa de Cala Nova. Less well known than other dive sites on the Costa Brava, the area is still relatively untouched. Divers can explore the area around Foralló

d'Aigua Xelida with the English-speaking outfit, Stolli's, Pg del Mar 26 (☎ & ℻972 620 245, ⓦwww.stollis–divebase. de; Easter–Oct).

Cala Pedrosa

The rugged inlets carved out of the shoreline between Tamariu and Llafranc – including the pretty and secluded Cala Pedrosa, 1km south of Tamariu – are most easily reached by boat. Paco Boats (☎607 292 578) rents out small motorboats from the beach; it takes about half an hour to reach Cala Pedrosa in one of these. Kayaking Costa Brava, also on Tamariu beach (☎972 773 806, ⓦwww .kayakingcb.com), rents kayaks and organizes excellent guided excursions to Cala Pedrosa and other hidden coves and caves in the area; especially atmospheric is their moonlight trip to the coves north of Tamariu.

An alternative is to head to the area on foot. The Camí de Ronda sets off from the southern corner of Tamariu beach and skirts the cove before climbing up to the treeline. The route from here hugs the cliff-edge to Cala Pedrosa (1hr away); the rocky terrain is treacherous in parts and you should only attempt it if you're a confident hiker and reasonably agile. At Pedrosa, the trail turns inland through less spectacular scenery as far as Llafranc's Far de Sant Sebastià (a further 30min away).

Hotels

Casamar

c/Nero 3, Llafranc ☎972 300 104, ℻972 610 651. Perched halfway up a flight of steps on the south

▲ CALELLA: NINETEENTH-CENTURY HOUSES ON PLATJA CANADELL

▲ LLAFRANC: LIGHTHOUSE

side of the cove, this place won a Catalan government quality award and has fabulous views over the beach and port from its terrace bar and bright, superb-value rooms. €82.

El Far

Far de Sant Sebastià, Llafranc ☎972 301 639, ✉hotelfss@intercom.es. Closed Jan. This tranquil eighteenth-century inn offers vast panoramas over the sea from its perch near the lighthouse on Llafranc's northern headland. The sumptuous rooms have air conditioning and spacious balconies. €140.

Hostal Plaja

c/St Sebastià 34, Palafrugell ☎972 610 828, ⊛www.hostalplaja.com. Oozing old-world charm, this town-centre *hostal* has large, comfortable rooms and is considerably cheaper than hotels by the beach. €50.

Mediterrani

c/Francesc Estrabau 40, Calella ☎ & ☎972 614 500, ⊛www .hotelmediterrani.com. Closed Sept–April. Overlooking the sea and very central, this old-fashioned hotel is good value, with airy rooms and friendly staff. €98.

Port-Bo

c/August Pi i Sunyer 6, Calella ☎972 614 962, ⊛www.hotelportbo.com. Closed Oct–Feb. Excellent value for money, about 200m from the sea, this hotel is run by very pleasant and helpful staff and has huge rooms; the price includes a copious buffet breakfast. €98.

Sant Roc

Pl Atlàntic 2, Calella ☎972 614 250, ⊛www.santroc.com. Closed Dec–Feb. This plush hotel's fabulous clifftop location affords it splendid views over the town and beaches. All rooms are well equipped and extremely comfortable, most with terraces. €110.

Tamariu

Pg del Mar 2, Tamariu ☎972 620 031, ⊛www.tamariu.com. Closed Dec–Feb. A fishermen's tavern in the 1920s and still in the same family, the Tamariu has an excellent seafood restaurant and seventeen large rooms, all beautifully furnished and some with sea views; pricier penthouses have large terraces. €150.

Shops

La Serra

Pl Nova, Palafrugell. Very helpful and charming wine shop with an impressive selection of Spanish and foreign wines at a wide range of prices.

▲ TAMARIU: EARLY EVENING ON THE SEAFRONT

▲ TAMARIU

PLACES

Palafrugell and its beaches

Restaurants

La Bella Lola

Pl Sant Pere 4, Calella. Daily noon–midnight; Oct–Easter closed Mon–Thurs. A lively restaurant and bar specializing in tasty *pà amb tomàquet* meals with hams, cheeses and salads. It's popular with the Havaneres crowd: the occasional impromptu singalongs are fun.

La Gavina

c/Gavina 7, Calella. Daily 7.30pm–midnight; Oct–Easter closed Mon–Thurs. One of the Costa Brava's most enjoyable Catalan restaurants, equally pleasant in the summer on the shaded terrace as in the winter in front of the open fire. The friendly owners serve superb *pà amb tomàquet* meals, freshly caught fish and char-grilled meats – all at prices that won't break the bank.

Llevant

c/Francesc Blanes 5, Llafranc ☎972 300 366. A seafront hotel with a busy terrace, well known locally for its moderately priced, generous fish and seafood dishes. Particularly appetizing is the pickled anchovy salad in cava sauce.

Pa i Raïm

c/Torres Jonama 56, Palafrugell ☎972 304 572. Just nine tables in the old living rooms of a former private house, this swanky restaurant serves a small selection of superb Catalan cuisine.

Tango

c/Voltes 8, Calella. Oct–Easter closed Mon–Thurs & Fri lunch. A small, reasonably priced Catalan restaurant, popular with a stylish crowd and serving excellent food, primarily fish, rice and vegetables.

El Tragamar

Pg del Canadell s/n, Calella. Easter & July–Sept daily noon–midnight; rest of year closed Tues and Mon, Wed & Thurs noon. Beautifully located on a stone walkway at beach level below the Canadell promenade, this smart, moderately priced establishment serves imaginative, modern Catalan cuisine, including exquisite fish.

Xerinola

c/Riera 23, Tamariu. Set well back from the sea, and consequently slightly cheaper than its seafront rivals, the *Xerinola* serves rice, pasta and local dishes on its comfortable terrace.

La Xicra

c/Sant Antoni 17, Palafrugell. Closed Tues pm & Wed. Excellent *mar i muntanya* fare at reasonable prices in this neighbourhood favourite.

Bars

Gelpí

c/Voltes 11, Calella. A popular, friendly establishment right on tiny Calau beach, serving the best *cremat* in Catalonia and perfect for a spot of wistful gazing out to sea.

Habana Café

Plaça Sant Pere, Calella. Inviting terrace café, albeit without the backdrop of the sea. It's very laid-back and attracts a cosmopolitan crowd.

Begur and its beaches

Nestling in the shadow of a ruined castle on a verdant headland 6km northeast of Palafrugell, the medieval hilltop town of Begur makes a great base for exploring the Baix Empordà region. Its narrow, history-steeped streets are home to a wide range of excellent bars and restaurants, not to mention exclusive shops, while nearby are some tranquil and stylish beaches, linked to each other by some stunning sections of the Camí de Ronda.

Plaça de la Vila

The heart of Begur is Plaça de la Vila, the venue for the Wednesday market, as well as *sardanes* most Saturdays in the summer, starting at 10.30pm. A smattering of terrace bars, which fill up during the early evening, occupy one side of the square, while a stone ledge known as Es Pedrís Llarg ("The Long Stone"), running the length of the adjacent church wall, has been used as a shaded meeting place and people-watching spot for as long as the church has been standing.

The simple lines of the seventeenth-century Església Parroquial de Sant Pere, renovated in 1996, belie its Gothic interior. A second nave parallel to the first was built in the eighteenth century in place of four side chapels and dedicated to Begur's co-patron saint, Santa

Reparada. In a side chapel to the right, a simple alabaster statue of the *Madonna and Child*, sculpted by Francesc Fajula in 1985, provides a pleasant contrast to the busy altarpiece, which depicts St Peter holding the keys to heaven.

From the square radiates a warren of charming pedestrianized streets, which achieved fleeting Hollywood fame when Elizabeth Taylor filmed a few short scenes in the town for her 1959 film, *Suddenly Last Summer*.

Castell de Begur

Built in the eleventh century, Castell de Begur was devastated twice by the French and subsequently rebuilt, being finally destroyed in 1810 by Spanish troops. The ruins that remain are scant testimony to such an eventful history, but the gentle climb up to the low walls is

Visiting Begur

It's best to leave your car in one of the clearly marked car parks near the old town. Buses stop by the Sarfa ticket office, within the Ribera bookshop at Pl Forgas 6 (☎972 622 446). From Easter to October, buses run from Pl Forgas in Begur to neighbouring beaches: to Sa Riera (daily 10am–8pm on the hour; 15min), and to Fornells and Aiguablava (daily 10.30am–7.30pm on the half-hour; 15–20min).

All the beaches are accessible via well-signposted roads from Begur, and while some are connected to each other by road or the Camí de Ronda, you'll occasionally have to trek back up to Begur to cross between beaches.

The helpful tourist office is at the rear of a small courtyard, Avgda Onze de Setembre 5 (June–Sept daily 9am–3pm & 5–9pm; Oct–May Mon–Fri 9am–2.30pm, Sat 10am–2pm & 5–8pm, Sun 10am–2pm; ☎972 624 520, ◉www.begur.org).

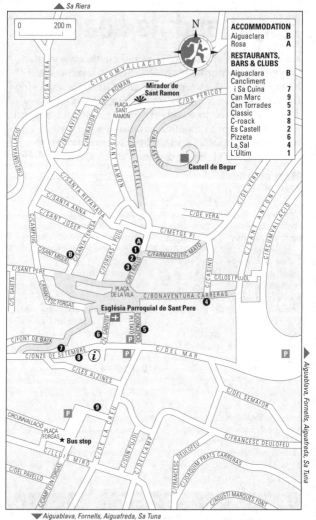

ACCOMMODATION

| Aiguaclara | B |
| Rosa | A |

RESTAURANTS, BARS & CLUBS

Aiguaclara	B
Cancliment i Sa Cuina	7
Can Marc	9
Can Torrades	5
Classic	3
C-roack	8
Es Castell	2
Pizzeta	6
La Sal	4
L'Últim	1

Aiguablava, Fornells, Aiguafreda, Sa Tuna

worth it for the spectacular views as far north as Cap de Creus. As you look north, the Gavarres mountains come into alignment with the hilltop castle of Torroella de Montgrí and the small escarpment at L'Estartit to create the illusion of a figure lying on its back; some see

a pregnant woman, others a sleeping bishop.

At the foot of the castle nestles the Mirador de Sant Ramon, where a tiny chapel stands on a low point offering equally impressive views out to sea. First documented in 1605, it was razed to the ground during the Civil War and rebuilt as an exact replica in 1951.

Aiguablava

The beautiful cove of Aiguablava shelters in the lee of the headland on which stands the Parador d'Aiguablava (see p.116). Popular with a chic local crowd, the sandy Blue Flag beach shelves quite steeply and offers fabulous views of neighbouring Fornells and the pine-covered hills. Overlooking the beach are a couple of *xiringuitos* and an excellent seafood restaurant (see p.118).

Fornells

Overlooked by fine villas and the luxury *Hotel Aiguablava* (see p.116), the minuscule beach of exclusive Fornells is more popular with yachters than bathers. For somewhere more secluded with better bathing, follow the Camí de Ronda north from Fornells (15min) until you come to a long, steep staircase winding down to the almost virgin Platja Fonda at the foot of a steep cliff; the swimming here in the deep water is wonderful.

Sa Tuna

One of the prettiest and most interesting beaches on the Costa Brava, Sa Tuna nestles in a small, steep-sided cove with a pebble beach and deep waters best suited to strong swimmers. With its picturesque jumble of old and new houses descending through pines to the beach, it's popular with a local crowd but seldom gets uncomfortably busy.

Sa Tuna's beauty is matched by its colourful history. A ruined watchtower on the northern headland bears witness to the damage wrought by General Doyle and his Spanish troops when they stormed the town in the war against the French. In more peaceful times, Sa Tuna became popular with Indianos returning from the Americas to Spain; their distinctive mansions – a blend of traditional and Modernista style – set amid the low, pine-clad hills on the water's edge, have contributed to the genteel and uniquely characterful ambience of the town today. More reluctant visitors were the crew of a French steamship carrying a cargo of hats which ran aground on the rocks at the entrance to the cove; for years after, the townspeople did a roaring trade in headgear.

Aiguafreda

With no beach to speak of, the sheltered inlet of Aiguafreda is more popular with boating people and divers than swimmers. Diving courses, equipment

▲ BEGUR: PLAÇA DE LA VILA

▲ BEGUR: CAP DE BEGUR

rental and excursions are offered by Gym Sub, Ctra Aiguablava km3.6 (☎972 622 659, ☺www .gymsub.com), and Sa Rascassa, beside the small jetty in Aigua-freda (☎972 624 247); the latter also has kayaks for rent.

By walking the thirty minutes to Aiguafreda on the Camí de Ronda from Sa Tuna, you'll pass the pretty and uncrowded Cova des Capellans (Chaplains' Cove), a secluded inlet where priests used to bathe in privacy.

Sa Riera

The largest of Begur's beaches, Sa Riera retains its fishermen's quarter on the south side of the sandy, Blue Flag beach. Backed by a short row of cafés and a couple of hotels, the beach is popular with local families, though rarely gets packed. It's signposted off the Sa Tuna road, or you can follow a spectacular but arduous stretch of the Camí de Ronda from Aiguafreda (1hr).

From the north end of the beach, steps take you on to a much gentler part of the Camí de Ronda, which is the only way to get to the minuscule and almost empty beaches between Sa Riera and the Platja de l'Illa Roja, 500m away, an idyllic

nudist beach framed by steep cliffs. The red island which gives the beach its name is, in fact, joined to the mainland by a short spit of sand. Next door to this is the longer sweep of Cala Moreta, with nude and clothed bathing plus a *xiringuito*.

Hotels

Aiguablava

Platja de Fornells ☎972 622 058, ☺www.aiguablava.com. Closed Dec & Jan. Plush hotel set in shady gardens right on the water's edge, with a seawater pool and tennis courts. The sumptuous rooms all have terraces giving onto the garden or the sea. €151.

Parador d'Aiguablava

Platja d'Aiguablava ☎972 622 162, ☺www.parador.es. The Costa Brava's only *parador* – the highest class of Spanish hotel – is a modern building set on the rugged headland overlooking the beach. It has a gym with sauna and an open-air pool, and the huge rooms, each with their own terrace, give onto the open sea or the coves of Aiguablava and Fornells. €126.

Aiguaclara

c/St Miquel 2, Begur ☎972 622 905,
ⓦwww.aiguaclara.com. Simple
luxury in a nineteenth-century
Indiano mansion close to the
centre, this beguiling hotel has
just two suites and six rooms
and a superb restaurant. €110.

Hospedería El Convent

c/del Racó, Sa Riera 2 ☎972 623 091,
ⓦwww.conventbegur.com. Set amid
pines on the road to Sa Riera,
and committed to sustain-
able tourism, this lovely hotel
occupies a seventeenth-century
former convent and makes a
relaxing base for exploring the
area. €135.

Hostal Sa Rascassa

Cala d'Aiguafreda 3 ☎972 622 845.
Closed Nov–Easter. This beautiful
old house a minute's walk from
the protected inlet of Aiguafreda has five peaceful, stylishly
decorated en-suite rooms and an
excellent restaurant. €95.

Hotel Sa Riera

Platja Sa Riera ☎972 623 000, ☎972
623 460. Closed Nov–Feb. Friendly
place set back from the beach,
with a good pool and pleasant restaurant. The simple but
stylish air-conditioned rooms,
all en suite, are large and
shaded. €74.

Hotel Rosa

c/Pi i Ralló 11, Begur ☎972 623 015,
ⓔhotelrosa@hotmail.com. Closed
Dec–Feb. Very hospitable hotel
in a lovely old building just off
the main square and far more
comfortable than its rates might
suggest. The rooms, with air
conditioning and hydromassage
bathrooms, are excellent value.
€69.

Hostal Sa Tuna

Platja de Sa Tuna ☎ & ☎972 622
198, ⓦwww.hostalsatuna.com. Closed
Oct–March. This welcoming *hostal*
on a tiny beach is deservedly
famous for its excellent seafood
restaurant. Its five tranquil
en-suite rooms have been refurbished, and all but one have a
seafront terrace. €130.

Apartments

AVI

Urb Residencial Begur 33–34 ☎972
622 505, ⓦwww.avi-inmobiliaria.
com. Agency with a decent
selection of villas and apartments for rent and sale in and
around Begur.

PLACES Begur and its beaches

▼ VIEW FROM AIGUABLAVA TO FORNELLS

▲ SA TUNA: VIEW OF COVE

Restaurants

Aiguaclara

c/Sta Teresa 3, Begur. ☎ 972 622 905. Daily 8–11pm. Set in an Indiano mansion, this is one of the priciest restaurants in town, known locally for its seafood. In summer, the walled garden provides an enchanting, torch-lit setting for an unhurried dinner, while the high-ceilinged interior is nice and bright.

Cancliment i Sa Cuina

Avgda Onze de Setembre 27, Begur. Closed June–Sept Mon; Oct–May Mon & Tues. This simple-looking, reasonably priced restaurant

▲ AIGUAFREDA: COVA DELS CAPELLANS

serves hugely imaginative dishes based on traditional local cuisine and prepared by a young chef rapidly making a name for himself.

Can Torrades

c/Pi i Tató 5, Begur. Daily 8pm–midnight; closed all Oct & Nov–April Mon–Thurs. For excellent, moderately priced, traditional Catalan cooking, follow the bright young things past the art gallery anteroom into the warmly lit stone courtyard of this deceptively large old house off Plaça de la Vila.

Es Castell

c/Pi i Ralló 5, Begur. In the modern interior of this old building you'll find a great variety of tapas and wines for a cobbled-together meal; inexpensive, although the price can mount up with your appetite.

Mar i Vent

Platja d'Aiguablava. Mon–Fri 8.30–11pm, Sat 1–3.30pm & 8.30–11pm, Sun 1–3.30pm; Oct–May closed Mon–Thurs. A sumptuous garden restaurant atop a staircase above the beach. The quality of the Catalan cuisine, including outstanding seafood, fish, rice and local cheeses, matches the high prices.

Pizzeta

c/Ventura Sabater 2–4, Begur. Daily 8pm–midnight; closed Jan & Feb. An unprepossessing entrance leads into a surprisingly large, colonial-style garden. Further pleasures are in store with the superb quality of the inexpensive, wide-ranging and imaginative Italian cuisine.

▲ AIGUAFREDA

Sa Rascassa

Cala d'Aiguafreda 3. Closed Nov–March. This old stone house with a shaded garden 50m from the beach serves imaginative variations on traditional Catalan cooking and offers a good choice for veggies.

Sa Tuna

Platja de Sa Tuna. Closed Oct–March. This lovely terrace restaurant on the beach is something of an institution and serves extremely good fish and seafood and solid Catalan fare, including some veggie dishes, all at reasonable prices.

Bars

Classic

c/Pi i Ralló 3, Begur. Daily 8pm–3am; Nov–March closed Mon–Thurs. This unusual nightspot – which claims, thankfully without apparent foundation, to be a karaoke bar – occupies the first-floor rooms of an old mansion, decorated in Indiano style.

C-roack

Avgda Onze de Setembre 7, Begur. Daily 8pm–3am; Nov–March closed Mon–Thurs. This lively bar has a lovely ramshackle terrace for late-night drinks enjoyed by a cosmopolitan crowd.

La Sal

c/Bonaventura Carreras 21, Begur. Daily 9pm–3am; Nov–March closed Mon–Thurs. A popular, trendy bar set apart from the main action in an old building on a street off Plaça de la Vila; it gets busy around midnight.

L'Últim

c/Pi i Ralló 13, Begur. Daily 9pm–3am; Nov–March closed Mon–Thurs. The last breathless stop in a short street heaving with bars and restaurants, this small place still has room for three areas. Behind the main bar is a terrace with an enormous Gothic font, while to the side is a dark dance floor, playing mainly house, with dimly discernible erotic art on the walls.

Clubs

Can Marc

c/Creu 5, Begur. Easter–Oct daily midnight–5am; Nov–March Fri & Sat 11pm–5am. Begur's only club, set in a lovely old building with a large garden overlooking the town and castle. Catering for all ages, it plays a mix of house and disco, while the garden's three bars are popular for chilling out.

Pals, Peratallada and Ullastret

The attractive medieval towns of Pals, Peratallada and Ullastret, set close together on the fertile Empordà plain between Begur and inland La Bisbal, can easily be toured in a day. The hilltop settlement of Pals was destroyed during the Civil War, and then painstakingly restored after 1948 by a local doctor in a thirty-year labour of love. The town's successful restoration has won it numerous architectural awards and attracted many wealthy second-home owners and day-trippers; the down side is that it can feel a bit like a showcase town. Some 5km away is its extensive beach, Platja de Pals, a modern, low-key development, good for bathing and watersports.

The medieval walled town of Peratallada, 6km west of Pals, has managed to preserve its rustic charm, but is no sleepy backwater, its labyrinth of narrow streets and squares full of craft shops and fine restaurants. The town is a great place for a pleasant stroll followed by a good meal, and its collection of charming hotels also makes it a good base from which to explore the whole Baix Empordà.

Further inland lies Ullastret, a peaceful walled town atop a low hill. Although it's an enjoyable

place for a stroll or a meal, its chief appeal lies in its proximity to the Poblat Ibéric d'Ullastret, a ruined Iberian settlement.

Pals

Pals is very compact and you can take in everything of interest in a couple of hours. To see it at its liveliest, arrive before lunch or in the late afternoon, when the craft and pottery shops are open.

On the main street into the old town is the intriguing Museu-Casa de Cultura Ca La Pruna, c/La Mina (Tues–Sat 10am–1pm & 5–7.30pm, Sun 10am–1pm; €1.50), a museum of local history, with exhibits on wine and cava production, a collection of offshore archeological finds, and

▼ PALS: VIEW OVER TOWN

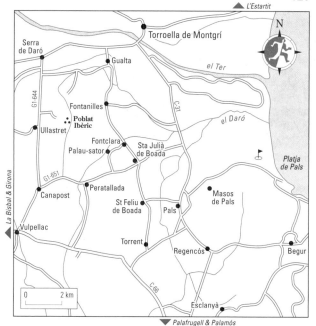

a small re-creation of an eight-eenth-century pharmacy.

The hub of the town is the Plaça Major, 100m northeast of the museum, home to craft shops and a café. From here atmospheric Carrer Major climbs uphill; pre-second-century-AD Visigoth graves were discovered here during Pals' restoration, and their shallow, boat-like shapes are clearly visible in alcoves set into house walls. Almost at the top of this rise is the architec-tural mishmash of the Església de St Pere, built using stones from the ruined castle that once stood here. The site of the church was first documented in 994, and the current build-ing has a Romanesque layout, with a fifteenth-century Gothic apse and nave, and an ornate Baroque facade topped by an eighteenth-century belfry. It's strangely austere inside, with an intricate vaulted ceiling framing a simple altar.

Visiting Pals

There's plenty of parking at the entrance to the medieval town and by Platja de Pals. In July and August, four buses a day run between Pals and Platja de Pals (€1.80).

The tourist office (June–Sept Mon–Sat 10am–2pm & 4–8pm, Sun 10am–2pm; Oct–May Mon–Sat 10am–2pm & 4–7pm, Sun 10am–2pm; ☎972 667 857) is by the roundabout on the north side of town at c/Aniceta Figueres 6 and is a good source of information on Pals and the region. There's a smaller branch in the town hall, Plaça Major 7 (Easter & June–Sept Mon, Tues & Thurs–Sun 10am–2pm & 4–8pm, Wed & Sat 9am–9pm; ☎972 637 380).

▲ PERATALLADA: PLACA DE LES VOLTES

Above the church rises the eleventh-century Romanesque Torre de les Hores clock tower. Some 50m north of here, a section of the old medieval walls survives; at a small gap in the walls, the minuscule Mirador de Josep Pla affords great views towards the offshore marine reserve of Les Illes Medes.

Platja de Pals

The golden sands of the Platja de Pals extend for 3.5km around the sweep of a bay. It's popular with a sporty set and can get crowded, but if you're prepared to walk 100m or so in either direction you'll usually find quieter areas. The beach shelves fairly gently and the sea is very good for swimming. Stands along the length of the beach rent out windsurfing equipment and kayaks. The red-and-white masts that frame the beach are all that is left of Radio Liberty, a US station that broadcast propaganda to the Eastern bloc during the Cold War.

Peratallada

Peratallada (which means "hewn stone") is separated from the outside world by a shallow moat carved out of the rock. In its medieval heyday, it was one of Catalonia's best-protected towns, with a defensive system comprising three ranks of walls, parts of which are still visible from the main road that runs around the town.

A good place to start a tour of the town is the lively Plaça de les Voltes with its low porticoes, terrace bars and craft shops. Adjacent is the larger Plaça del Castell, on which stands the Castell de Peratallada, the ancient palace of the Barons of Peratallada; the atmospheric ruins of the Torre d'Homenatge dels Cavallers (Knights' Homage Tower), a five-storey tower with dungeons, refectory and defences, are currently closed, and whether they re-open or not depends on the new owners. From July to September, both Plaça de les Voltes and Plaça del Castell host Saturday crafts and produce markets.

Outside the walls and across the main road to the northeast of the town is the thirteenth-century Romanesque Església de Sant Esteve, remarkable for its imposing facade with four bells. It's rarely open outside

▲ PERATALLADA: FACADE OF ESGLESIA DE SANT ESTEVEST ESTEVE

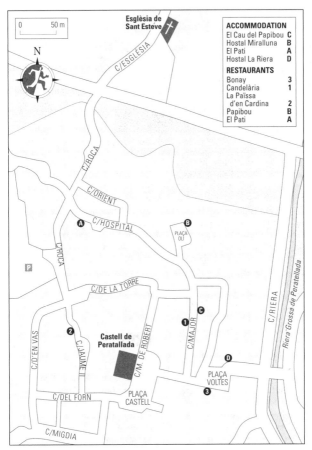

ACCOMMODATION

El Cau del Papibou	C
Hostal Miralluna	B
El Pati	A
Hostal La Riera	D

RESTAURANTS

Bonay	3
Candelària	1
La Païssa d'en Cardina	2
Papibou	B
El Pati	A

services, but it's worth getting in to see the unusual double nave and the Gothic ossuary in the north nave, dated 1348 and containing the bones of Gilabert de Cruïlles, lord of Begur.

Ullastret

A burgeoning crafts centre, full of potters and artists, Ullastret makes for a pleasant half-day's wandering among the maze of shops around the central Plaça de l'Església. This is the venue for the town's lively Festa Major on the second weekend

in August and site of the eleventh-century Església de Sant Pere, a charming Romanesque church adorned with an elaborate Baroque facade. Parts of the original Romanesque facade were re-used inside, such as for the bases of the arches – one is carved with a lion, another with mermaids.

Poblat Ibéric d'Ullastret

Tues–Sun: Easter & June–Sept 10am–8pm; Oct–May 10am–2pm & 3–6pm. €1.80. Parking at the base of the hill and near the main entrance (drive

▲ ULLASTRET: VIEW OVER PLAIN, FROM THE MUSEUM

through the first gate past the ticket booth). Sited amid olive groves and cypresses atop the Puig de Sant Andreu, the Poblat Ibéric d'Ullastret (signposted 3km east of the medieval town) is the most significant and extensive settlement in Catalonia of the Iberians, considered Spain's earliest civilization: they had their own system of writing – as yet undeciphered – and money, as well as agriculture, metallurgy and pottery. The Ullastret settlement, located in what is thought to have been the heartland of the Indiketa tribe, was populated between the sixth and second century BC; there's still a great deal left to unearth, including a second site 500m across the plain, which probably formed part of the same settlement.

Running north from the entrance, the sixth-century-BC walls, the oldest and one of the largest Iberian defences in Catalonia, are punctuated with seven circular towers. Some 50m from the gate there's a newer square tower, at the base of which traces of a stairway from an earlier round tower are visible. The most striking feature of the settlement is its modern-looking layout: you can easily make out the streets, including a beautifully preserved cobbled roadway leading to a water cistern, flanked by the foundations of rectangular houses.

Outside the museum, at the top of the hill, you can discern the outlines of two temples; it's still not known which gods were worshipped here.

The superbly laid-out site museum chronicles the history of the settlement and uses finds to explain Iberian life. The most fascinating exhibits are some lead tablets marked with writing, recording commercial transactions, along with coins for trading with other tribes and – more gruesomely – the skulls of victims of ceremonial execution, pierced by spikes. You can pick up a free returnable booklet, containing an English translation of the display panels, at the entrance.

Hotels

El Cau del Papibou

c/Major 10, Peratallada ☎ & ☏ 972 634 018, ✉ peratallada@hotelcau.net. A small, friendly hotel with just seven stylishly decorated rooms grouped around an interior patio in an old house; it also has a very good restaurant. €100.

Hostal Miralluna

Pl de l'Oli 2, Peratallada ☎ 972 634 304, ⊛ www.hostalmiralluna.com. A thoroughly charming private hotel in an eighteenth-century house set back from the street. All six rooms, including two suites, are individually and beautifully designed, though its main attraction is the splendid tranquillity of its carefully tended garden. €135.

El Pati

c/Hospital 13, Peratallada ☎ 972 634 069, ⊛ www.hotelelpati.net. A tastefully decorated hotel in an eighteenth-century mansion near the church. All five rooms give onto a sunken garden, with hammocks and loungers, and breakfast (included in the price) is served beneath fig trees and bougainvillea. €120.

Sa Punta
Platja de Pals ☎972 636 410, ⓦwww.hotelsapunta.com. Sumptuous blend of traditional and modern, with airy rooms and terraces set around a swimming pool and gardens, a short walk from Pals beach. €140.

Hostal La Riera
Pl de les Voltes 3, Peratallada ☎972 634 142, ⓕ972 635 040. A friendly hotel occupying a seventeenth-century building under the arches at the entrance to the village. The huge rooms give onto a private garden. €60.

Turisme rural

Can Pere Ni
Barri Bernagar 7, Masos de Pals ☎972 636 116, ⓦwww.ruralplus.com/can-pereni. A private house between Pals and the beach, offering fifteen comfortable double rooms around a swimming pool. A peaceful base for exploring the area. €36.

Restaurants

Bona Vista
c/Muralla 5, Pals. Closed Mon & Jan. One of the very few options in Pals, this terrace restaurant in an old house in the town walls north of Plaça Major serves excellent local rice dishes and desserts at moderate prices.

Bonay
Pl de les Voltes 13, Peratallada. Closed Mon & Nov. This antiques-cluttered restaurant, founded in 1936, specializes in Catalan cooking at reasonable prices, with some *mar i muntanya* dishes, and is good for game in winter. Don't miss the mouthwatering dessert buffet.

Candelària
c/Major 9, Peratallada. July–Sept daily 8pm–midnight; Oct–June Fri–Sun 8pm–midnight, plus Sat 1–4pm; closed Feb. A slightly surreal cavern, with dried corn and St John's Wort – Salvador Dalí's favourite flower – hanging from the ceiling and a hotchpotch of mirrors and paintings cluttering the walls. The pricey dishes are imaginative and delicious.

La Païssa d'en Cardina
c/Jaume II 10, Peratallada. Mon–Fri 7pm–12.30am, Sat & Sun 1–4pm & 8pm–12.30am; Nov–March closed Wed & Thurs. A superb and moderately priced Italian pizzeria with a hugely stylish interior and terrace. There are 33 different pizzas, complemented by an imaginative choice of fresh pasta, salads and grilled vegetables.

Papibou
c/Major 10, Peratallada. Closed Wed. Inexpensive restaurant serving Empordà cuisine in a subtly lit stone-vaulted interior or on the cosy terrace off the street. Interesting selection of cod specialities.

El Pati
c/Hospital 13, Peratallada ☎972 634 069. Nov–March closed Mon–Thurs. Even more inviting than the eighteenth-century interior is the lush, shaded garden at this restaurant, specializing in traditional Catalan fare. Some veggie options, too.

Central Baix Empordà

County seat of the Baix Empordà, the medieval town of La Bisbal is famous for its distinctive ceramics, produced here since the seventeenth century; visitors come from all over the region to buy ceramic ware and antiques from a string of outlets in the new town. The old town's main draws are the imposing and beautifully preserved Castell Palau de La Bisbal and a seventeenth-century bridge spanning the River Daró.

Lying 6km northwest of La Bisbal, the enchanting and peaceful medieval village of Monells is perfect for an afternoon's wander or a longer stay at one of its small hotels.

Nearby Púbol is the site of the castle that Salvador Dalí bought and renovated for his Russian wife Gala and that he himself lived and worked in for a couple of years after her death in 1982; the Castell Gala-Dalí is now a museum, affording a fascinating insight into the couple's life together.

Accommodation in La Bisbal is limited, but the outlying area has more than its fair share of picturesque villages with exceptional restaurants and some very enticing hotels.

La Bisbal's Barri Nou

The new part, or Barri Nou, of La Bisbal is divided into two and connected by a road bridge. To the northwest lie all the ceramics shops, most of which offer similar stock, although you'll also find some contemporary variations on traditional designs and methods, as well

▲ LA BISBAL: OLD BRIDGE

as good-quality tableware and ornaments.

If you're taken by the ceramics and want to discover more, the fascinating Museu Terracota (July–Sept Mon–Sat 10am–1pm & 5–9pm, Sun 10am–1pm; €3), c/Sis d'Octubre 99, is a must. Housed in a cavernous building – a former factory dating from 1922 – the museum offers an engaging insight into La Bisbal's ceramic and tile-making

Visiting La Bisbal

The small but informative tourist office is inside Castell Palau de La Bisbal on Plaça Castell (Easter–Sept Tues–Sat 10.30am–1.30pm & 4.30–8.30pm, Sun 10.30am–1.30pm; Oct–March Mon–Fri 5–8pm, Sat 11am–2pm & 5–8pm, Sun 11am–2pm; ☏972 645 166, ⊛www.labisbal.org).

La Bisbal ceramics

The characteristic colours of La Bisbal pottery are blues, greens and mustards. Traditional items include plates depicting the winds as points on a compass, tiles portraying traditional trades, and the "auca", a framed and painted tile showing crafts such as winemaking or baking.

industry, tracing its development from early manual techniques to the machine methods of the 1930s. The tiles exhibited range from purely artistic works to functional domestic and industrial wares, and a variety of moulds is displayed along with the fiendishly complicated machinery used to create them.

La Bisbal pottery was popular with Modernista architects, and a display of prototypes for constructions built by Rafael Masó shows how traditional materials were adapted to create the distinctive Modernista style.

Huge brick kilns and glass floor inserts showing the colourfully tiled underground *nevera* (fridge), where clay was stored to keep it malleable, serve as a reminder that this was once a busy working factory.

The area on the other side of the bridge is home to a variety of antiques shops selling all manner of objects, from two-thousand-year-old amphorae and medieval doors to petrol pumps and dentures.

La Bisbal's Barri Vell

La Bisbal's compact old town has been host to a Friday market since 1322 and was once the home of an important Jewish quarter, the sole remnant of

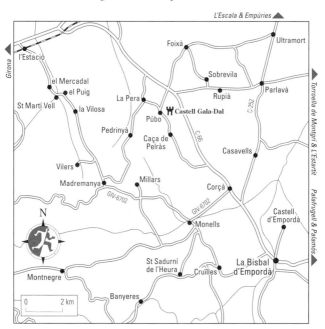

which is the rather drab Carrer del Call, where you can still see the grooves for the enclosures that sealed the ghetto at night.

On the northwestern edge of the old town, the seventeenth-century Renaissance Pont Vell stands on the site of an earlier Romanesque bridge washed away by the once-raging torrent – hard to imagine on the evidence of the meagre trickle of the river today. The bridge was originally planned with a single arch, but the bishop of the time feared it would be swept downstream a second time and insisted on a solid two-arched design.

The focus of the Barri Vell is the imposing eleventh-century Castell Palau de La Bisbal (Easter–Oct Tues–Sat 10.30am–1.30pm & 4.30–8.30pm, Sun 10.30am–1.30pm; Nov–March Mon–Fri 5–8pm, Sat 11am–2pm & 5–8pm, Sun 11am–2pm; €2), Plaça Castell. It was once the palace of the bishops of Girona and is remarkable for its fortified rooftop chapel and heavy defences, including a large machicolation over the main door. A fourteenth-century extension to the palace added outer walls and a parade ground, two sides of which, complete with embrasures, still stand, marking the present Plaça Castell.

Inside, to the left of the entrance, are stables and stone troughs, in excellent condition. In a room opposite the entrance, excavations in 1993 turned up the original well, covered over in the fifteenth century and still containing water, while a section of wall and two silos provide evidence of a building predating the palace by up to two hundred years. To the right of this room are two

▲ LA BISBAL: STREET WITH ANTIQUES SHOPS

perfectly preserved eighteenth-century wine presses connected to a stone collection pool. The remains of a small dungeon are visible off this chamber.

Steps lead up to the crenellated roof, offering terrific views over the countryside. In one corner stands the chapel, a very simple building with a rounded stone apse; it has a trapdoor which once communicated directly with the bishop's quarters below.

Monells

The compact, medieval fortified village of Monells is a warren of unspoilt tiny squares and streets, at the centre of which lies the impressive, porticoed Plaça de Jaume I. Under the arches opposite the town hall is a reminder of the village's medieval splendour – an 1818 reproduction of the Mitgera de Monells, a standard grain measure which Jaume I decreed in 1234 was to be used for markets throughout the see of Girona. Monells has some great hotels (see p.130), making it an ideal base for exploring the area.

Púbol: Castell Gala-Dalí

ⓦwww.salvador-dali.org. Mid-June to mid-Sept daily 10.30am–7.15pm; March to mid-June & mid-Sept to Nov Tues–Sun 10.30am–5.15pm. €4.20.

Dalí bought and restored this dilapidated fourteenth-century castle – consisting of three storeys around a courtyard – in the 1960s to fulfil a promise he'd made to Gala, his wife, decades earlier – to provide her with a place that she could retreat to and that he claimed he would never visit without her permission. Although it was very much Gala's domain, Dalí couldn't resist stamping his own sense of mischief on the place, preserving, for example, all the cracks, most notably a huge one running down the main facade.

This mischievousness runs throughout the place. Gala had insisted on the radiators being covered up, so Dalí painstakingly created an alcove in the **Saló del Piano** (Piano Room), only to paint it to look like a radiator, while the **Sala dels Escuts** (Room of the Escutcheons) is dominated by an elaborate false door. Also in the Sala dels Escuts is Dalí's haunting *Camí*

a Púbol, featuring a narrow trail leading to the castle of Púbol and tall poplar trees (the name of the village is derived from the Catalan word for "poplar").

Other highlights on this floor are the **Blue Room**, originally Gala's bedroom and where Dalí took to sleeping after her death – it was here that he was badly burned in an accidental fire in 1984 and forced to move to Figueres, where he lived until his death in 1989 – and the **Lost Library**, containing a chess set designed by Dalí and dedicated to Marcel Duchamp.

Highlights on the upstairs floor are an exhibition of Gala's dresses, featuring creations by Givenchy, Christian Dior, Pierre Cardin and Elizabeth Arden, and the elegant **Dining Room**, where the easel on which Dalí's last works were painted stands against a wall.

The most poignant moment of the visit is the sight of two tombs side by side in the **crypt**. Gala is buried in one, but the other, where Dalí insisted he wanted to be interred, lies empty: the executors of his estate instead laid the artist to rest in a mausoleum in Figueres.

PLACES Central Baix Empordà

▼ MONELLS: PLAÇA JAUME 1

Hotels

Pensió Adarnius

Avgda de les Voltes 7, La Bisbal ☎972 640 957, ℻972 600 112. Handily situated for both the old town and the shops. The en-suite rooms are small, and some can get noisy, but they're comfortable enough for a short stay. €50.

Arcs de Monells

c/Vilanova 1, Monells ☎972 630 304, ⓦwww.hotelarcsmonells. com. A lovely hotel in a fourteenth-century former hospital surrounded by lawns and boasting a superb restaurant and a three-tier swimming pool. Choose from huge, luxurious air-conditioned rooms (some with Jacuzzis) within the cool stone walls of the original building, or modern ground-floor bedrooms on the edge of the lawns. €160.

Castell d'Empordà

Castell d'Empordà ☎972 646 254, ⓦwww.castelldemporda.com. Dominating the bluff-top hamlet of Castell d'Empordà, this 800-year-old castle, once lived in by Pere Margarit, one of Columbus's captains, boasts sumptuous bare-stone rooms warmly decorated with tapestries and rugs. €160.

Hostalet 1701

Pl Jaume I 1, Monells ☎972 630 012, ⓦwww.hostalet1701.com. An old curiosity shop of a hotel on the main square, combining six charming antique-decorated rooms – plus pool, Jacuzzi and garden terrace – with an antiques shop. The owners claim that guests are welcome to buy any piece of the hotel furniture. €132.

La Plaça

St Esteve 17, Madremanyà ☎972 490 487, ⓦwww.laplacamadremanya. com. Idyllic private hotel in a rambling *masia* outside a hilltop village with fabulous views of the Gavarres mountains. Choice of rooms from spacious doubles to apartment-sized suites, all beautifully designed. A superb restaurant makes it complete. €92.

Turisme rural

Mas Masaller

c/Rabioses 5, Cruïlles ☎ & ℻972 641 046, ⓦwww.masmasaller. com. Pleasant *masia* with six spacious double rooms and a garden with pool. Breakfast included. €50.

▼ CASTELL GALA-DALÍ: STATUE OF ELEPHANT IN GARDEN

▲ CRUÏLLES: MEDIEVAL TOWER

Castell and the river, serving modern variations on Empordà cooking, with a good choice for veggies.

Mas Pastor

Ctra Girona km20, Corçà. Closed Wed & Feb. Run by a larger-than-life owner, this moderately priced restaurant in an old *masia* is very popular with locals, thanks to its generous servings of traditional Catalan cooking; the baked fish is particularly recommended.

Monells

c/Vilanova 11, Monells. Closed Tues & July. An inexpensive restaurant in an atmospheric old house, specializing in cod – such as cod baked in honey – and hearty Catalan meat dishes.

La Plaça

St Esteve 17, Madremanyà ☎972 490 487. Easter–Oct Mon–Fri 8–11.30pm, Sat & Sun 1–3.30pm & 8–11.30pm. The fabulous and fairly pricey Empordà cooking by the passionate and perfectionist chef of this lovely restaurant and hotel is a rare treat you should allow yourself at least once on holiday. Book ahead.

La Riera

St Martí Vell ☎972 490 211. Tucked away on a winding road, this excellent, moderately priced restaurant serves extraordinary Catalan cuisine, with fresh market produce determining the day's menu.

Shops

"El Rissec" Valls i Llenas

c/L'Aigüeta 92-102, La Bisbal. Rambling ceramics shop with easily the best and most extensive selection of well-crafted traditional and modern pieces, from "wind" plates to dinner services.

Rogenca

c/L'Aigüeta 112, La Bisbal. A small establishment specializing in tasteful contemporary, designer-made ceramics ornaments and tableware.

Restaurants

La Cantonada

c/Bisbe 6, La Bisbal. Closed Tues. Small, stylish, but inexpensive restaurant between the Palau

Torroella de Montgrí and L'Estartit

The history of inland Torroella and its coastal extension, L'Estartit, is a familiar one throughout the Costa Brava. Torroella enjoyed glory days when King Jaume I declared it a royal port in 1273, making it one of the most important in medieval Catalonia, falling into decline, however, when the king's rivals diverted the course of the Ter River. L'Estartit was originally Torroella's fishing quarter and in the nineteenth century grew into a port, exporting rice and wine. With the advent of tourism, L'Estartit expanded and the inland parent was overshadowed by its coastal offspring.

Today, Torroella is a compact and sedate medieval town retaining a strongly Catalan feel; the best time to visit is during the summer music festival (see box opposite), when the whole town comes alive. L'Estartit, on the other hand, has a deserved reputation for being a classic pack-'em-in tourist spot. Parts of it are an unsightly sprawl of high-rises and bars serving all-day English breakfasts, but the area around the port, favoured by the locals, has retained much of its original identity.

In recent years L'Estartit has also become a magnet for divers and watersports enthusiasts in general, on account of the proximity of Les Illes Medes marine wildlife reserve, a group of islands 1km offshore, hosting an extraordinary variety of species of flora and fauna.

Torroella de Montgrí

Torroella de Montgrí stands in the shadow of the Castell de Montgrí, which dominates the town and surrounding area from its vantage point on the summit of the Massis de Montgrí. The town's grid-plan streets – a beautifully preserved example of thirteenth-century town planning – radiate from the porticoed Plaça de la Vila, which was designed as a meeting point on the model of the Greek agora and Roman forum. The square boasts the fifteenth-century Ajuntament and a huge sundial dating from 1725, and is the site of the town's bustling Monday market.

Visiting Torroella de Montgrí and L'Estartit

Torroella's tourist office is on c/Ullà 1 (July & Aug Mon 10am–2pm & 6–9pm, Wed–Sat 11am–2pm & 6–9pm, Sun 11am–2pm; Sept–June eves 5–8pm), and features exhibits on Mediterranean life. In L'Estartit, the tourist office is at Pg Marítim 47–50 (May Mon–Fri 9am–1pm & 4–7pm, Sat & Sun 10am–2pm; June & Sept Mon–Sat 9.30am–2pm & 4–9pm, Sun 10am–2pm; July & Aug as June but eves 4–9pm; Oct–April Mon–Sat 9am–1pm & 3–6pm, Sat 10am–2pm).

Festival Internacional de Músiques

Every July and August, Torroella de Montgrí stages the renowned Festival Internacional de Músiques, featuring chamber, orchestral and world music performed in several venues around town. Tickets (€14–40) are available from the festival office (☎972 761 098, ⊛www.festivaldetorroella.org), c/Ullà 26. At the same time, a lively free festival of music and crafts markets is held in various squares around the town.

On the narrow Carrer Església lies the Museu de Pintura Palau Solterra, at no. 10 (June–Sept Mon & Wed–Sun 5–9.30pm; Oct–May Sat 11am–2pm & 4.30–8.30pm, Sun 11am–2pm; €3), a sumptuous medieval mansion that displays temporary exhibitions of contemporary Catalan paintings and is also a venue for the music festival. A passage at the northern end of the broad Passeig de l'Església leads to the imposing Gothic Església de St Genís. Started during the prosperous years of the fourteenth century, it was intended as a cathedral – which explains its size and outward splendour – but the town's fortunes declined and the eighteenth-century belfry was never finished. The interior is contrastingly simple, the only highlight being the medieval font. North of the church, the fourteenth-century Portal de Santa Caterina is the only remaining part of the town wall.

Heading south towards Palafrugell, you cross a road bridge built in the summer of 1942 by the slave labour of 300 Republican prisoners of war, and subsequently known as "The Bridge Over the River Ter". A road off to the left after this leads to the sweeping Platja de la Gola, a less crowded extension of L'Estartit's sandy beach.

L'Estartit

L'Estartit feels like it's divided into two unequal parts. There's no reason to linger in the first, larger, section, which includes the unsightly high-rise development at the entrance to the town from Torroella and the sprawling residential district of Griells to the south. In contrast, the port area is attractive and characterful, framed by the pine-covered Roca Maura escarpment, where the Gavarres range drops into the sea. It's home to some good bars and restaurants, and is also a thriving fishing concern and leisure marina from where diving expeditions and boat trips (€13–24) leave for Les Illes Medes.

Beyond the port, the windswept Cap de Barra headland

▲ TORROELLA DE MONTGRÍ: DETAIL OF SUNDIAL IN MAIN SQUARE

PLACES | Torroella de Montgrí and L'Estartit

Torroella de Montgrí and L'Estartit **PLACES**

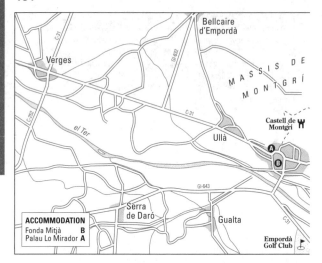

affords excellent views of Les Illes Medes and the choppy waters and gull-strewn cliffs of the Molinet cove.

Adjoining the port, the town centre is surprisingly small, centring on the Plaça de l'Església, a short section of the pleasant Passeig Marítim and the fairly ordinary shopping street of calle Santa Anna. At the end of this street, on Plaça Santa Anna, the Església de Santa Anna, built in 1920 and open during the day, is beautiful in its simplicity: its whitewashed walls and sturdy belfry are set off by a single palm beside the door and the backdrop of the escarpment. Inside, two stained-glass windows illuminate both ends of the transept. Crowned by a

A walk to the Castell del Montgrí

Overlooking the town, the thirteenth-century Castell del Montgrí was only ever partially completed, and all that stands today are the walls and towers. The steep but relatively easy kilometre-long walk from Torroella de Montgrí to the castle is best tackled early or late in the day, to avoid the midday sun and the haze which can obscure the summit views.

Signposts lead from the roundabout on Plaça Lledoner to a footpath, showing red-and-white GR92 markings. Follow this for half-an-hour to three tiny, derelict chapels either side of the track, originally used for worship of Santa Caterina and later occupied by shepherds. About ten minutes further, the path divides at a stone cross; to the right is a scrambling detour to El Cau del Duc (The Eagle's Lair), one of a series of fifty-odd caverns hereabouts; archeological finds have shown that this strategic site – named after the eagle owls that used to nest on the massif – was occupied by humans 300,000 years ago. Heading straight on at the stone cross, you've got another 50m to go before you come out onto a plateau and you're faced with the castle's massive walls. Inside, steps lead up to the walls, from where you'll be rewarded with a breathtaking panorama of the coastline from Begur in the south to Cap de Creus in the northeast, and the Pyrenees to the northwest.

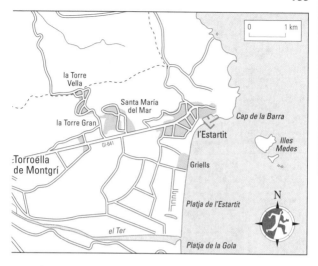

wrought-iron representation of
the town's seafaring history, the
marble altar and pink marble
altarpiece with a wood and glass
insert are supremely elegant.

From the town centre and the
port, L'Estartit's beach stretches
some 5km south, boasting fine
golden sand all the way along,
with very gently shelving
water. It gets pretty crowded in
August, although you can
find quieter areas if you're prepared to walk away from the
town.

Les Illes Medes

Comprising seven islets and
a scattering of reefs, Les Illes
Medes archipelago is the most
important marine reserve in
the western Mediterranean,
home to over 1300 animal
and plant species. During the
early days of tourism, lack of
controls on diving and fishing
led to large tracts of coral reef
being destroyed, but subsequent
laws passed by the Catalan
government seriously restrict
all activity around the islands,
and this has gone a long way

towards redressing the ecological
balance.

All boating, diving and snorkelling in the area is strictly
regulated. Only 450 divers are
allowed to dive here each day,
and then only if accompanied
by a certified instructor or

▼ L'ESTARTIT: BARS AND CAFÉS IN THE PORT

Torroella de Montgrí and L'Estartit

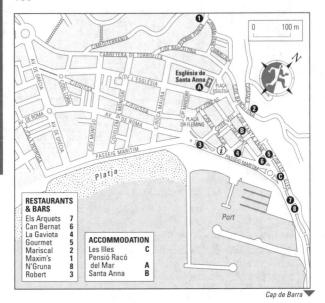

Cap de Barra ▼

RESTAURANTS & BARS

Els Arquets	7
Can Bernat	6
La Gaviota	4
Gourmet	5
Mariscal	2
Maxim's	1
N'Gruna	8
Robert	3

ACCOMMODATION

Les Illes	C
Pensió Racó del Mar	A
Santa Anna	B

divemaster. Consequently, for novices and experts alike, it's essential to use only a recognized PADI or CSL diving centre. Best of the bunch are Poseidon, Pg Marítim 82 (☎972 750 204); Medaqua, Pg Marítim 13 (☎972 752 043, ⓦwww.medaqua.com), which also offers a variety of activities including sailing, parasailing and bird-watching; and El Rei del Mar, Avgda Grècia 5 (☎972 751 392).

The largest island, Meda Gran, can be visited on boat trips (not March–June), but you must stick to the signposted paths, which lead to the belvedere at the topmost part of the rock. Nesting birds here include cormorants and shags, and you can also spot kestrels, hoopoes and linnets. The most common species of fish include amberjack, barracuda, conger eels and groupers; more exotic fish, such as marbled electric rays and angler fish, are found over 20m down.

Hotels

Les Illes

c/Illes 55, L'Estartit ☎972 751 239, ⓦwww.hotellesilles.com. Closed Feb. Top choice for serious divers, offering a wide range of reasonable packages that include diving lessons or excursions; half or full board is compulsory. Rooms are a little dark, but are all en suite with a balcony. €63 half board; €98 full board.

Fonda Mitjà

c/Església 14, Torroella ☎ & ☎972 758 003. Closed Nov–Jan. Very good-value en-suite rooms in this charming, small hotel in the heart of town, with a fine restaurant attached. €46.

Palau Lo Mirador

Pg l'Església 1, Torroella ☎972 758 063, ⓦwww.palaulomirador.com. The former royal palace of Jaume I, this fabulous hotel provides

Dance of the dead

A moated medieval town with a charming central square, Verges, a little way west of Torroella, is most famous for its macabre Ball dels Morts (Dance of the Dead), that sees skeleton figures – fathers and sons – dance through the narrow streets every Easter.

king-sized luxury rooms and a swimming pool set in lush grounds. €210.

Pensió Racó del Mar

c/Església 12, L'Estartit ☎ 972 751 085, ⑲ 972 750 674. Closed Nov–April. Simple but comfortable *pensió* near the church, with a terrace garden and airy, balconied rooms. €52.

Santa Anna

c/del Port 46, L'Estartit ☎ 972 751 326, ⑩ www.hotelsantaanna.com. Smart hotel near the port with comfortable en-suite rooms, some with balcony. Organizes golfing, diving and cycling holidays. Prices include breakfast. €79.

Restaurants

Els Arquets

Pg Marítim 21, L'Estartit. Daily 1pm–midnight; closed Nov–Easter. The best pizzas and pasta in town, as borne out by the queues. There's

a pleasant terrace downstairs, and a more private upstairs balcony with great views of the port.

La Gaviota

Pg Marítim 92, L'Estartit. Closed mid-Nov to mid-Dec. One of the town's most traditional and pricey restaurants, famous throughout Catalona for its seafood – including some *mar i muntanya* dishes. It also has an impressive wine list.

Gourmet

c/de les Illes 21, L'Estartit. Closed Feb. Inexpensive, modern Catalan cuisine that is very popular with the locals and serves upbeat versions of traditional fare; particularly recommended are the rice casserole, roast lamb and seafood tapas.

Robert

Pg Marítim 59, L'Estartit. Nov–March closed Mon–Fri. Occupying a Modernista house dating from 1917, with a beautiful shaded

PLACES

Torroella de Montgrí and L'Estartit

▲ TORROELLA

garden on the seafront, this imaginative Catalan place is excellent value for money, offering a range of *menús del dia* from €9 to €18.

Bars

Can Bernat

c/del Port 2, L'Estartit. Daily 10am–2am. Traditional fishermen's tavern founded in 1926, serving torrades during the day; at night, the terrace is a great place to kick back with cocktails or a cremat.

Mariscal

c/Barcelona 51, L'Estartit. Dust off your air guitars for the best craic in town. Ageing and not-so-ageing rockers, both locals and tourists, flock to this hugely enjoyable bar playing 60s, 70s and 80s rock. Two or three live bands play each week – watch for posters around town or in the tourist office.

N'Gruna

Pg Marítim 20, L'Estartit. By day, a terrace bar serving an excellent range of tapas and one of the best breakfasts in town; at night it doubles up as a trendy bar attracting bright young locals.

▲ OLD WALLED GATES, TORROELLA

Clubs

Maxim's

c/Primavera s/n, L'Estartit. A five-minute walk from the centre, along the road leading to the rock overlooking the town, this huge club – spread over four floors and playing mainly house – caters for a young crowd. The large garden is a welcome respite from the packed dance floors.

L'Escala and Empúries

Catering primarily for locals, the inviting seaside town of L'Escala remains quite unspoilt – spared over-development by the construction of the outlying suburb of Riells, where most of the tourist activity is concentrated. What makes L'Escala really special are the stunning Greek and Roman ruins at Empúries, one of the most important archeological sites in Spain. A visit to the ruins can easily be combined with a stroll around the picturesque medieval hamlet of Sant Martí d'Empúries or a dip in the sea at one of the pristine sandy coves nearby.

L'Escala

At the heart of old L'Escala is its charming historic port, previously the main fishing harbour until the new one south of Riells was built in the 1960s. Fishing boats still pull up onto the small beach, while on the quayside are medieval mooring posts and towering stone mounds built in the eighteenth century – the square-topped ones for mooring, the round-topped ones for salting anchovies. Techniques of anchovy fishing and salting, first used by the Greeks, who colonized the area in the sixth century BC, are still followed today.

All the buildings lining the port were once related to the fishing industry. Many of the old whitewashed cottages, built around patios for storing nets and tools, are still lived in, while former fishermen's taverns are now bars and shops. At

Port d'en Perris, south of the main beach, which was once a secondary port and housed the anchovy warehouses, there's still a number of family fishmongers dotted about, where you can buy the local delicacy; it also has a pleasant beach, good for swimming.

On the corner of the seafront and the busy shopping street of calle Alfolí, the imposing Casa de la Punxa was built in 1919 as an ice factory, while further along the same street stands the towering seventeenth-century Alfolí or salt warehouse. The small street to the right from

▼ L'ESCALA: CANNONBALL EMBEDDED IN WALL

Visiting L'Escala

The main tourist office is at Pl de les Escoles 1 (daily 9am–9.30pm; ☎972 770 603, ⊛www.lescala.org), while there's an equally well-stocked information point (June–Sept daily 9am–8.30pm) at the northwestern entrance to town by the roundabout on Ctra Viladamat, and a touch-screen stand on the beach at Riells.

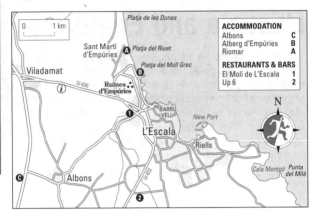

here houses Can Maranges, the fortified family seat of the Maranges family, a dynasty of famous local politicians, soldiers and writers.

On the north side of the harbour, at c/Joan Massanet 2, a cannonball – fired in May 1809 – is embedded in the wall of a house that subsequently belonged to Surrealist artist Joan Massanet.

L'Escala's lively market is held in the streets of the Barri Vell every Sunday morning.

Riells and Montgó

L'Escala is linked to its beach suburb, Riells, by the Passeig Marítim, a kilometre-long seafront promenade lined with craft stands in summer. Developed in the 1960s to cater for the influx of tourists, Riells is a small, if rather brash, beachfront concentration of restaurants, bars and hotels that attracts mostly foreign family tourism.

Various operators on Riells beach offer windsurfing, ski-bus, water-skiing and kayaking; the best is Funtastic (☎972 774 184, ⓦwww.funtastic-emporda. com). Boat tours run by Mare Nostrum, c/Maranges 3 (☎972 773 797), head from the new port, beyond Riells, north to Cap de Creus and south to Palamós.

Rows of villas extend from Riells to Cala Montgó, a crystal-clear, deep and sheltered bay with fine sand. Tiny inlets and beaches and sunken wrecks make it popular with divers and kayakers, equipped by Montgó Sub, Avgda Montgó 297 (☎972 771 307), and Kayaking Costa Brava (☎972 773 806, ⓦwww. kayakingcostabrava. com). It's worth the half-hour walk up to the top of Punta Montgó for the superb views of the coastline.

▲ L'ESCALA: ANCHOVY SHOP AT PORT D'EN PERRIS

Riells' Little Prince

The French author and World War II pilot Antoine de Saint-Exupéry was shot down over the Golf de Roses, and in commemoration the Riells seafront has been charmingly themed on his most famous story, *The Little Prince*. At the eastern end of the promenade, a haunting statue of the little prince sits on a seafront wall, on the other side of which is a slithering chain symbolizing the snake. Further on there are palms planted to re-create constellations, a small stone amphitheatre with a statue of the fox, bronze asteroids set into the ground and, at the far end of the promenade, a baobab tree and rose next to tiny volcanoes emerging from the pavement.

Empúries

Daily: Easter & June–Sept 10am–8pm; rest of year 10am–6pm. €2.40.
Enjoying a fabulous setting on the seashore, the ruins of Empúries – an ancient Greek city and a later, Roman, settlement – comprise one of Spain's most important and engaging archeological sites. The Greek settlement has been extensively excavated, and foundations and streets give a good idea of the layout. Much less of the Roman city has been unearthed, although intact mosaics and columns clearly mark out individual buildings. A beautifully presented museum (admission free with site ticket) houses all the finds from the site, including funeral urns, coins and jewellery. There's also an award-winning twenty-minute audiovisual exhibition (every 30min; €1.50), offering a neat potted history of the development and decline of the cities.

You can cover everything in half a day, and still have time for a dip at one of the beautiful beaches below the site (see box on p.143). Parking is free with your admission ticket. An audioguide, available in English, is worth shelling out an extra €3.60 for.

The first city that the Greeks founded in the area – known as the Palaiopolis, or old city – was in the early sixth century BC on the site of Sant Martí d'Empúries, then a small island and now joined to the mainland. Shortly afterwards, they built a new city, or Neapolis, nearby, known as Emporion (literally "Trading Post"), which grew thanks to flourishing trade with tribes around the Iberian peninsula.

In 218 BC, at the outbreak of the Second Punic War, a Roman army, commanded by Scipio, landed at Emporion to block the Carthaginians, and effectively began the Romanization of Iberia. In 195 BC, Marcus Portius Cato established an army camp at Empúries,

▼ L'ESCALA: MEDIEVAL FISH SALTING POSTS IN THE OLD PORT

▲ Empúries

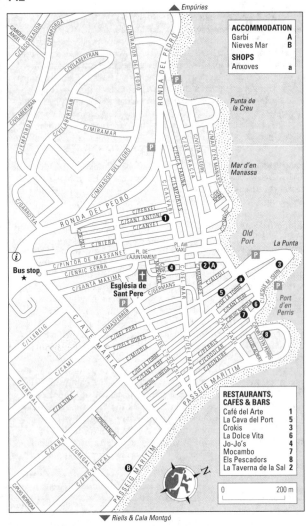

ACCOMMODATION
Garbí	A
Nieves Mar	B

SHOPS
Anxoves	a

RESTAURANTS, CAFÉS & BARS
Café del Arte	1
La Cava del Port	5
Crokis	3
La Dolce Vita	6
Jo-Jo's	4
Mocambo	7
Els Pescadors	8
La Taverna de la Sal	2

Bus stop ★

Església de Sant Pere

0   200 m

▼ Riells & Cala Montgó

nucleus of the city that was founded anew in around 100 BC. Under Emperor Augustus, the Greek and Roman settlements were united under the name Municipium Emporiae. However, whereas Roman settlements such as Barcino (Barcelona) and Gerunda (Girona) flourished, Emporiae declined and was abandoned in the third century AD.

The Greek city (Ciutat Grega)

Empúries. The Greek city is reached through an impressive gateway, cut into the southern defensive walls. This

Camí de les Dunes

Part of the Camí de Ronda, the paved and partly shaded Camí de les Dunes is a two-kilometre-long footpath leading from the old port past a string of outstanding sandy beaches, below the Empúries ruins and Sant Martí d'Empúries; both are easily accessible from the path. The most interesting beach is Moll Grec, by Empúries, where part of the remains of the original Greek dock stands proud above the dunes. Where the path turns away from the main road towards the beaches, a huge statue of a hand brandishing a torch commemorates the arrival here in 1992 of the Olympic Torch from Greece.

leads directly into a religious quarter, which includes the Serapeion, a sanctuary dedicated to the Egyptian deities Isis and Zeus Serapis, and the more interesting Asklepeion, consecrated to the Greek god of medicine. In the middle of the latter stood a small temple with a statue of Aesculapius – the original statue, preserved nearly intact, is in the museum and a copy now stands in its place – next to which are some open-based amphoras, which acted as water filters for purifying the sick.

Further along the main path, six different-sized tanks mark the site of a **salting factory**, precursor to the fish-salting industry that subsequently made the area's fortune. On from here past family residences is a large public cistern, which would originally have stood in the centre of a **macellum**, or small market; its sloping roof channelled rainwater into the cistern for use by the small businesses in the building. At the end of this street, little but the ground plan remains of the **agora** – the public square and hub of the city – and stoa, a porticoed building housing shops and businesses.

The Roman city (Ciutat Romana)

Empúries. The Roman city is more extensive and potentially much more splendid than its Greek counterpart. The city was divided into seventy blocks, or insulae, due to be excavated by 2008, although to date, only ten percent of it has been unearthed.

The first area contains **Domus 1**, one of the largest houses that has been uncovered, remarkable for its abstract symmetrical mosaics. Nearby lies Insula 30, where latest excavations have revealed an extensive **public baths** complex, complete with a hypocaust and a mosaic of Triton. Unfortunately, an abstract black-and-white mosaic was sliced in two by an anti-aircraft trench dug during the Spanish Civil War.

The path leads from here

▼ EMPÚRIES: DETAIL OF MOSAIC

▲ EMPÚRIES: RUINED GREEK QUAYSIDE

to the forum, the political, religious and financial heart of the city. The north side of the square was dominated by temples, most notably the Capitoline temple, of which only the outline and some stones remain. Directly opposite, on the south wall, a reconstruction of the high porticoes gives some idea of what the forum would have looked like in its heyday; plans are underway for further reconstruction of this area. On the east wall were the basilica and curia, which included the law courts and legal offices.

South of the forum, the **city walls** are well preserved, while the low main gate has a deeply rutted threshold, showing the passage of traffic. Outside the wall and to the left, a carved phallic symbol at head height invoked the protection and prosperity of the city.

To the right (west) of the gate is the base of the **amphitheatre**, probably constructed on an earlier wooden structure. Built in the first century AD, when the city had begun its decline, it lacks the usual underground chambers, indicating a considerable shortage of funds.

Sant Martí d'Empúries

Site of the original Greek settlement of Palaiopolis, Sant Martí d'Empúries was founded in the sixth century BC. Regarded as the oldest town in Catalonia, it has been occupied without interruption since the Bronze Age and was the first capital of the region at the time of Charlemagne, a position it held until the eleventh century. Its medieval walls mark the original Greek enclosure, while its rather austere sixteenth-century church stands on the site of a tenth-century pre-Romanesque temple. The town withstood numerous attacks between the thirteenth and seventeenth centuries by the French, while its separate fishing quarter subsequently grew to become the town of L'Escala.

For all its fascinating history and picture-postcard looks, the hamlet is ultimately something of a disappointment, attracting as it does hordes of visitors, who crowd the tiny, café-lined main square, and its buildings look as though they've been renovated just a tad too zealously. Still, it's a pleasant place for a short stroll or an evening drink, and it has some superb beaches (see box on p.143) and fine views of the bay.

Hotels

Albons

Ctra La Bisbal–Figueres km18, Albons ☎972 788 500, ⊛www.hotelalbons. com. A convivial four-star hotel on a bluff 6km southwest of L'Escala. The low, modern buildings are grouped around the sunny lawns and swimming pool. All rooms are huge, some with four-poster beds, and have air conditioning and stunning countryside views. €142.

Garbí

c/Sta Màxima 7, L'Escala ☎ & ☎972 770 165. Closed Feb. Located in a small street near the old port, this tastefully renovated old merchant's house offers good value. The loquacious owners are very helpful and cheery, while the simple but comfortable en-suite rooms, some facing the sea, are bright and cool. €48.

Nieves Mar

Pg Marítim 8, L'Escala ☎972 770 300, ⓦwww.nievesmar.com. Closed Nov–Feb. Between the old port and Riells, the modern Nieves Mar is famous for its excellent restaurant, open to non-guests too, and has large gardens, tennis courts and a swimming pool. All of the spacious, brightly decorated bedrooms have sitting areas and balconies with sea views. €110.

Riomar

Platja del Riuet, Sant Martí d'Empúries ☎ & ☎972 770 362, ⓦwww .riomarhotel.com. Closed Oct–April. Good for families, this sprawling hotel and gardens is right on the beach near Sant Martí. The simple en-suite rooms are airy and comfortable. €76.

Hostels

Alberg d'Empúries

Ctra del Museu 38–40, Empúries ☎972 771 200, ⓦwww.tujuca.com. Closed Jan & Feb. A friendly hostel in a renovated mansion near the Empúries ruins. Accommodation ranges from dorms for up to twenty to smaller rooms in a new extension for six people. €18.10.

Shops

Anxoves

c/de la Torre 20. In the heart of the Barri Vell, this is one of the best fishmonger's in town in which to buy traditionally prepared anchovies.

Restaurants

La Dolce Vita

Port d'en Perris 1. One of the most popular places in town, this inexpensive restaurant serves great fresh pasta, pizzas and local meat dishes in a brightly lit upper-floor dining room with splendid sea views.

El Molí de L'Escala

Camp dels Pilans ☎972 774 727, ⓦwww.el-moli.com. Nov–March closed Wed. Near the roundabout at the western entrance to L'Escala, this sumptuous and expensive Catalan restaurant occupies a rambling sixteenth-century watermill in lush gardens. The top-range fish and seafood are superb, while

▼ RIELLS: STATUE OF LE PETIT PRINCE

PLACES L'Escala and Empúries

there's also a reasonable selection for vegetarians and a list of over 150 wines. It's best to book.

Els Pescadors

Port d'en Perris 5 ☎972 770 728. Closed Nov. The pricey *Els Pescadors* is a traditional restaurant renowned for the quality of its excellent seafood, almost matched by the range of imaginative vegetable and meat dishes.

La Taverna de la Sal

c/Sta Máxima 7. Bustling place in the same building as *Hotel Garbí*, with a welcoming pavement terrace. A great selection of tapas and *pà amb tomàquet* meals is served alongside an extensive meat, fish and salad menu, all at very low prices.

Bars

La Cava del Port

c/del Port 33. A lively bar in an old cottage, serving a huge range of tapas washed down with cava. Worth trying are the *flautes* (tiny, thin sandwiches)

▼ EMPÚRIES: WHEEL RUTS THROUGH SIDE GATE

and the platters of cheeses, pâtés and local anchovies.

Café dell'Arte

c/Calvari 1, L'Escala. Daily 5pm–1am. This small, friendly bar, cluttered with antiques, is a great place for a laid-back drink. It also serves fondues and tapas.

Crokis

Pl de la Punta, L'Escala. Daily 9.30pm–2.30am. The trendiest spot in town, occupying a terrific position atop the small La Punta headland overlooking the main beach. Downstairs is noisy with a small dance area playing anything from house to salsa, while the upstairs bar, with a pantile-roofed terrace, is perfect for relishing the sea views.

Jo-Jo's

c/del Mig 3, L'Escala. Daily 8pm–2.30am. A laid-back, enjoyable dive in the old town with something of the atmosphere of the ageing hippy about it.

Mocambo

Port d'en Perris 3. Daily noon–2.30am. In the western corner of Port d'en Perris, this small, modern bar in an old fisherman's cottage serves an enticing range of cocktails to accompany a selection of salads and sandwiches.

Clubs

Up 6

Ctra Torroella, 2km southwest of L'Escala. Daily 10pm–6am. One of the most popular clubs in the region, with two distinct areas and a chill-out bar. One part plays house and features visiting DJs from Ibiza, while the other has a buzzing salsa dance floor. Admission (€8) includes one drink.

The Golf de Roses

Bordered by the rocky coves of the Baix Empordà to the south and the craggy wilderness of the Cap de Creus to the north, the Golf de Roses is where the fertile Empordà plain, full of lush fields and orchards, turns into a sweep of fine sand around a hooked bay.

Crowning the bay, the 3000-year-old town of **Roses** has exploited the beauty of its natural setting and thrown itself body and soul into the tourist industry. Halfway around the Golf de Roses is the **Parc Natural dels Aigüamolls de l'Empordà**, a magnet for bird-watchers and walkers that also boasts a splendid beach. The park's main town, **Sant Pere Pescador**, lies 3km inland, surrounded by acres of apple orchards.

North of the park sits the fascinating Gothic town of **Castelló d'Empúries**, dominated by its would-be cathedral and skeined with cobbled alleys. The nearby modern development of **Empuriabrava** went up in the 1960s around a giant marina and 30km of canals, instantly turning it into a favourite with yachties.

Roses

Shaded by palm trees, Roses occupies a grand position at the head of its broad, sandy bay. It was founded in the eighth century BC by Greek colonists, who named it Rhodes after their home, and was subsequently developed by the Romans, who established a fishing industry, still very active today. After Roses had been sacked in 1543 by the Turkish pirate Barbarossa, Carlos I of Spain ordered the building of a citadel, the Ciutadella, later dismantled by French troops and the remains of which are now virtually the only trace of the town's illustrious past. Much of Roses today is geared towards tourism; it makes the most of its attractive four-kilometre sandy beach and tranquil, tree-lined beachfront, and the jumble of busy streets in its old town is awash with generic tourist shops and restaurants.

▼ ROSES: CASTELL DE LA TRINITAT

Visiting Roses

The tourist office in Roses is at Avgda Rhode 101 (daily: June–Sept 9am–9pm; Oct–May 9am–7pm; ☎972 257 331, ✉www.roseswebinfo.com).

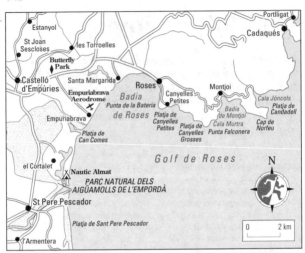

Protected behind its imposing Renaissance gate, the vast pentagonal **Ciutadella** (April–Sept daily 10am–8pm; Oct–March Tues–Sun 10am–4pm; €3) is currently undergoing a facelift, part of which includes the construction of a museum highlighting its history. The grounds of the citadel, a curious mishmash of eras, includes the layout of the original Greek streets on which it was erected and

▼ EAST OF ROSES: CALA JÓNCOLS

the remains of a seventeenth-century monastery built within the extensive, moat-lined walls.

West of town, **Platja Salatar** and **Santa Margarida** are lined with rows of apartments and hotels, while the pine-clad coves of Canyelles Petites and Almadrava to the east are much prettier, but get very crowded.

About 1km east of town, on the Cap de Norfeu road (see below), is the peaceful Creu d'en Cobertella, the oldest dolmen in Catalonia, dating from 3000 BC and topped by a huge four-ton granite slab.

Cap de Norfeu

East of Roses, a partly unmade road snakes up through the hills to the desolate Cap de Norfeu headland and some of the northern Costa Brava's most rugged and stunning coves.

Many are set below the road, meaning you'll have to park and then clamber down rough hillside paths to reach them, a fact that has helped keep them relatively unspoilt. The coves can also be accessed via the arduous,

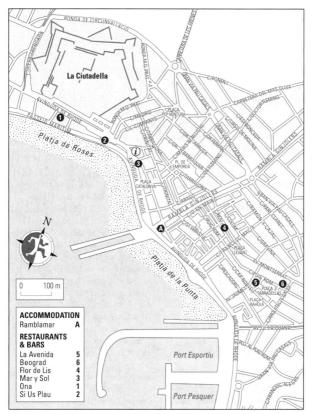

ACCOMMODATION
Ramblamar   A

RESTAURANTS
& BARS
La Avenida   5
Beograd   6
Flor de Lis   4
Mar y Sol   3
Ona   1
Si Us Plau   2

coast-hugging Camí de Ronda: from Roses allow four hours to reach the furthest, Cala Jóncols.

The first of the coves, Cala Murtra, is a horseshoe-shaped cove, popular with snorkellers and yachties, while alongside it is the even more idyllic, pine-clad Cala Rostella, with turquoise waters, a pebble beach and steeply shelving waters excellent for swimming. Both are popular with naturists. Picturesque Cala Montjoi – location of the famous *El Bullí* restaurant (see p.154) – is dominated by a Spanish holiday camp, though you can rent kayaks here. Further on, the headland itself is a deceptively long sixty-minute walk from the road, but offers spectacular views of the coves and Golf de Roses from a ruined tower on the summit, and has the pebbly Cala Canadell down below. At the end of the track is the wonderful, secluded Cala Jóncols, whose sheltered waters are perfect for swimming and scuba diving.

Parc Natural dels Aigüamolls de l'Empordà

The Parc Natural dels Aigüamolls de l'Empordà (Empordà Wetlands Park) comprises two areas of marshland either side of the modern development of Empuriabrava.

Almost a hundred bird species nest in the park, and a further two hundred have been observed; the most common are moorhens, coots and mallards. The reserve is also active in protecting endangered species, such as the garganey, a rare breed of duck found only on the Iberian peninsula, and in reintroducing others such as the purple gallinule, previously not seen in Catalonia for fifty years.

▲ PARC NATURAL DELS AIGÜAMOLLS WITH EGRETS

Mammals you might spot include water voles and otters, as well as weasels, polecats, badgers and red foxes.

The largest number of birds can be seen during the two migration periods (March–May & Aug–Oct), when herons, flamingoes and the occasional crane also pass through.

Entrance to the park (unlimited access; free) is at the excellent El Cortalet information centre (daily: April–Sept 9.30am–2pm & 4.30–7pm; Oct–March 9.30am–2pm & 3.30–6pm; ⓦwww.aiguamolls.org), where you can also rent binoculars.

There are two routes through the park, both of which set off from the information centre.

The La Massona route (2hr round-trip) takes in the most interesting areas, following a shaded track to the beach and back. Dotted along the way is a series of hides; in the summer, nos. 5 and 7 attract

huge numbers of birds, as the watering holes here don't tend to dry up. Between these are four towering silos used to dry rice grown in the paddy fields nearby; one of the silos has been turned into an observatory. The last part of the track, from a gate leading into a dusty road alongside a campsite, has little to offer, making the observatory a good point to turn back if you don't mind missing out on the beach.

The other track, Can Comas, is a loop walk for serious walkers that takes about five hours (or 1hr 30min on a bike); if you're attempting it in summer it's best to set off in the early morning before the heat hits. The first part is exposed, with fewer sightings of birds, although it eventually doubles back along the beach to join the La Massona route for the last stretch.

Sant Pere Pescador

Sited amid orchards on the banks of the pretty River Fluvià, Sant Pere Pescador is the main town in the Parc Natural dels Aigüamolls. Built 3km inland to escape the attentions of pirates, it was passed by during the tourist boom and makes its

Visiting St Pere Pescador

The tourist office is at c/Verge Portalet 10 (June–Sept Mon–Fri 10am–1.30pm & 4–6pm, Sat 10am–noon; ☏972 520 050, ⓦwww.santpere.org).

Visiting Castelló d'Empúries

The tourist office is at Pl dels Homes 1 (Easter–Sept Mon–Sat 9am–1pm & 4.30–8pm, Sun 10am–1pm; ☎972 250 426, ⊛www.castellodempuries.net).

living from fruit growing.

The centre is tiny, with narrow pedestrianized streets converging on the quiet Plaça Major, graced by an ornate Gothic-style fountain and a simple seventeenth-century Baroque church. The town's real draw, though, is its outstanding beach. At the end of a signposted three-kilometre road past fruit orchards, the spectacularly long Platja de Sant Pere Pescador, with its beautiful golden sand, stretches off into the distance. There's plenty of parking space amid the dunes, and, although it gets busy, the beach is so expansive that a short walk away from the cars and campsites will find you a relatively isolated spot.

There are several windsurf rental operators on the Platja de Sant Pere Pescador, or you could have a go at flysurf – dangling on a surfboard from a parachute; get information from Ventilador, next to Camping Amfora (☎972 521 063, ⊛www.ventilador. com).

Castelló d'Empúries

The delightful town of Castelló d'Empúries is characterized by cobbled alleys and fine Gothic buildings, many dating back to the eleventh century, the town's golden age, when it became the home of the Counts of Empúries. Much of the old town is still partly surrounded by a medieval wall and some of the towers are still intact.

At the heart of Castelló d'Empúries is the porticoed Plaça dels Homes, from which narrow streets radiate, their

names, such as c/Sabateries (Cobblers Street), invoking the old trades practised here.

A two-minute walk south of the square is Castelló's medieval prison (daily 9.30am–1pm & 4–8pm; €2), on c/Presó, worth a look for the graffiti that prisoners scratched on the walls of its tiny cells, counting off the days or recording prayers.

The town's most remarkable sight, though, is the giant Església de Santa Maria, often referred to as the Cathedral of the Empordà. In the thirteenth century it was intended by the Counts of Empúries to be the centre of an episcopal see, but opposition from Girona, who didn't relish a rival bishopric so close, meant that this never came about, and Castelló d'Empúries was left with a huge church out of all proportion to the town. Evidence of the church's change in fortune

▼ PARC NATURAL DELS AIGÜAMOLLS: LA PLATJA DE LES DUNES

PLACES

The Golf de Roses

can be seen in the unfinished belfry to the right of the facade. Note the statue of Judas Thaddeus, on the far left of the facade, a hundred-year-old copy of the original, damaged by medieval townspeople, who would hurl rocks at it in the mistaken belief that it represented Judas Iscariot. You can see the original in the church museum (€2). Other exhibits of note include a Hebrew gravestone found in the church, evidence of a medieval Jewish community in the town.

Inside the church itself look out for the unique eleventh-century double font, one half for children and one for adults, and the ornate but ungilded fifteenth-century alabaster altarpiece, towering more than six metres over the altar, framed by windows made of alabaster slivers.

Butterfly Park

Ctra de Castelló a Empuriabrava. Daily 10am–sunset. €5.25. The enchanting Butterfly Park is one of the largest in Europe, beautifully laid out under an arched roof to resemble a tropical rainforest. There's no set route, just a maze of paths weaving between trees and ponds. A free leaflet details the different butterflies; the most impressive specimens are the Blue-banded Swallowtail and perfectly camouflaged Indian Leaf. The giant atlas moths and owl butterflies spend most of the day resting by the water; in the late afternoon, staff shutter the windows to allow them to fly – a spectacular sight as they swoop through tunnels of palm leaves.

Empuriabrava

Built in the 1960s, Empuriabrava was conceived as a little Venice of canals, low houses and apartment blocks by the sea, and has since become a fairly upmarket destination for sporty types and families. Row upon row of whitewashed buildings snake back from the lovely sandy beach following the 30km of interlinking canals, where boats of all shapes and sizes are moored. It's the ideal base for lazy holidays pottering about the canals or taking advantage of the excellent watersports facilities (contact the tourist office for information). Motorized boats can be rented from Eco Boats, c/Poblat Típic (☎972 454 946). Empuriabrava also has its own aerodrome, and so has become a favourite with skydivers: Skydive Empuriabrava (☎972 450 111,

▼ SANT PERE PESCADOR: APPLE ORCHARDS

▲ CASTELLÓ D'EMPÚRIES: CHURCH FACADE

ⓦwww.skydiveempuriabrava.
com) offers tandem jumps for
beginners (and jumps for more
experienced folk), as well as
plane trips.

The town has a decent selection of restaurants and an
ebullient nightlife: the best
atmosphere is on and around
Avinguda Carles Fages de
Climent, where a string of bars
thumps out live and recorded
music of all types.

Hotels

Briaxis

Port Principal 25A–30C, Empuriabrava
ⓣ972 451 545, ⓕ972 451 889.
Much more luxurious than its
exterior would suggest, the
swish *Briaxis* boasts spacious
rooms with waterside balconies
and a terrific pool on the edge
of a canal. €135.

Cala Jóncols

Cala Jóncols, Roses ⓣ972 253 970,
ⓦwww.calajoncols.com. Set in a
secluded, rugged cove at the
end of a dirt track. A cheerful,
sprawling place, with simple
but comfortable rooms around
a pool, a good restaurant and a
diving school attached. €75.

Can Ceret

c/Mar 1, St Pere Pescador ⓣ & ⓕ972
550 433. Originally a farmhouse,
built in 1723, this enchanting
hotel occupies a cool stone
building with large gardens and
has a marvellous restaurant. All
its beautifully decorated rooms
have sumptuous bathrooms and
air conditioning. €95.

Hotel de la Moneda

Pl Moneda 8–10, Castelló d'Empúries
ⓣ972 158 602, ⓦwww
.hoteldelamoneda.com. Delightful,
newly opened hotel occupying
a seventeenth-century mansion
in the heart of the old quarter,
with vaulted ceilings and pool.
The brightly coloured rooms
are elegantly decorated and air-
conditioned. €100.

Ramblamar

Avgda Rhode 153, Roses ⓣ972 256
354, ⓕ972 256 811. Best-value
hotel on the seafront in the
heart of town, with pleasant,
airy rooms, most with beach
views. €82.

Campsites

Nautic Almatà

Ctra Castelló km11, St Pere Pescador
ⓣ972 454 477, ⓕ972 454 686. The
handiest site for the Aigüamolls

PLACES The Golf de Roses

Visiting Empuriabrava

The tourist office is at c/Puigmal 1 (June–Aug daily 9am–9pm; ⓣ972 450 802,
ⓦwww.empuriabrava.com).

park, this large complex is mostly shaded, with a landscaped pool, shops and restaurants.

Restaurants

La Avenida

c/Jaume I, 28, Roses. Small, friendly restaurant near the fishing port, specializing in fresh cod. Also does a good range of tapas.

El Bullí

Cala Montjoi ☎972 150 457. Closed Oct–March. Idyllically located in beach-view gardens, Ferran Adrià's establishment was voted third-best restaurant in the world in 2004 by *Restaurant Magazine*, and boasts three Michelin stars for his superb original take on traditional Catalan cuisine. It's astronomically expensive; one of the best-value deals is the five-and-a-half-hour tasting menu at €125.

Hotel Canet

c/Joc de la Pilota 2, Castelló d'Empúries. Central hotel with a sunny terrace that serves very tasty Catalan food at reasonable prices and a good *menú del día*.

▼ EMPURIABRAVA: BOAT TRAFFIC IN THE CANALS

Flor de Lis

c/Cosconilles 47, Roses. Easter–Sept daily 7–11pm. Set in a beautiful stone cottage, the *Flor de Lis* has earned a Michelin star for its French nouvelle cuisine. It's worth trying the *menú degustació*, which includes a sample of everything.

Mar y Sol

Pl Catalunya 20, Roses. Tasteful seafront restaurant offering excellent fish and seafood, including regional rice dishes and local prawns and anchovies at moderate prices.

Bars

Beograd

c/Puig Rom 106, Roses. Bustling, trendy bar in the town centre that attracts a glittering local and weekender set.

Si Us Plau

Pg Marítim 1, Roses. A café by day, this pleasant place comes to life in the evenings, drawing in the pre-clubbing crowd and last-drink revellers. There's a varied programme of live music every summer weeknight.

Clubs

Ona

Avgda Rhode 66, Roses. A curious spot, offering snacks and cocktails at the beach bar or a night of hedonism at the fun, extravagant club with visiting DJs.

Passarel.la

Pg Marítim, Empuriabrava. June–Sept daily 11pm–5am. A happening beach club, with several bars grouped around a large dance floor and pool. Mainly house and dance, with visiting DJs from Ibiza.

Figueres and around

Figueres is forever destined to be associated with Salvador Dalí, who was born here and whose extravagant Teatre-Museu Dalí attracts more visitors than any other museum in Spain, apart from Madrid's Prado. Dalí's colourful and eccentric legacy rather puts the rest of Figueres in the shade, but a stroll around town reveals a pleasant and prosperous old centre, as well as two other worthwhile museums. Figueres also boasts the largest fortress in Europe, Castell de Sant Ferran.

The building of the fortress, as well as a burgeoning wine industry, saw a rise in Figueres' standing in the eighteenth century. Occupied by Napoleon's troops in the early nineteenth century, it was eventually recovered by the Catalans and saw a period of steady growth until the end of the century when phylloxera wiped out the vineyards.

Figueres has always been renowned in Catalonia for its republican and federalist ideals; it was the last stronghold to fall during the Civil War, and was the seat for seven days in 1939 of the last parliament of the Spanish Republic.

Of Figueres' outlying villages, the most attractive are Vilabertran, with its beautiful eleventh-century monastery, and the more cosmopolitan Peralada, boasting a Renaissance castle, casino and vineyards.

The Rambla and Barri Vell

Defining the southern edge of the old town, the short Rambla, lined with plane trees, is more of a traffic island than a pedestrian thoroughfare, surrounded by shops and glass-fronted terrace

▲ FIGUERES: LA RAMBLA

cafés. A regular Thursday market is held here, as well as other fairs and events throughout the year. Between the Rambla and the Museu-Teatre Dalí, the streets of the Barri Vell harbour a hotchpotch of designer shoe-shops, fashion boutiques, Dalí memorabilia and traditional food and houseware shops.

Visiting Figueres

Figueres is just off the A7 and the N-II, with underground parking at Plaça Catalunya. It is served by regular trains on the Portbou–Barcelona line, and buses from Girona and towns on the northern stretch of the Costa Brava.

The tourist office is on Plaça del Sol (July & Aug daily 9am–9pm; Sept–June Mon–Sat 9.30am–1pm & 4–7pm, Sun 9.30am–1pm; ☎972 503 155, ✉www .figueres.net, ✉www.figueresciutat.com). There are also small information points by the Teatre-Museu Dalí and at Plaça Estació 7 (July–Sept Mon–Sat 9.30am–1pm & 4–7pm).

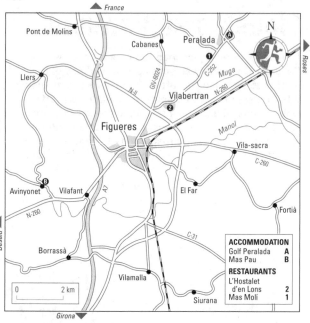

Map showing: France, Pont de Molins, Cabanes, Peralada, Roses, C-252, Muga, Llers, GIV-6024, N-II, Vilabertran, N-260, Figueres, Manol, Vila-sacra, C-260, Avinyonet, Vilafant, El Far, Fortià, Besalú, N-260, A7, C-31, Borrassà, Vilamalla, Siurana, Girona, 0 — 2 km

ACCOMMODATION	
Golf Peralada	A
Mas Pau	B

RESTAURANTS	
L'Hostalet d'en Lons	2
Mas Molí	1

Teatre-Museu Dalí

Plaça Gala-Salvador Dalí 5. July–Sept daily 9am–7.45pm; Oct–June Tues–Sat 10.30am–5.45pm, plus open Mon in June. ⓦ www.salvador-dali.org. €9.

The wildly extravagant Teatre-Museu Dalí went up in 1974 on the site of a ruined theatre where Dalí had staged his first exhibition in 1918 at the age of fourteen. Although the museum houses a representative selection of his works, you shouldn't expect to find his most famous paintings here, as they are dispersed far and wide, but that's not to say you won't get a strong sense of his bizarre vision and genius from the works that are on display.

The moment you set foot in the door, you enter a fantasy world of one man's fevered imagination, ghosts and paranoia. The first sight to greet you is an open courtyard, where a buxom bronze statue rises above the bonnet of the *Rainy Taxi*, a Cadillac in which the rain falls inside onto two figures shrouded in ivy and snails. Towering above it is a totem pole of tyres crowned by Gala's rowing boat, from which hang pendulous drops of water.

▼ FIGUERES: SHOP SELLING DALÍ SOUVENIRS

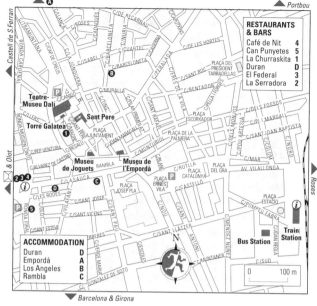

RESTAURANTS
& BARS
Café de Nit   4
Can Punyetes   5
La Churraskita   1
Duran   D
El Federal   3
La Serradora   2

ACCOMMODATION
Duran   D
Empordà   E
Los Angeles A
Rambla   C

The dome area behind the courtyard houses one of Dalí's many trompe l'oeil paintings, which at first glance resembles a pixillated jumble with a portrait of Gala; viewing it through the inverted telescope placed in front reveals the face of Abraham Lincoln. Adjoining this is the Mae West Hall, in which a pink sofa in the shape of lips and some carefully arranged drapes come together to form a giant portrait of Mae West. In the crypt below the dome area, a simple marble stone marks the artist's tomb; sadly, his body rests here and not in Púbol with Gala as he had wished.

Among all the playfulness and love of illusion on display, there are some superb paintings where Dalí's consummate practical skill comes shining through. The Palau del Vent on the first floor, representing his idea of an artist's home – studio, living room and bedroom – is dominated by the ceiling painting of the huge feet of Gala and Dalí ascending to heaven, while beautiful pictures, such as Dalí's haunting self-portrait in oils, go almost unnoticed. Other rooms house a series of variations inspired by Millet's *Angelus* and some enigmatic portraits of Gala, particularly *Gala Nude from Behind* and the lovely *Galatea of the Spheres*.

Museu de l'Empordà

Rambla 2 ⊕ www.museuemporda.org.
Tues–Sat 11am–7pm, Sun 11am–2pm.
€3. The Museu de l'Empordà holds local archeological finds and an outstanding art collection – mainly nineteenth- and twentieth-century Catalan paintings and some Spanish contemporary art. On the second level, the sombre works of Vayreda and the Olot School stand in stark contrast to the vibrancy of Sorolla's expansive Mediterranean scenes. Equally

▲ CASTELL DE SANT FERRAN: OLD STABLES

engaging is the third floor's exhibition of abstract and figurative depictions of the region's landscape, including some by the ubiquitous Dalí. On the same floor is a small but eye-catching array of contemporary art by Spain's big guns, featuring Joan Miró's broad brushstrokes, the louring swirls of Antoni Tàpies and the attractive textured abstract portraits and depictions of nature by Modest Cuixart.

Museu de Joguets

c/St Pere 1 ⓦ www.mjc-figueres.net. June–Sept Mon–Sat 10am–1pm & 4–7pm, Sun 11am–1.30pm & 5–7.30pm; Oct–May closed Sun eve & Mon. €3. Occupying the old *Hotel Paris*, a mansion dating from 1767, the Museu de Joguets is a delightful collection of over four thousand antique toys, including some that once belonged to famous names such as Dalí, Federico García Lorca and Joan Miró.

Castell de Sant Ferran

Daily: July–Sept 10.30am–7pm; Oct–June 10.30am–2pm. €3. The Castell de Sant Ferran was considered in its day to be one of the most impressive fortresses in Europe and is still the most extensive. You can choose to roam among the buildings and battlements at your own pace, but it's more rewarding to opt for an audioguide (€2) and follow the marked itinerary.

The castle was built in 1753 to defend the town against the French, but an unpromising start saw it fall twice to their arch enemy in the early nineteenth century without a single shot being fired. In the Spanish Civil War, it was used as a barracks for the International Brigades and was the last home of the Spanish Republic before its leaders fled into exile in 1939. Most recently used as a prison for Colonel Tejero, who staged an attempted coup in 1981, it was opened to the public in 1997.

An imposing gateway leads through the defensive outer walls, over 3km in circumference, and the wide, earth-filled moat to the inner walls, which conceal a vast parade ground. On the eastern side are the atmospheric underground stables, an enormous double-galleried nave, which was able to shelter a cavalry regiment of five hundred. The real wonder lies 8m beneath the parade ground, where cavernous cisterns store water in a sabotage-proof marvel of hydraulic engineering designed to last out a year-long siege. Dinghy trips through the cisterns are available, preceded by a jeep ride around the walls; book on ☏972 506 094; €15.

Vilabertran

June–Sept Tues–Sat 10am–1.30pm & 3–6.30pm, Sun 10am–1.30pm; Oct–May closes 1hr earlier & closed Sun; €3, free on Tues. Dominating the village of Vilabertran is the former Augustinian monastery of Canònica de Santa Maria de Vilabertran. At its heart is its beautiful Romanesque church, the setting for the marriage on Christmas Day in 1322 of the Catalan queen, Elisenda de Montcada, to King Jaume II of Aragon, who chose the town for the simple reason that royal weddings bestowed tax-free status on the town hosting it, and Vilabertran was small enough for this not to be a loss in income for the royal coffers. The church is crowned by a magnificent Lombard belfry, consisting of three tiers of double arched windows on all four sides, and has a tranquil twelfth-century cloister. The interior's highlight is an ornate fourteenth-century gold and silver cross, almost 2m high.

The church is the venue for Vilabertran's prestigious Schubertiada festival (☏972 508 787; €18–32), a series of concerts devoted to Schubert, held in late August and early September.

Peralada

The fortified medieval town of Peralada is best known for its splendid, moated Renaissance Castell de Peralada, containing vineyards, Catalo-

nia's most stylish casino and a museum (July–Sept daily, tours hourly 10am–noon & 4–8pm; Oct–June Tues–Sun, tours hourly 10am–noon & 4.30–6.30pm, closed Sun pm; €3.60); this holds a fine collection of glass and ceramics and a magnificent library containing 80,000 volumes, including 1000 versions of *Don Quixote* in dozens of languages; the ticket includes entry to the adjacent fourteenth-century Convent de Sant Domènec with its beautiful Romanesque cloister. You can buy wines produced by the castle, including good cavas, at the Museu de Caves de l'Empordà (same site & hours).

Hotels

Duran

c/Lasauca 5, Figueres ☏972 501 250, ⓦwww.hotelduran.com. This lovely old-world hotel, founded as a carter's tavern in 1855, is handy for the Rambla and Teatre-Museu Dalí, and is famous for its fine restaurant. The air-conditioned rooms are on the

▲ CASTELL DE SANT FERRAN: VIEW OF OUTER RAMPARTS

dark side, but very comfortably furnished. €86.

Empordà

N-II km 763, Figueres ☎972 500 562, ⊚www.hotelemporda.com. An extremely comfortable hotel set around a shaded courtyard about five minutes' walk north of the centre. All the spacious, modernized rooms have large terraces. €119.

Golf Peralada

Camí Garriga ☎972 538 830, ⊚www .golfperalada.com. Unabashed luxury in a modern five-star complex with its own top-flight golf course; rooms are as stunning as you'd expect. €325.

Los Angeles

c/Barceloneta 10, Figueres ☎972 510 661, ⊚www.hotelangeles.com. Friendly, family-run hotel

tucked away in a quiet street behind the Teatre-Museu Dalí. The en-suite rooms are simply but pleasantly decorated, and are quiet despite the central location. €45.

Mas Pau

Avinyonet de Puigventós ☎972 546 154, ⊚www.maspau.com. Enchanting sixteenth-century *masia* in a village west of Figueres, with gardens, pool and a lovely terrace restaurant. The super-stylish suites are luxurious and superbly equipped. €105.

Rambla

Rambla 33, Figueres ☎972 676 020, ⊚www.hotelrambla.net. Relaxing, modern hotel in a Neoclassical building right in the centre, with spacious, air-conditioned rooms, all elegantly designed. €75.

▼ VILABERTRAN: EXTERIOR OF THE MONASTERY

Restaurants

Can Punyetes

Ronda Firal 25, Figueres. Bustling place with rustic decor, serving excellent Catalan food at eminently reasonable prices, specializing in *pà amb tomàquet* meals and chunky grilled meats.

La Churraskita

c/Magre 5, Figueres. Closed Mon. Busy Italo-Argentinian restaurant on a narrow backstreet, offering huge steaks and extremely good pizzas and fresh pasta at moderate prices.

Duran

c/Lasauca 5, Figueres. Pleasantly cluttered old-world dining hall in a hotel off the Rambla, with well-cooked traditional Catalan fare, including a wide selection of meat and fish at surprisingly moderate prices.

▲ VIEW OVER SUNFLOWER FIELDS TO FIGUERES

farmhouse by the roadside, this delightful, if pricey, restaurant dishes up extremely good traditional Catalan cuisine.

Bars

Café de Nit
Pl Sol 2, Figueres. Favoured by stylish thirty-somethings, the *Café de Nit* has a large dance floor and covers music from 1980s pop to salsa.

El Federal
Pl Sol 4, Figueres. A lively bar, with surreal decor, including a living room clinging upside down to the ceiling. There's also a fabulous interior garden.

La Serradora
Pl Sol 7, Figueres. A young, local crowd packs this place, set in an old sawmill and thumping out house with a mixture of Latin pop.

L'Hostalet d'en Lons
c/Concha 6, Vilabertran. Closed Mon. A deceptively large, and popular, restaurant inside a welcoming old house, offering fine Catalan fare, all at reasonable prices.

Mas Molí
Ctra Vilabertran, Peralada. Closed Mon. In a lovingly restored

Cadaqués and Cap de Creus

Often referred to as an island on the coast, the beautiful fishing village of Cadaqués has been protected from mass tourism by the tortuous route in through the mountains. Distinctly bohemian in feel, the town was discovered by the likes of Picasso and Marc Chagall in the early 1900s, but its star quality was assured when Salvador Dalí settled in neighbouring Portlligat in 1930. His home, a rambling collection of fishing huts, has now been turned into a fascinating museum.

Cadaqués' old town, set on a low hill, is a delightful warren of flower-decked narrow streets leading down to a string of pretty pebble coves lining the bay. In keeping with the general bohemian-chic feel of the town, nightlife is a pleasurable blend of laid-back supping on the seashore and stylish hobnobbing in the streets of the old town. From Cadaqués you can easily make a trip to the wild and tumbling **Cap de Creus** headland to the north.

Cadaqués Barri Vell

The most impressive way to enter Cadaqués is to climb up to the Barri Vell from the car park at the entrance to town; you'll find a picturesque maze of rough cobbled alleys and chaotic layers of whitewashed buildings scaled by rich pink and purple bougainvillea. Come here on a Monday and you'll pass through the market held on Riera Sant Vicens.

Near the bottom is the Museu de Cadaqués, c/Narcís Monturiol 15 (opening hours and prices vary), a gallery staging some excellent exhibitions of local art or displays relating to Dalí's work.

A short path climbs uphill to the sixteenth-century Església de Santa Maria, with a simple exterior and tall belfry.

▼ CADAQUÉS: DETAIL OF CHURCH FACADE AND CYPRESSES

Visiting Cadaqués

The small tourist office, c/Cotxe 2 (Mon–Sat 10am–1pm & 4–8pm; Easter–Oct also Sun 10am–1pm; ☎972 258 315), is in an office behind the seafront Casino building.

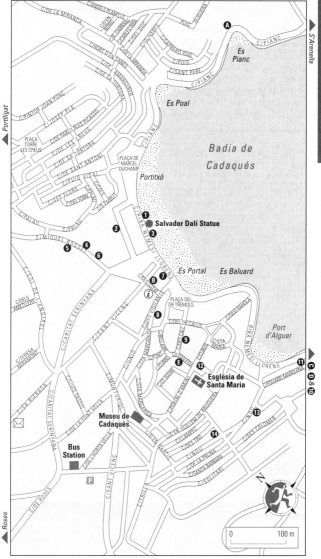

ACCOMMODATION		RESTAURANTS & BARS					
Hostal Cristina	B	El Barroco	14	Casino	7	Pizzeria Cesar	12
Llané Petit	C	Boia	3	Celeste	13	La Sirena	9
Playa Sol	A	Café de la Habana	10	La Frontera	4	Si Té 7	11
Rocamar	D	Can Tito	8	L'Hostal	2	Tropical	5
Hostal Vehí	E	Casa Anita	6	Marítim	1	Vehí	E

A wrought-iron door bearing symbols of the town and the sea opens to the ornate eighteenth-century altarpiece; among the gilded carvings are Atlas supporting the world, St Rita, patron saint of the impossible, and St Barbara, protector from storms and shipwrecks. The third side chapel on the left was painted by Dalí. The church hosts classical music concerts every summer; for information and tickets (€12–32), contact the tourist office.

Below the church, the pretty streets around Dr Callis and des Call gradually become busier with smart clothes shops, restaurants and artists' studios and galleries before emerging into the tiny Plaça Dr Trèmols, where a narrow archway leads down to the seafront.

▼ CADAQUÉS: UNEVEN STREETS IN THE OLD TOWN

Cadaqués seafront and beaches

On the seafront a bronze statue of Salvador Dalí, standing with his back to the pebble beach, stares down haughtily on all the artists, shoppers and street musicians; flanking the statue are two very popular cafés, *Boia* and *Casino* (see p.167), good for a daytime refresher or night-time socializing.

The small but busy Passeig is lined with bars and restaurants, including the celebrated *L'Hostal* (see p.169), where – it is said – Dalí once spent a legendary night drinking with Gabriel García Márquez and Mick Jagger. Behind the Passeig, the bar- and restaurant-lined c/Miguel Rosset is a hot night-time spot.

At the southern end of the seafront, some 300m along the road to the right of *Hotel Llané Petit*, lies the sheltered Platja Sa Conca. Along the shore, a footpath to the east leads through a slate and cactus gully to the ruined Capella de Pius V, built to commemorate the 1571 Battle of Lepanto. The tranquil little chapel has an intact domed roof and a bas-relief of Pope Pius V discernible on the back wall.

A stretch of the Camí de Ronda climbs steeply from Sa Conca for a thirty-minute trek and scramble to some good

Cadaqués activities

There are some great diving spots around the Cap de Creus; the best of the English-speaking diving schools, offering excursions, are Scuba World, c/Font Vella 5 (☎629 491 380, ☎972 259 163, ☻www.scubaworld-cadaques.info) and Diving Center Cadaqués, at Hotel Rocamar (☎972 258 989). Kayaking Costa Brava at Portlligat (☎972 773 806, ☻www.kayakingcb.com) runs monitored excursions along the coves and rents kayaks. Scooters and boats can be rented at Bikes&Boats, Es Poal (☎972 258 027), while boat trips to Cap de Creus run from Portitxó, organized by Creuers Cadaqués, Ctra Portlligat 28 (☎972 159 462). You can also rent Gala's boat in Portlligat for the couple's favourite jaunt to Cap de Creus (☎617 465 757).

swimming at the medium-shelving beach of Cala Nans, nearly always virtually empty. Five minutes south of here, a lighthouse marks the boundary of the Badia de Cadaqués and gives wonderful open views.

Casa-Museu Dalí

Portlligat. Mid-June to mid-Sept daily 10.30am–9pm; mid-Sept to mid-June Tues–Sun 10.30am–6pm; closed Jan & Feb; last entry 50min before closing. ☎972 251 015, ⊛www.salvador-dali.org. €8. The artist's main residence for some fifty years, the superb Casa-Museu Dalí has now been converted into by far the most engaging of the three Dalí museums in the region (see p.156 and p.129 for the others). Dalí and his Russian wife, Gala, set up home in 1930 in an old fisherman's hut, subsequently buying up all the huts around to create a labyrinthine house.

Visitor numbers are strictly limited: always book a day or two in advance by phone. Small groups get ten minutes with a guide in each of four areas, which is ample.

Access to the first area, which includes the Dining Room and Library, is through the Hall of the Bear, the first hut the artist bought, where a stuffed bear greets visitors. Pictures of moustached men are dotted throughout the house, reflecting one of Dalí's obsessions, while yellow St John's Wort, one of Gala's touches, is also in abundance.

The second area, on the first floor, is where Dalí worked, housing the Models' Room and his Studio, displaying two unfinished original works on easels. Above this, the Yellow Room is remarkable for the view of the natural beauty of the surroundings – in sharp contrast with the surreal art; to the left of the window is a mirror angled so that the couple could watch the sun rise without getting out of bed.

The third area features the Bird Room and the Bedroom. The tiny cages in the former were for cicadas from Olot (Dalí felt they sang the most sweetly). The Photo Room, originally used as a dressing room, displays photographs of celebrities visiting Dalí. The last indoor room, the domed Oval Room, built to resemble a sea urchin, was Gala's retreat and has remarkable acoustics.

The final area, the Summer Dining Room and Patio, was

PLACES Cadaqués and Cap de Creus

▼ CAFÉ IN CADAQUÉS

where the couple would entertain: the inside of the house was reserved for very close friends. The shaded garden, protected by a wall topped with giant eggs (to symbolize life), gives on to the phallic-shaped swimming pool, built to resemble the fountains in Granada's Alhambra and surrounded by some splendid examples of 1960s pop art using everyday objects.

Portlligat

Besides the Casa-Museu Dalí, tiny Portlligat boasts nothing more than some minuscule coves and a brace of hotels. The beach at Portlligat isn't suitable for swimming, but the enticing pebble coves immediately to the north, known respectively as Platja S'Alqueria Petita and Platja S'Alqueria Gran, both shelve steeply and are ideal for some lazy swimming. Idyllic little inlets to the north of the latter are much favoured by nude bathers.

Cap de Creus

The wild Cap de Creus headland, where the Pyrenees crash down to the sea, is the easternmost point in the Iberian peninsula; dawn revels take place here every New Year's Day. A lighthouse dating from 1853 stands in juxtaposition with the fake lighthouse built nearer the edge of the cliff for the 1971 film, *The Light at the End of the World*. Crowning the clifftop, the Cap de Creus bar and restaurant has a great terrace for soaking in the stunning views and tranquillity. The only sounds you're likely to hear are seagulls calling and the gentle chugging of fishing boats down below, while sailing boats glide lazily from turquoise cove to rock-strewn beach.

Hotels

Hostal Cristina

c/Riera 5 ☎972 258 138. This cheerful *hostal* occupies an old veranda-fronted building a short distance from the main beach. The rooms are small but well furnished and have en-suite bathrooms. €55.

The road to Cap de Creus

The spectacular six-kilometre road **from Portlligat** to the Cap de Creus climbs tortuously through a lunar landscape, past some stunning views of barren headlands and the jagged coastline. Along the way, the route passes secluded coves and after about 4km a sand-coloured rock formation known as El Camell on account of its shape, said to resemble a haughty, seated camel.

Walkers can take the breathtaking and demanding Camí de Ronda footpath, which follows the rocky shoreline from Portlligat and offers lots of opportunities along the way to take a dip.

From Cadaqués you can get to Cap de Creus by minibus (contact Passarella, Avgda Caritat Serinyana 23 ☎972 258 771; €14) or by the mini-train from Portitxó beach (daily 10am–6pm, hourly; 2hr round trip; €10).

Best of the beaches en route are **Platja de Sant Lluís**, reached by a twenty-minute signposted footpath from the road through olive terraces, where bathers (both nude and not) enjoy an uncrowded pebble beach. Almost at the headland, a yellow rambler sign by a crash barrier signals a parking place for the climb down to a pair of wind-battered coves – **L'Infern** ("Hell") and the prettier **Cala Jugadora**, where calm, crystalline waters contrast with the savagery of the rocks.

▲ CAP DE CREUS: VIEW FROM CAP DE CREUS BAR

Llané Petit

c/Dr Bartomeus 37 ☎972 258 050, ⓦwww.llanepetit.com. Smart, friendly hotel that makes for a relaxing option overlooking a less crowded beach at the south end of town. Half of the rooms have splendid sea views, and all have air conditioning and spacious terraces. €105.

Misty

Ctra Portlligat ☎972 258 962, ⓕ972 159 090. The low buildings of this hacienda-style hotel, in a residential area between Cadaqués and Portlligat, are grouped around a small swimming pool and well-tended gardens. Most bedrooms give onto the garden. €70.

Playa Sol

Pianc 3 ☎972 258 100, ⓕ972 258 054. Closed Oct–Dec. Tasteful colonial-style place with a large pool, located on a curve in the seafront north of the centre. Rooms with a sea view give the best panorama in town, although the alternative, looking over tranquil gardens behind, is almost as appealing. €155.

Port-Lligat

Portlligat ☎972 258 162, ⓕ972 258 643. Closed Nov–Dec. At the top of a flight of steps overlooking the Casa-Museu Dalí, this tranquil hotel with a pool is ideal for exploring Cadaqués or the Cap de Creus. €85.

Rocamar

c/Verge del Carme s/n ☎972 258 150, ⓦwww.rocamar.com. Tucked away in a cove south of town, this pleasant hotel with tennis courts, a large pool and diving school is full of oak-beamed charm, its pleasant, airy rooms giving onto either the sea or the gardens. €121.

Hostal Vehí

c/ Església 6 ☎972 258 470. Friendly, excellent-value *hostal* in a lovely central location near the church. Most of the rooms have great views, but all share bathrooms. €32.

Cafés

Boia

Pg del Mar. Daily 9pm–2am. Friendly beach bar to the south of the Dalí statue, serving good breakfasts and fruit juices.

Casino

Riba Nemesi Llorens s/n. This old-fashioned locals' haunt features high ceilings and subtle lighting. The conservatory-style front room is great for morning breakfast or evening cocktails, while modernity is encroaching with an Internet room off the bar.

Marítim

Pg del Mar. Daily 9pm–2am. The other side of the Dalí statue from *Boia*, this beach bar is frequented by a trendy set and ideally suited to a late-night tipple by the sea.

Restaurants

El Barroco

c/Nou s/n. Nov–March closed Sun–Tues. With a logo designed by Dalí, who used to dine here in the summer, this extravagantly decorated and reasonably priced restaurant has a garden full of jasmine and geraniums and serves a range of local and Italian dishes, plus some veggie choices.

Can Tito

c/Vigilant s/n. Nov–March closed Mon–Thurs. In what appears to be a small warehouse hollowed out of a building, this superb, if expensive, establishment specializes in innovative Catalan cuisine, with especially good grilled fish dishes.

Cap de Creus

Cap de Creus headland. Mon–Thurs noon–8pm, Fri–Sun 11am–midnight. An inviting bar and restaurant, with a fabulous terrace overlooking the coastline, serving a wide range of dishes, from Catalan to Indian, and attracting an equally diverse crowd.

Casa Anita

c/Miquel Rosset 16 ☎972 258 471. Another of Dalí's favourite haunts, this rustic-chic restaurant is in the heart of Cadaqués' night quarter and is always heaving. Huge portions of traditional and filling Catalan food are accompanied by slabs of *pà amb tomàquet*.

Celeste

c/Nou 1. Nov–March closed Wed. A cheap and cheerful old-town bar-restaurant, decorated with wicker furniture and abstract paintings and specializing in four types of pasta in eleven types of sauce. They also serve great cocktails.

Pizzeria Cesar

c/Curós 11. Daily 8pm–midnight; Nov–March closed Sun–Tues. This labyrinthine restaurant is set in

▲ CAP DE CREUS: FAKE LIGHTHOUSE

a former cottage, with a white-washed stone interior. Serving a wide selection of delicious pizzas and imaginative salads – notably chicory and walnut – it's justly popular.

La Sirena

c/Es Call s/n. Closed Feb & Nov. Owned by a perfectionist Croatian chef, this superb and not at all pricey restaurant, in a tiny street, serves some of the best fish dishes in town. Especially good is the *suquet*, while the desserts are fabulous.

Vehí

c/Església 6. Closed Nov–Feb. This lovely restaurant has views of the town and bay, and serves tasty traditional local cuisine. It's not cheap unless you choose from the range of *menús del dia* from €9 to €14.

Bars

Café de la Habana

Porta d'en Pampà. Rustic Cuban furnishings and eclectic paintings help create the atmosphere in this cool bar serving an amazing selection of cocktails. Live music by a singer-songwriter every night at 11pm adds to the mellow tone.

La Frontera

c/Miquel Rosset 20. Closed Nov–Easter. One of the trendiest places in town, this lively, friendly bar serves top cocktails. The noisy interior contrasts nicely with a pleasant garden bursting with flowers.

L'Hostal

Pg del Mar 8. Nov–March closed Mon. The first night-time bar in Catalonia when it opened in 1901 and a favourite haunt of Dalí's, *L'Hostal* retains a vaguely surreal air, with bizarre artworks jostling for wall space with photos of the rich and famous who have passed through its doors. Live jazz and rock plays every night in the summer, while the outdoor terrace is the coolest place on the block.

Si Té 7

Riba d'en Pixot. Nov–March closed Mon & Tues. In a great location overlooking the beach at Port d'Alguer, this tiny bar – with an amiable Catalan owner – is perfect for late-night chilling to jazz, blues and reggae.

Tropical

c/Miquel Rosset 19. A lush, candle-lit garden leads into a cavernous interior where fish painted on driftboard line the natural rock painted to resemble the sea bed. In all, a fun place to sip a cocktail and listen to Spanish Caribbean tunes.

▼ CADAQUÉS: INTERIOR OF L'HOSTAL BAR

Port de la Selva

Tucked away in a small, near-circular bay, Port de la Selva is a charming collection of low-rise whitewashed buildings set round a fishing port and marina. Either side is a string of picturesque coves, rugged to the north, gentler to the west. The inland parent town of Selva de Mar is quieter still and makes for a pleasant afternoon's visit. Also worth a detour are the imposing Monèstir de Sant Pere de Rodes and the even more atmospheric Castell Sant Salvador, atop the craggy Serra de Rodes.

The town

The town hugs the southern and eastern shores of its bay, and is barely more than two streets deep; walking from one end to the other takes a good thirty minutes, but it's an enjoyable stretch of charming whitewashed buildings, and wandering amongst these is the chief appeal of the town.

The town's Blue Flag Platja Gran is a popular beach despite its steep shelving and occasional jellyfish warnings. Nearby is the café-lined Plaça Dr Oriol and the short promenade, truncated by the bustling fishing port, which juts out squarely into the bay.

The northern coves

The seaside road north of Port de la Selva passes the leisure marina before coming to a string of small beaches. The first, Platja d'en Pas, a steeply shelving pebble beach, boasts some of the cleanest water in the Mediterranean, and inevitably attracts the crowds. Some 200m north from here, the road ends and a footpath takes over, leading to Cala Tamariua, a sheltered pebble cove favoured by clothed and nude bathers. The path picks up again on the far side of the beach, skirting the shoreline for 700m until it reaches the tiny Cala Cativa inlet, where a fishermen's refuge stands on the water's edge. A quarter-hour of scrambling along the less stable path from here culminates in the delightful pebble beach of Cala Fornells, where an ancient limekiln made of stones still stands.

The best way to see the isolated coves further east towards Cap de Creus is to take a cruise from Llançà (see p.178).

The western coves

The beaches to the west of town can be reached along the

Visiting Port de la Selva

The tourist office is on the seafront at c/Mar 1 (July–Sept daily 8am–10pm; Oct–June Mon–Fri 8am–3pm, Sat 9am–1pm; ☎972 387 025, ✆www.ddgi.es /porselva). A small summer tourist office operates from Selva de Mar town hall, c/Camp de l'Obra (July & Aug Mon 9.30am–1pm & 4–8pm, Wed 4–8pm, Tues, Thurs & Fri 9.30am–1pm; ☎972 387 228).

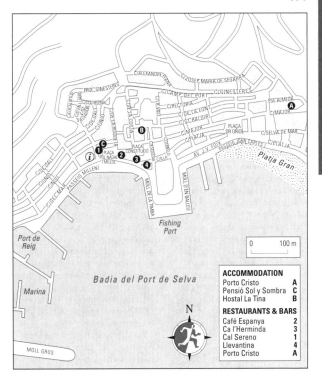

ACCOMMODATION

Porto Cristo	A
Pensió Sol y Sombra	C
Hostal La Tina	B

RESTAURANTS & BARS

Café Espanya	2
Ca l'Herminda	3
Cal Sereno	1
Llevantina	4
Porto Cristo	A

Camí de Ronda, starting at the western end of Platja Gran. By road, some 2km from the town a signposted turning to the right leads to a rough-and-ready parking area on the Punta de S'Arenella, a scrubby headland surmounted by a solitary lighthouse; the quiet little coves here are good for snorkelling.

Selva de Mar

Selva de Mar's setting in the foothills of the Pyrenees has contributed to preserving this medieval village's unhurried pace of life; the best place to take this in is from one of the shaded terrace cafés on Plaça Camp de l'Obra. From here a warren of streets meanders through the village past six-teenth-century watchtowers converted into homes. Each street sign bears a little epithet; the one accompanying Cantó del Puig, for example, a precarious, rocky ascent, claims that the elderly flee rather than face climbing it.

Turning right into the street at the top of the steps on Plaça Camp de l'Obra leads you past a fortified house and through a narrow alley to the start of a thirty-minute walk (signposted); this gives you a complete tour of the outskirts and affords a pleasing blend of fine views of the countryside and some tranquil spots for a short breather. Follow the signs along a track leading uphill past vineyards until you come to an ancient stone bench decorated with carved lions. The trail leads down from here to the remains of a small water mill and the steep waterfall that fed it – an idyllic spot. Across a bridge by a small square with a fountain, the path climbs again through evergreen oaks to the twelfth-century fortified Església de Sant Sebastià, directly aligned with the church in Port de la Selva. The track back to the centre skirts the church to the right, descending past cultivated terraces to the edge of the village, where three tiny and ancient stone bridges span the rocky river bed running through Selva de Mar.

From the Església de Sant Sebastià you have the option of making a fairly arduous, but rewarding, waymarked ascent (4hr) to the monastery at Sant Pere de Rodes.

Sant Pere de Rodes

Monastery Tues–Sun: June–Sept 10am–8pm; Oct–May 10am–2pm & 3–5.30pm. €4, free on Tues. Inland from Port de la Selva, a tortuous road of hairpin bends climbs 675m to a complex of ancient buildings, dominated by the rambling Benedictine Monèstir de Sant Pere de Rodes. There's space for parking (€1.50) about 500m before you reach the monastery, from where you'll have to proceed on foot.

Legend has it that, in the seventh century, in the face of barbarian threats on Rome, Pope Boniface IV ordered a safe haven to be found for countless holy relics. They were hidden in this region by a trio of hapless monks, who then forgot where, and so they built a monastery rather than return to face the pope's wrath. Historians, though, claim that this was the site of an ancient temple of Venus. By the tenth century the monastery had become wealthy: four centuries of splendour ended in 1789 with the site's abandonment.

Sant Pere de Rodes used to be one of the most romantic ruins in Catalonia, but over-zealous restoration is robbing it of a great deal of its charm. No original columns or capitals

▼ PORT DE LA SELVA: CALA TAMARIUA

Port de la Selva

PLACES

▲ PORT DE LA SELVA: THE SEAFRONT

remain in the cloister and the new pantiled roofs are just too tidy. The redeeming feature, apart from the superb views, is the church, which retains tenth- to fourteenth-century stonework in its three naves, including delicate carvings of animals on the capitals. Below the church are atmospheric lower cloisters; excavations have turned up traces of pre-Roman-esque murals.

In July (Sun 8pm), there are piano recitals in the Monèstir de Sant Pere de Rodes; information and tickets are available from the Port de la Selva tourist office.

Castell Sant Salvador

Far more spectacular than Sant Pere de Rodes is the louring silhouette of the ruined Castell Sant Salvador, perched on the summit of the mountain and reached by a steep uphill footpath from outside the monastery. You'll need to be reasonably agile to make the thirty-minute ascent, especially the last few metres and the hop up into a gap in the castle walls; once at the top, you should take extreme care as there are no barriers between parts of the ruins and a sheer drop. What remains today dates from the tenth and eleventh centuries, primarily the perimeter walls and alternate semicircular and square towers. The views of the Cap de Creus and the Golf de Roses are breathtaking.

Hotels

Porto Cristo

c/Major 59 ☎972 387 062, ☎972 387 529, ⓦwww.hotelportocristo .com. This sumptuous con-verted merchant's mansion on a quiet backstreet is excellent value and boasts the best res-taurant in town. Each room is unique, furnished with king-size beds, marble floors and circular baths. €82.

Pensió Sol y Sombra

c/Nou 8–10 ☎972 387 060, ©solisombra@teleline.es. On a tiny street near the port, this friendly *pensió* offers generous-sized rooms with air conditioning; ask for an attic room as they have huge balconies with sea views. €56.

Hostal La Tina

c/Sant Baldiri 16 ☎972 126 444. A cheerful *hostal* one street back from the beach, with a broad choice of spacious rooms, and a copious buffet breakfast thrown in; the owners also have apartments and a house for rent. €42.

Casa Felip

Plaça Camp de l'Obra 15, Selva de Mar. ☎972 387 271. An atmospheric old house in the heart of town, with a good traditional restaurant and airy double rooms, both en suite and shared. €30.

Restaurants

Ca L'Elvira

c/Baix 1, Selva de Mar. Closed Oct–Easter. An ordinary-looking house conceals a charming

▼ SELVA DE MAR: MAIN SQUARE

restaurant serving excellent Catalan home cooking and an inexpensive *menú del dia*.

Ca l'Herminda

c/Illa 7. Sept–June closed Mon & Tues. In the cellars of an old fisherman's house near the fishing port, this bustling restaurant specializes in seafood and fresh fish, serving very good *suquet* and *sarsuela*.

Llevantina

c/Illa s/n. Daily 10am–11pm; Sept–June closed Mon. With a terrace on the water's edge between the fishing port and the marina, this relaxing bar has tranquil views and serves great tapas.

Porto Cristo

c/Major 59. Closed Jan & Feb. This cavernous restaurant in a nineteenth-century town mansion is hugely atmospheric and surprisingly inexpensive. Specializing in Catalan cuisine, it is rightly famous for the chef's superb daily specialities and the delicious homemade desserts.

Bars

El Celler de la Selva

Plaça Camp de l'Obra, Selva de Mar. An extraordinary, laid-back bar in a five-century-old tied house, which stages live music in the summer amid surreal art and luscious cocktails. This was a favourite haunt of Dalí's and the setting for one of his preferred pastimes of autographing women's bottoms.

Café Espanya

c/Illa 1. Daily 10am–3am; Sept–June closed Mon–Thurs. This old-fashioned seafront café appeals to

▲ SANT PERE DE RODES: VIEW FROM THE MONASTERY

all sorts, from domino-playing elderly men to stylish youngsters. In the summer, it has a great terrace on the water's edge and serves anything from tapas to a late-night drink.

Cal Sereno

c/Cantó dels Pescadors 4. Sept–June closed Wed. In a narrow street between the fishing and leisure ports, this semi-surreal bar gets joyously packed in the early hours. Set in the cellar of a 250-year-old fisherman's cottage, it's named after the former owner, who would serenade his wife on returning from sea so that she would let him in.

Mackintosh

Ctra Cadaqués. Sept–June closed Mon–Thurs. This unpretentious disco has all the spontaneous fun of a Catalan small-town nightspot, where a diverse group of locals, with one or two tourists thrown in, strut their stuff to an eclectic range of music.

The Serra de l'Albera and north coast

Occupying the hinterland between Figueres and the French border, the Serra de l'Albera mountains have the lowest passes anywhere in the Pyrenees and have always been an important thoroughfare between France and Spain. The Parc Natural de l'Albera, covering 4108 hectares, provides a safe haven for indigenous flora and fauna and helps to preserve an unspoilt environment of sheer escarpments and hidden villages. Perfect walking country, the region is home to secluded monastic ruins, Neolithic dolmens and a stunning variety of wildlife, including tortoises, a protected species of Albera cow, golden eagles and wild boar.

Just 14km south of the French border is the peaceful seaside town of Llançà. North of here, the coast starts to feel a bit like a through route, with the tiny, rather unattractive village of Colera, redeemed by its craggy beaches, and the old border town and railway terminus of Portbou, trying to come to

▲ PARC NATURAL DE L'ALBERA: FONT DEL ROURE BURIAL CHAMBER IN ESPOLLA

terms with change after the removal of border controls in 1995.

Espolla

The best place to begin a visit to the Parc Natural de l'Albera is Espolla, a mountain village with crisp air, set around its eighteenth-century Església de Sant Jaume, and site of the excellent Centre d'Informació del Parc de l'Albera, c/Mossén Amadeu Sudrià (May–Oct Mon–Fri 8am–3pm, Sat 9am–2pm & 4–6pm, Sun 10am–2pm; Nov–April Sat 9am–2pm & 3–5pm, Sun 9am–2pm; ☎972 545 039); fascinating display panels of flora, fauna and human history are complemented by a range of detailed maps and itineraries for any number of walks in the area.

Just 1km southwest of Espolla stands the atmospheric Cabana Arqueta dolmen, shaded by tall oaks and dating from 2500 BC; it's a ten-minute walk along a footpath off the GI602 road towards Sant Climent Sescebes.

Garriguella

The thousand-year-old village of Garriguella is remarkable for its disproportionately large Església de Santa Eulàlia de Noves. First recorded in the tenth century, the present church was built in 1722 of unworked stone, belying its ornate interior. Based on the original Romanesque building, the large central nave is crowned by a pronounced vault supported on three arches.

Centre de Reproducció de Tortugues de l'Albera

Santuari del Camp, Garriguella. July–Sept daily 10am–6pm; closed Nov–March; April–June hours vary. ☎972 552 245. €4. The fascinating Centre de Reproducció de Tortugues de l'Albera (Mediterranean Tortoise Reproduction Centre) sets out to protect the creatures in their last remaining natural habitat in the Iberian peninsula. Over two hundred tortoises a year born in the centre are released with transmitters, in order to monitor them in an environment devastated each summer by forest fire, the main factor endangering their existence. The centre is laid out to re-create the different ecosystems in which the tortoises thrive, revealing them to be surprisingly endearing animals in their movements and social behaviour. The circular path (about 90min) begins with the appealingly tiny newborns

and moves through dryland and wetland habitats, taking in other endangered breeds such as shy pond turtles and massive African spurred tortoises.

The Santuari de Santa Maria del Camp, outside the tortoise centre, marks the site where Charlemagne is said to have fought a great battle against the Moors in the eighth century. The chapel holds an intricate sixteenth-century mural relating the story.

Sant Quirze de Colera

The Benedictine monastery of Sant Quirze de Colera was founded more than a thousand years ago. The solitary ruins nestle in the basin of a lush valley, dwarfed by the

▼ PARC NATURAL DE L'ALBERA: SANTUARI DE SANTA MARIA DEL CAMP

A short walk in the Serra de l'Albera

The village of Rabós d'Empordà, on the Espolla-Garriguella road, provides the starting point for one of the most rewarding circular walks (10km) in the park, taking in the breathtakingly set ruined monastery of Sant Quirze de Colera, well signposted northeast. The route follows a tortuous, dusty track, also passable by car, and winds through pine-carpeted valleys amid the stunning natural arena of the foothills; your only companions are likely to be cicadas and the odd hoopoe.

The Serra de l'Albera and north coast **PLACES**

sheer height of the escarpment framing them. The building is undergoing renovation and is currently closed to the public, but you can still view the facade, including the perfectly preserved arched windows of the cloisters; the four blocks visible above the main building are thought to have been part of the tenth-century church. An enterprising soul has located a restaurant (Easter–Sept daily 1–5pm) in the nearby stables, which serves good Catalan cooking in a perfect setting.

Llançà

The quiet town of Llançà is divided between the original tenth-century settlement, the

▼ LLANÇÀ: FISHING PORT

Vila, built inland to escape the attentions of marauding pirates, and its port. Site of the Wednesday market, the port area is sandwiched between the modern Passeig Marítim, which follows the curve of the sandy beach, and the shops and restaurants of Carrer Castellar. Where the two meet is the fishing port – much older and livelier than the rest of the quiet seafront. Crowning the southern end of the port, the craggy Es Castellar point is a favourite place for an evening stroll; below it, the quiet Platja de la Gola, a medium-shelving beach, is good for swimming, but its waters get very choppy when the wind is up.

The small Vila revolves around the animated Plaça Major, where pavement cafés sit in the shade of the Arbre de la Llibertat, a huge plane tree planted in 1870 to commemorate freedom from France, and where locals flock for *sardanes* and live music through the summer. Adjacent to the square is the imposing fourteenth-century defensive Torre de la Plaça (Mon–Fri 5.30–9pm, Sat 6.30–9pm), crowned by battlements and a pyramid-shaped roof; the remnants of a roof halfway up show that it was once part of a larger construction. During restoration work, medieval stocks were unearthed and are now on display on the ground floor; higher floors feature temporary exhibitions and afford great views of the surrounding

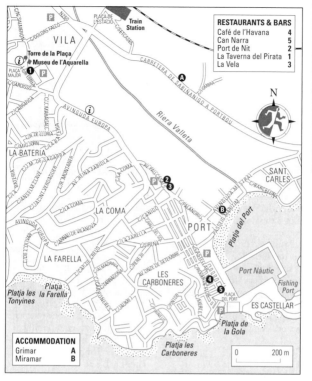

RESTAURANTS & BARS

Café de l'Havana	4
Can Narra	5
Port de Nit	2
La Taverna del Pirata	1
La Vela	3

ACCOMMODATION

Grimar	A
Miramar	B

countryside. To the right of the tower, the Museu de l'Aquarella Martínez Lozano (June–Sept Mon–Sat 7–9pm, Sun 11am–1pm & 7–9pm; Oct–May Sat & Sun 11am–1pm & 6–8pm; €1.80), the first museum in Spain devoted purely to watercolours, is a small-scale gem, featuring a surprising variety of twentieth-century Catalan works, from some fabulously bold abstracts to more traditional landscapes.

Cap Ras and Platja Garbet

The beaches north of Llançà can be reached by the Camí de Ronda, which hugs the water's edge, or by the main N260 road, which swoops in and out of the shoreline.

Some 3km from town, past the uninspiring Platja Grifeu, a signposted turn-off on the brow of a hill leads to the cluster of coves on the Cap Ras headland. Don't be put off by the number of cars, as the warren of little

Llançà activities

Centre d'Immersió Cap de Creus (☎972 120 000, ⊛www.cicapcreus.com) operates scenic cruises among the hard-to-reach coves around Llançà and Port de la Selva, as far east as Cap de Creus; they also run diving courses. SK Kayak (☎627 433 332, ⊛www.skkayak.com) runs rewarding kayak excursions from the port.

beaches can accommodate a good number of sunbathers. Tracks crisscross the headland amid low pines, bamboo and scrub, dipping down to the sea on the south side. The pebble beaches here have shallow waters, great for splashing about in. The tip of Cap Ras – almost always deserted – is thoroughly wild, with craggy inlets and trees bent horizontal by *tramuntanes*. Around the point, the trails descend sharply to sheltered sandy beaches on the north side, which are more steeply shelving and are very much the domain of nude bathers.

Past Cap Ras, the road picks up the shoreline again before descending to Platja Garbet, a pebble beach that gets extremely crowded – largely because of a superb seafood restaurant (see p.182) on the water's edge.

Colera

The sleepy seaside town of Colera is a rather unprepossessing place, overshadowed by the huge iron railway bridge passing high overhead, but it does have some inviting rugged beaches. The core of the town, Plaça Pi i Margall, is 200m back from the beach; here a pair of pavement cafés sit under the Arbre de la Llibertat. Walking north along the sheltered pebble beach brings you to the Platja d'en Goixa. Steep steps climb up to a small road, which leads about 650m north to wild, windblown Punta de l'Escala; a public footpath descends precariously from

here to the rocks below. The solitude is rewarding, but you need to be a confident swimmer to cope with the underwater currents.

Portbou

Portbou lies on the border between Spain and France. Once a semi-deserted haven, where fishermen would pull their catch ashore, safe from storms, Portbou was transformed by the construction of a huge railway station in 1872. For more than a century, the town made its living from border traffic, and old money is still evident in the grand, if faded, Modernista buildings. In 1995, however, the eighty-odd customs agencies disappeared almost overnight following the elimination of border controls, and Portbou is slowly trying to redefine itself as a holiday town.

The bay, a natural amphitheatre of granite and water, shelters an uncrowded pebbly beach. The small, café-lined promenade provides a picturesque backdrop for the *sardanes* and *havaneres* held here throughout the summer.

An easy five-minute climb from the beach to the south cliff overlooking the bay takes you to Israeli sculptor Dani Karavan's abstract Passagen, or Walter Benjamin Memorial, a bleak testimony to the plight of refugees. The German Jewish philosopher committed suicide in a hotel in Portbou in 1940 rather than be handed over to the Gestapo. A claustrophobic brown metal tunnel leads down

Visiting Colera

Colera's tiny tourist office is at c/Labrun 34, at the top of a flight of steps off Plaça Pi i Margall (Easter–Sept Mon–Fri 10am–2pm & 4–8pm; ☎972 389 050).

Visiting Portbou

The small tourist office in Portbou (May–Sept daily 9am–8pm; ☎972 390 284) is centrally located in a cabin on the seafront, Pg Sardana.

to the sea, open to the sky only for the last few metres, before coming to a glass barrier etched with an inscription by Benjamin in five languages: "It is more arduous to honour the memory of the nameless than that of the renowned. Historical construction is devoted to the memory of the nameless." Through the glass, all you can see is the sea crashing on the rocks below, while the only way out is back up through the stifling tunnel. The philosopher's grave is in the town cemetery, a few metres away, on the second terrace on the right.

Hotels

Grimar

Ctra Portbou, Llançà ☎972 380 167, ⊛www.hotelgrimar.com. Closed Oct–Easter. This plush hotel outside town is set in its own extensive lawns, with tennis courts and a large pool. The rooms are simple but airy, boasting ceiling fans and wicker decor. €100.

Miramar

Pg Marítim 7, Llançà ☎972 380 132, ⊛972 121 008. One of the longest-established hotels in Llançà, in a perfect setting on the seafront. It's family-run and has been extensively renovated, with the added benefit of a very good restaurant. €77.

Hostal Juventus

Avgda Barcelona 3, Portbou ☎972 390 241. A good-value *hostal*, which has airy rooms and modern shared bathrooms, with a bar serving appetizing, inexpensive snacks and pizzas. €40.

La Masia

Pg Sardana 1, Portbou ☎972 390 372. Giving onto the beach and pos-

▲ LLANÇÀ: PLATJA GARBET

▲ PORTBOU: GUARDIA CIVIL HEADQUARTERS

sessing a fairly good restaurant, this friendly place has airy rooms with large balconies. €72.

Turisme rural

Cal Pastor

c/Pont 3, Rabós d'Empordà ☎972 563 247, ⊕www.cal-pastor.com. Lovely old house in a pretty little village in the Serra de l'Albera, offering good self-catering facilities for up to nine people. €590 per week.

Can Garriga

c/Figueres 3, Garriguella ☎972 530 184, ⊕www.cangarriga.net. Large house with garden offering airy double rooms on a B&B basis, or a spacious top-floor three-bedroom apartment. €600 per week.

Campsites

Vell Empordà

Ctra La Jonquera, Garriguella ☎972 530 200, ⊕www.vellemporda.com. Excellent family-run site with shaded pitches and a good shop, restaurant and pool.

Restaurants

Art in Café

c/Mercat 11, Portbou. This laid-back establishment near the train station makes tasty crêpes, salads and juices while you surf the net.

Can Batlle

Plaça de Baix, Garriguella. Oct–May closed Sun–Thurs. In the centre of town, this enjoyable family restaurant is prized by locals for its tasty fish and traditional cuisine.

Can Narra

c/Castellar 37, Llançà. Sept–June closed Sun eve & Mon; also closed Oct. The best of the traditional fish restaurants, overlooking the beach and serving top *suquet* and a huge *graellada de peix*.

Can Tomas

Pl Pou Nou, Rabós d'Empordà. Closed Wed. An extremely popular, unfussy country restaurant serving hearty portions of wholesome mountain food.

Garbet

Platja Garbet, Llançà. In a fabulous windswept beachfront setting, this highly regarded and expensive restaurant serves superb fresh fish dishes on a terrace that just invites you to linger; also a good selection of tapas.

La Vela

Avgda Pau Casals 23, Llançà. Sept–June closed Mon; also closed mid-Oct to mid-Nov. A plush restaurant, decorated in crisp white throughout, serving superb fish – try the *graellada de peix* – and seafood, plus a range of local meat dishes with an innovative twist, all at moderate prices.

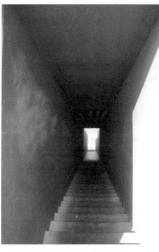

▲ PORTBOU: WALTER BENJAMIN MEMORIAL

Bars

Café de l'Havana

c/Castellar 40, Llançà. Daily 10am–3am. The walls of this small, laid-back bar are covered in photos of old Llançà, Havana and Che Guevara. A pavement terrace overflows with patrons of all ages savouring *mojitos*.

Port de Nit

Avgda Pau Casals 25, Llançà. Sept–June closed Sun–Thurs. Abstract art in this designer bar reflects the trendy image of the twenty- and thirty-something clientele on the techno dance floor, while the summer terrace attracts a more diverse crowd.

La Taverna del Pirata

c/Rafael Estela 19, Llançà. Off the Vila's Plaça Major, this place is decorated with a hotchpotch of surrealist-inspired objects. A favourite late-night haunt, especially for the live rock and reggae at weekends.

Clubs

Rachdingue

Ctra de Pau, Vilajuïga. Easter–Oct daily 11.30pm–5am. Once a favourite of Salvador Dalí, who designed the logo, this surreally decorated house boasts a pool and two dance areas, playing techno, house, jungle and trip-hop; the mixture of Dalí and music gives it a broad appeal.

Essentials

Arrival

The easiest and cheapest way to reach the Costa Brava is to **fly**; there's a broad choice of flights and many package options to Girona; Barcelona, 100km south of Girona; and Perpignan, 70km north in France. From Britain, **rail** travel is relatively quick, although not cheap, and in recent years **driving** has steadily increased in popularity owing to easier access to the continent with the Eurotunnel.

By air

Increasing numbers of **scheduled flights** are finding their way to Girona, primarily with no-frills airlines from regional airports in the UK. A more flexible option is to get one of the many regular flights to Barcelona and then take the train for the two-hour ride from Barcelona airport to Girona or rent a car. A less obvious alternative is to fly with one of the budget airlines to Perpignan in France and then take a train from there to the northern Costa Brava, Figueres or Girona.

Numerous **charter flights** operate in summer to Girona (often referred to simply as "Costa Brava airport"). It's also possible to find flights in the winter, especially around Christmas and New Year. Although many are block-booked by travel agents, there are normally seats free; last-minute deals can be as low as £80, although expect to have to travel at any time of the day or night.

If you don't have a package with a free transfer to your hotel included, there are scheduled **buses** from Girona airport to Girona (€1.75), while a **taxi** will cost around €20.

By car

Going by **car**, the main decision is whether to take two days to schlep all the way across France or pay more for the 18- or 24-hour **ferry** crossing (Feb–Oct only) to the Spanish coast. Ferry prices vary depending on the day and period of travel, but a return to Bilbao or Santander for a car and two adults, including a cabin, is likely to be around £700. Add at least €60 for motorway tolls: both arrival ports are a full day's drive from the Costa Brava (roughly 600km). By contrast, crossing to and from France costs around £260 by ferry or £329 (£100 for low-season promotions) by **Eurotunnel**, to which you should add €400–700 for *autoroute* tolls, meals and accommodation on the long drive there and back.

By train

Trains from London arrive in Paris at the Gare du Nord, from where you'll have to cross the city: night trains to Girona depart from the Gare d'Austerlitz, day trains from the Gare de Lyon. You may also have to change midway (at Narbonne or Montpellier). Journey time from London is at least 12 hours, and point-to-point return fares start at around £260; a **rail pass** might work out cheaper. Note, though, that exploring the Costa Brava by train is not a viable option (see p.189).

Information

The **Spanish National Tourist Office** (SNTO) has information on general matters such as accommodation and climate, but virtually nothing of practical help on Girona and the Costa Brava. Far better information is available from the **Patronat de Turisme Costa Brava Girona**, either directly or via their website.

Local **tourist offices** (Oficines de Turisme), sponsored by the Patronat de Turisme, are very efficient; we've listed them in the guide text where relevant. They stock free, top-quality information and maps and generally have helpful staff who can advise on accommodation, trips and activities.

Most towns have official **websites**, as well as unofficial ones. Besides the Patronat de Turisme, there's a handful of general sites in English – plus plenty in Catalan – with information on the region.

Maps

Our **maps**, and the free maps handed out by the tourist offices, should be enough for most needs, although a **road map** will help you explore more fully. The best are Catalunya Comarques, covering the whole of Catalonia, or the more detailed Costa Brava Comarques de Girona, both published by Distrimapas Telstar and available at most local newsagents for around €4.60.

Detailed 1:30,000 maps of the **natural parks** can be had free from each park's information office. The most reliable 1:50,000 **walking** maps are the series of sheets covering each *comarca*, or area (Baix Empordà, Alt Empordà, La Garrotxa, and so on), published by the Institut Cartogràfic de Catalunya (around €8) and available at better newsagents.

Transport

The Costa Brava has a very good **public transport** system, with **buses** linking all the minor and major towns, main-line **trains** running through the region and **boats** plying almost the full length of the coast. If you want to explore the region in depth, though, you'll really need a **car** or **motorbike**.

Bus

The region's extensive **bus** network is reliable and inexpensive. All inter-town services are run by the **Sarfa** company (☎ 902 302 025, ✆ www.sarfa.com). Between the main towns comfortable buses run roughly hourly 7am–9pm, with between two and ten buses a day to smaller towns. In summer, additional local services run to some of the beach towns.

Timetables are available from Sarfa ticket offices (*taquilla*), bus stations and tourist offices. It's possible to buy **tickets** for inter-town services on the bus, but to be sure of a seat it's best to buy them in advance at the bus station (some tourist offices also sell tickets). **Fares** average out at around 12c per kilometre: a one-way fare (*anar*) from Girona to Cadaqués is €7.10, Barcelona–Begur is €12.90, and L'Escala–Palamós is €3.75. Return tickets (*anar i tornar*) cost exactly double.

Larger towns also have good **local buses**, going around town and to outlying beaches. Tickets – bought from the driver – are very cheap, generally around €0.75 flat rate.

Sarfa bus company offices

Begur Pl Forgas 6 ☎972 622 446; **La Bisbal** c/Voltes 10 ☎972 640 964; **Cadaqués** c/St Vicens ☎972 258 713; **Castelló d'Empúries** Hotel Emporium ☎972 250 593; **L'Escala** Avgda Ave Maria 26 ☎972 770 218; **Girona** Estació Autobusos ☎972 201 796; **Lloret de Mar** Estació Autobusos ☎972 364 295; **Pals** Turisme, Pl Major 1 ☎972 637 380; **Palafrugell** c/Torres Jonama 73–79 ☎972 300 623; **Palamós** c/López Puigcerver 7 ☎972 600 250; **Platja d'Aro** Estació Autobusos ☎972 826 787; **Roses** Gran Via Pau Casals ☎972 150 585; **St Antoni de Calonge** Turisme, Avgda Catalunya ☎972 661 714; **St Feliu de Guíxols** c/Llibertat 1 ☎972 321 187; **Tossa de Mar** Estació Autobusos ☎972 340 903.

Car or motorbike

Driving your own vehicle, you're able to reach the most secluded – and attractive

– towns and beaches. The fastest **road** is an *autopista*, for which you pay at a staffed or automatic toll (*peatge*). The **A7** is the main route, running inland from Barcelona to the French border (and on to Perpignan as the French A9), while the **A19** hugs the coast from Barcelona to Blanes. All other roads are free.

Fuel is the cheapest in Europe. There are two types of unleaded (*sense plom*), usually labelled "98" and "95" and always with green pumps; leaded Super-Plus (97 octane); and diesel (sometimes *gas-oil*), usually with black pumps.

Dozens of companies offer **car rental**, which is cheaper than in most European countries. **Prices** vary greatly; for a small saloon, budget on €36–42 a day with unlimited mileage, although you can sometimes get better rates with agencies that deal with local firms, such as Autos Abroad. **Fly-drive** deals can be good value: in the UK, for example, Iberia offers cars from around £140/200 a week (low/ high season).

A **motorbike** lets you explore areas that might otherwise be inaccessible, and is especially good for some of the rougher tracks in the north of the Costa Brava and inland areas. You can rent from local agencies in most large towns.

Boat

Numerous **boats**, ranging from large open-topped water-buses to simple craft with room for a dozen people, chug up and down the coast between Easter and the end of October. They usually operate on short stretches and count less as an efficient means of getting around than as an unhurried way of trying out new beaches while getting a passing view of the coastline. **Tickets** are available from booths on the beach, where you'll also find timetables. Fares vary depending on the type of boat, but as a guide, a trip from Blanes to Sant Feliu de Guíxols – nine stops and three main towns away – costs €14.40 return.

Accommodation

The Costa Brava boasts a wide range of **accommodation**, from campsites of all prices and sizes, through self-catering apartments to luxurious, spectacularly sited hotels. In addition, there's a growing number of enticing, individually owned boutique hotels, often in farmhouses or town houses of historic interest, and a network of *turisme rural* houses, an imaginative alternative to more traditional forms of self-catering. Accommodation is cheap in comparison with other European countries and normally of a high standard.

A lot of hotel rooms in more popular towns are block-booked by agencies, but this still leaves plenty for independent travellers – along with the range of self-catering accommodation. Although it's possible to turn up and find a place to stay even in high season (July, Aug & Easter), it's highly advisable to reserve. Cheaper hotels in coastal towns tend to close in winter. The hotels listed in "Places" either accept or are geared more towards the independent traveller, and although walk-in rates are often substantially higher than a pre-booked package price, discounts are occasionally available, especially in June and September.

Accommodation agencies

Four local associations monitor quality across types of accommodation. The **Provincial Hotel Federation** (ⓔ fphg@gna.es) is the only one that doesn't offer online booking, while the **Tourist Apartment Association** (ⓦ www.apartamentos-ata.com), **Girona Rural Tourism** (ⓦ www.costabrava. org/rural) and the **Girona Camping Association** (ⓦ www.campingsgirona. com) all do.

You can also make online reservations for local hotels, apartments and *turisme rural* houses through **Eoland** (💻 www. eoland.com) and **Dlleure** (💻 www. dlleure.com). Reservations at some of the new boutique hotels can be made through **Petits Grans Hotels** (💻 www. petitsgranshotels.com).

Activities

You'll find countless opportunities for outdoor pursuits in the Costa Brava, including mountain trekking, scuba-diving and paragliding – plus, of course, the waters are some of the cleanest and clearest in the Mediterranean. The Costa Brava boasts one of Europe's greatest concentrations of Blue Flag beaches, an international standard awarded for the cleanliness of the water and coast and quality of facilities.

Walking

You're spoilt for choice in the number and type of walks you can try. A network of signposted trails, following a clearly defined **footpath** (*sender*), crisscrosses the region. Split into three categories according to their length, the routes are colour-coded: parallel horizontal yellow-and-white lines for short local paths; green-and-white lines for medium-distance paths; and red-and-white lines for the very long trails. The two major long-distance routes touching on the Costa Brava are the **GR92**, which runs along the French border to Portbou before cutting south to Barcelona; and the **GR11**, which runs east from Andorra to a trailhead on the Cap de Creus headland. Local tourist offices stock free leaflets and maps outlining dozens of walks in their area.

The Camí de Ronda

Among the loveliest routes is the **Camí de Ronda**, made up of old coastguards' and farmers' trails that hug the coastline. Meaning "patrol walk", it originally referred to any coastal path, but now means – in the Costa Brava region, at any rate – the long-distance coastal route linking these paths into one trail.

In the bad old days of the tourist boom, the paths were built over or simply allowed to crumble into the sea, but now the Catalan government is gradually restoring them: it will soon be possible to walk the entire coast from the French border to Blanes. For now, the path is intermittent and varies from a single-file dirt track to wide, paved sections on the edges of towns. Parts cut across well-used beaches or follow a road for a short distance, while others snake over desolate headlands and can be quite arduous, although they're often the best – or only – way to reach some of the more isolated coves. You'll also sometimes find yourself on parts of the GR92, which cuts in and out of the Camí de Ronda.

Cycling

Long-distance **cyclists** will enjoy the **Ruta del Carrilet**, which follows the old railway line from Olot to Girona and on to Sant Feliu de Guíxols through rolling countryside. When it's eventually completed some time in the near future, it will connect Olot with the mountains at Ripoll, enabling you to cycle from the Pyrenees to the Mediterranean. You can rent a bike at several points along the way; tourist offices in Girona, Olot and Sant Feliu de Guíxols have details. There's also a network of good off-road tracks, indicated by red signs with a bike symbol, and some footpaths – marked on the rambler sign by a small bike symbol – are open to cyclists. A word of warning: be alert even on minor roads, since motorists are often oblivious to cyclists.

Golf

Recently voted by the International Association of Golf Tour Operators as the best emerging **golf** holiday destination, the Costa Brava staged the 2000 Spanish Open at the demanding PGA Catalunya course, designed by Neil Coles. The region boasts nine top-class courses and a further eight pitch-and-putt courses. You don't have to become a member, but you will need to be one of a club in your own country; a round is expensive, at about €60 for eighteen holes in high season. The best way to get around both issues is to take advantage of one of the **golf packages** offered by tour operators (eg Golf in the Sun @www.golfinthesun. co.uk and Longmere Golf @www.atlgolf. demon.co.uk) and some hotels.

Golf courses

PGA Golf de Catalunya Caldes de Malavella ☎972 472 577, @www.pgacatalunya.com.
Club de Golf Girona Sant Julià de Ramis ☎972 171 641, @www.golfgirona.es.
Empordà Golf Club Gualta ☎972 760 450, @www.empordagolfclub.es.
Club de Golf Costa Brava Santa Cristina d'Aro ☎972 837 150, @www.golfcostabrava.com.
Golf Serres de Pals Pals ☎972 637 375, @www.golfserresdepals.com.
Club de Golf Pals Pals ☎972 636 006, @www.6tems.com/golfpals.
Peralada Golf Club Peralada ☎972 538 287, @www.golfperalada.com.
Club de Golf d'Aro-Masnou Platja d'Aro ☎972 816 727, @golfdaromasnou@retemail.es.

Diving and snorkelling

Numerous **diving** schools offer a range of services from beginners' courses to boat excursions and equipment rental. The main areas of interest are around the Illes Medes Maritime Reserve, famous for its fauna and coral beds, and the tiny inlets of the Cap de Creus and the coves near Begur and Palafrugell, where there are over three hundred species of fish, including barracuda and seahorses, drifting among coral and shipwrecks. Always dive with a school (all closed Nov–Easter) registered with the local Association of Diving Centres (@www.costabrava.org/guisub). A single dive will cost around €50, which includes equipment; a six-dive week's pass is €145, a ten-dive voucher €240. A six-day beginner's course is €400.

Many schools also organize **snorkelling** excursions to the more inaccessible coves. With your own gear, you could head for easier-to-reach inlets in the southern Baix Empordà and northern Alt Empordà.

Watersports

Windsurfing is very popular, and there are plenty of operators renting equipment (around €22/hr) and running courses (€30/hr). Summer is relatively calm, but pay keen attention, as squalls can sweep windsurfers out to sea. Most towns have **sailing** clubs, and the area runs a number of competitive events, the most famous being Palamós's impressive Christmas Race of big yachts. In most beach towns, watersports possibilities include **jet-skiing** (around €15 for 15min), **waterskiing** (roughly the same), being dragged behind a boat on a giant **banana** (about €8), as well as a more sedate **pedalo** (around €4/hr). **Parasailing** costs around €40/hr.

One of the best ways to explore coves is by **kayak**, which cost about €15 for half a day (plus a large deposit). A handful of operators can also rent you a small **inflatable** or rigid **motorboat** for about €24 an hour.

Aerial sports

In Empúriabrava is one of Spain's best **sky-diving** centres, offering tandem jumps and a range of courses. **Sightseeing flights** over the rocky shoreline or the volcanoes of La Garrotxa set off from Girona airport, bookable through local operators (prices vary according to route and number of passengers). There are **ultralight** clubs in Empúriabrava and L'Escala (around €40 for 30min), or you could try **ballooning** in Platja d'Aro or La Garrotxa for about €140: two balloonists do all the work, while you just enjoy the ride.

ESSENTIALS

Public holidays and festivals

Horse riding

Both the coast and the hinterland have a long tradition of **horse riding**, and the better stables keep well cared-for Spanish and Arabian breeds. The tough choice is whether to plump for La Garrotxa or to try one of the few beach-side riding spots, primarily around L'Estartit and Pals. Half a day's excursion will cost about €65.

Public holidays and festivals

Spain has ten national **public holidays** a year, supplemented by five regional ones; in addition to this, each town and village has its own Festa Major, or patron saint's day. On a public holiday (*festiu*) all shops and businesses close, public transport runs one-third of its normal service, and museums and public buildings follow Sunday hours. In coastal towns, though, most businesses trade as usual.

Combining religious ceremony with surprisingly large doses of pagan ritual, each Catalan town's **Festa Major** involves noise, merrymaking and plenty of dancing. Many include traditions such as the *gegants* ("giants"), originally mascots for craftsmen's guilds – pairs of effigies up to 12m tall (a king and queen, or shepherd and shepherdess) swirling through the streets, attended by the *capgrossos* ("bigheads"), smaller effigies with oversized caricature heads, to the tune of ancient wind instruments and drums.

Fire plays a significant role, especially around Sant Joan's Eve on June 23, when bonfires are lit and spectacular firework displays are held; the best is the week-long fireworks festival in Blanes. More eye-catching still are the *correfocs* ("fire runs"), when bands of devils prance through the streets under a rain of sparks while drummers beat out a hypnotic rhythm.

Two annual festivals stand out. **Setmana Santa** (Easter) is marked by elaborate and colourful processions in most towns, while **Carnestoltes** (Carnival), in February, is a frenzy of pure hedonism.

All through the year, you're likely to stumble across the **sardana**, the traditional dance, being performed in the open. A highly social dance, it's created by dancers forming circles, which then either join with others to form larger circles or split off into smaller rounds when they become too unwieldy. The steps are much more complicated than they look, and dancers keep time by counting them. Accompanying them is the *cobla*, a band made up of five woodwind musicians, five brass players and a double-bassist, who create the distinctive keening shrill of *sardana* tunes.

National and regional holidays

Jan 1 New Year's Day (*Any Nou*)
Jan 6 Epiphany (*Reis*)
Good Friday (*Divendres Sant*)
Easter Monday (*Dilluns de Pascua*)
May 1 Labour Day (*Festa de Treball*)
June Corpus Christi
June 24 St John's Day (*Sant Joan*)
Aug 25 Assumption (*Assumpció*)

Sept 11 Catalan National Day (*Diada*)
Oct 12 Spanish National Day (*Pilar/Hispanitat*)
Nov 1 All Saints (*Tots Sants*)
Dec 6 Constitution Day (*Constitució*)
Dec 8 Immaculate Conception (*Immaculada Concepció*)
Dec 25 Christmas Day (*Nadal*)

More stirring still are the **havaneres**, sea shanties brought back from Cuba by sailors, which tell of lost loves and faraway ancestors. Concerts are staged throughout the summer, the top event being the stunning *cantada d'havaneres* festival held every June in Calella de Palafrugell.

The Costa Brava hosts a wide range of **food festivals**, in which the main restaurants in all the towns create traditional dishes with local ingredients. Celebrations normally run over a period of around four weeks, and are the perfect opportunity to sample the best in regional cooking. Festivals include the **Setmana Gastronòmica Gironina** (Gastronomy Week), which takes place in the second week of April in Girona; and the **Tastets de Mar** (Seafood Tasting Festival) held in L'Estartit and Torroella de Montgrí from mid-May to mid-June.

Festival calendar

January
20–21 Tossa de Mar celebrates its *Vot del Pelegrí* (the Pilgrim's Vow), a colourful maritime procession commemorating the end of the plague in the fifteenth century.

February
Lent *Carnestoltes* (Carnival). Banned under Franco, the reinstated celebrations are especially fun at Platja d'Aro, its glittering procession one of the most spectacular in Spain.

March/April
Setmana Santa (Easter). The most interesting celebrations are the colourful *Manaies* procession in Girona, dating from 1566, when superbly attired Roman soldiers march through the Barri Vell on Wednesday of Easter week and Good Friday, preceding the procession of the Virgin. A more macabre celebration is the *Ball dels Morts* (Dance of the Dead) in Verges, when five people dressed as skeletons dance through the streets. Besalú's Good Friday procession features Jesus and the Apostles chanting a haunting hymn.

May
Corpus Christi St Feliu de Guíxols, L'Estartit and Tossa de Mar are decorated with colourful *catifes de flors* (flower carpets): millions of petals are meticulously laid out in front of churches and on avenues to create mosaics.
First fortnight Flower Festival in Girona's Barri Vell.
Last weekend Palafrugell's Spring Festival, started as a way of getting past Franco's ban on Carnival, features music and a procession.

June
June & July The castle square in Calella's Jardí Botànic Cap Roig is the perfect setting for the town's prestigious Jazz Festival, which attracts big international names.
24 The *Festa de Sant Joan* sees bonfires lit all over Catalonia; celebrations are especially lively in Palamós, where music, dancing and fireworks run from the previous Friday to the Sunday following June 24.

July
July & Aug Peralada Music Festival, with an eclectic programme including leading classical musicians and cabaret stalwarts.
All month Maritime processions in Palamós, Llançà and Lloret de Mar.
First Sunday Tossa de Mar's bay fills with lateen sailing boats in the *Vela Llatina* festival.
First weekend International bagpipe festival in Olot.
First Sat Calella de Palafrugell's *Havaneres* festival, where the sea shanties attract 40,000 spectators.
Second Sun Olot's *Aplec de la Sardana* is one of the largest *sardana* festivals in the region.
Second week Begur tunes in to its week-long Jazz Festival in various venues around town.
Last two weeks International Fireworks Competition in Blanes.
Last two weeks Figueres Jazz Festival.
24–26 Lloret de Mar's *Ball dels Almorratxes*, as part of the town's *Festa Major*, features an ancient ritual dance between couples, culminating in the girl dashing a jar to the ground to fend off the boy's advances.

August
All month International Music Festival in Torroella de Montgrí.
First three weeks Cadaqués classical music festival.

September

All month Sant Feliu de Guíxols' Porta Ferrada Music Festival.
7–8 Olot's *Ball dels Gegants* (Dance of the Giants) is the high point of the lively local *Festa de la Tura* festivities, famed for its high jinks and procession.
11 Catalonia's national day *La Diada*.
Second weekend Cadaqués' spectacular *Regates de Llaguts i de Vela Llatina* fills the bay with billowing sails.

October

29 The holidays of the patron saint of Girona, Sant Narcís, run from the Friday before Oct 29 to the Sunday after. A cultural programme is complemented by music together with craft stalls, funfair and *sardanes*.
31 The eve of All Saints is celebrated everywhere with the *castanyada*, a feast of roast chestnuts and moscatel wine.

Directory

Addresses Abbreviations follow a standard format: c/Balmes 9 is no. 9 on Carrer (street) Balmes; Pl Catalunya 21 is no. 21 on Plaça (square) Catalunya; Ctra is Carretera (highway); Avgda is Avinguda (avenue). Plaça Catalunya 21, 5-2, means Flat 2 on the 5th floor at no. 21 Plaça Catalunya. S/n means *sense número* ("no number"). Ctra Barcelona km2,3 means that the address is 2.3km along the Barcelona road beyond the town.
Banks and exchange The currency on the Costa Brava is the euro. Spanish banks are slow, bureaucratic and expensive, but they're still the best places to change money, with lower commissions than elsewhere. Normal banking hours are Mon–Sat 9am–2pm, except between June and September, when they close on Saturdays; ATMs are widely available in larger towns.
Consulates Australian, Pl Descubridor Diego de Ordas 3, 28003 Madrid ☎914 419 300, ✆www.embaustralia.es. Canadian, c/Nuñez de Balboa 35, 28001 Madrid ☎914 233 250, ✆www.canada-es.org; consulate in Barcelona, ☎933 170 541. Irish, Paseo de la Castellana 46-4, 28046 Madrid ☎915 763 500. New Zealand, Pl de la Lealtad 2-3, 28014 Madrid ☎915 310 997. UK, c/Fernando el Santo 16, 28010 Madrid ☎917 008 200, ✆www. ukinspain.com; consulate in Barcelona, ☎933 666 200. US, c/Serrano 75, 28006 Madrid ☎915 872 200, ✆www.embusa. es; consulate in Barcelona ☎932 802 227.
Emergency numbers Medical, fire & police ☎112; local police ☎092; national police ☎091.
Health For minor complaints, go to a pharmacy (*farmàcia*); there are plenty in the major towns, identifed by a green or red cross outside. Most keep usual shop hours (Mon–Sat 9am–1pm & 4–8pm), and they

all display the rota indicating which one locally is open 24 hours. For more serious cases, head to the CAP (*Centre d'Atenció Primària*, or Primary Healthcare Centre) in larger towns, where you'll often find English-speaking staff, or to a hospital (*hospital* or *urgències* in Catalan).
Post Postal services work fairly well through the year, but get clogged in the summer, when you should allow a week for items to reach places in Europe, two weeks or more for elsewhere. All large towns have a post office (*Correus*; generally Mon–Sat 9am–1.30pm), which spawn long queues but are the only places from which you can send parcels. For stamps and sending letters or postcards, you're better off going to a tobacconist (*estanc*; Mon–Fri 9am–1pm & 4–8pm, Sat 9am–1pm).
Telephones Phonecards can be bought from any tobacconist for €5 or €10. Mobile phones work on the Costa Brava, but you'll be charged hefty surcharges for both receiving and making calls. There are no area codes in Spain: you dial all nine numbers for landlines (which start with a 9) and mobile phones (which start with a 6). Off-peak rates apply Mon–Sat 8pm–9am, and all day Sunday.
Time Spain is 1hr ahead of London and Dublin, 6hr ahead of New York and 9hr behind Sydney. Clocks go forward by 1hr on the last Sun in March and back 1hr on the last Sun in Oct.
Tipping Give about 5 percent for taxis and restaurants, about €0.20 in a café and €1 for a hotel porter. Tipping is uncommon in bars unless you're being served on a terrace. A *menú del dia* normally includes service (look for *Servei (no) inclós* – "Service is (not) included"), but it's polite to leave a small tip as well.

Catalan

The vast majority of people on the Costa Brava speak Catalan as their first language: Girona, even more than Barcelona, is the heartland of Catalan culture and almost all schooling is now in Catalan, although, thanks to Franco – who outlawed the language and prohibited its teaching in schools and use in the media – many over-35s have difficulty in writing.

Many people working in the tourist industry speak English and most young people learn English at school, so all along the coast you'll be able to get by with little difficulty; inland, though, it's rarer to find English-speakers.

Pronunciation

Catalan is pronounced quite differently from Castilian (Spanish), with much more neutral sounds, similar to those found in English. In Catalan, "c" and "z" aren't lisped as they are in Spanish.

Rules of stress are convoluted, but as a rule of thumb, emphasis lies on the last syllable unless the word ends in a vowel or an "s", or if there's an accent (which marks the stress). Plurals of masculine nouns simply add "s", while feminine nouns ending in "a" drop it and add "es", so *cervesa* ("sairvaisa") becomes *cerveses*. Adjectives add a final "a" in the feminine.

a as in m**a**t when stressed, as in **a**lone when unstressed.

e as in g**e**t when stressed, as in fath**e**r when unstressed.

i is long, as in pol**i**ce.

o varies, but usually as in d**o**g when stressed and t**oo** when unstressed.

u somewhere between sch**oo**l and r**u**le.

c followed by *e* or *i* is soft as in fa**c**ile; otherwise hard as in ba**c**on.

ç is always soft, as in fa**ç**ade.

g followed by *e* or *i* is like the "s" in plea**s**ure; otherwise hard as in wa**g**on.

h is always silent.

ig as in do**dg**e.

ix as in ba**sh**.

j is like the "s" in plea**s**ure.

l.l occurs in the middle of words, as in "aquarel.la", and doubles the ordinary *l* sound.

ll is like the sound in the middle of co**lli**ery.

nt has a silent *t*: the word *cent* is pronounced "sen".

ny as in o**ni**on.

qu before *e* or *i* sounds like *k*; before *a* or *o* as in **qu**it.

r is rolled at the start or in the middle of a word; at the end, it's silent.

rr is doubly rolled.

s at the start or in the middle of a word as in **s**ee; at the end, as in **z**oo.

tx as in ba**tch**.

tz as in ba**ts**.

v is very soft, as if you're trying to say *b* without closing your lips.

w is similar to *v*.

x is halfway between *s* and *x*.

z as in **z**oo.

Words and phrases

si	yes
no	no
val	OK
sisplau	please
gràcies	thank you
de res	not at all
hola	hello
adéu	goodbye
bon dia	good morning
bona tarda	good afternoon
bona nit	good evening
adéu bona nit	good night
ho sento	sorry
perdoni	excuse me
(no) entenc	I (don't) understand
Parla anglès?	Do you speak English?
(No) parlo català	I (don't) speak Catalan
obert	open
tancat	closed
ahir	yesterday
avui	today
demà	tomorrow

Numbers

u, un	1
dos, dues	2
tres	3
quatre	4
cinc	5
sis	6
set	7
vuit	8
nou	9
deu	10
onze	11
dotze	12
tretze	13
catorze	14
quinze	15
setze	16
disset	17
divuit	18
dinou	19
vint	20
vint-i-un	21
trenta	30
quaranta	40
cinquanta	50
seixanta	60
setanta	70
vuitanta	80
noranta	90
cent	100
doscents	200
mil	1000

Hotels, shops and directions

Voldria...	I'd like...
Teniu...?	Do you have...?
una habitació (doble)	a (double) room
amb dutxa	with shower
per a una persona /dues persones	for one/two people
per a una nit /dues nits	for one/two nights
per a una setmana	for one week
Quant val?	How much is it?
On ès...?	Where is ...?
l'estació d'autobussos	the bus station
l'estació de trens	the train station
el correu	the post office
el lavabo	the toilet
a l'esquerra	left
a la dreta	right
tot recte	straight on
D'on surt l'autobus a Olot?	Where does the bus to Olot leave from?
Un bitllet (d'anar i tornar) a Portbou	A (return) ticket to Portbou
Una taula per a dos	A table for two
carta	menu
La compte, sisplau	The bill, please
Em cobra, sisplau?	How much is it? (in a bar)

Food and drink

a l'ast	spit-roasted
a la brasa	chargrilled
a la planxa	grilled
a la romana	deep-fried in batter
aigua (mineral)	(mineral) water
al forn	oven-baked
albergínies	aubergine
all	garlic
amanida catalana	salad with cold cuts and cheeses
amanida verda	green salad
amb/sense gas	sparkling/still

arròs a banda	rice cooked in fish broth
arròs a la cubana	boiled rice with tomato sauce, egg and banana
arròs negre	rice cooked in squid ink
bacallà	cod
berberetxos	cockles
bikini	toasted cheese and ham sandwich
bistec de vedella	veal steak
botifarra	Catalan sausage
café (amb llet)	(white) coffee
calamars	squid
canalons	cannelloni
cargols	snails, often served in a spicy sauce
cebes	onions
cervesa	beer
chupito	tot of liqueur
cloïsses	clams
cogombre	cucumber
conill	rabbit
crema catalana	egg custard with a caramelized topping
cremat	rum, brandy, cinnamon and lemon peel served aflame in an earthenware bowl to which you add a cup of coffee per person
dinar	lunch
embotits	cold cuts and cured sausages
entremesos	hors d'oeuvres of mixed meat and cheeses
entrepà	sandwich
escalivada	roasted aubergine, red pepper and onion salad, drizzled in olive oil
escamarlans	king prawns
escudella	broth with rice or pasta
esmorzar	breakfast
espàrrecs	asparagus
espinacs a la catalana	spinach sautéed in olive oil with raisins and pine-nuts
esqueixada	salad of dried cod, red pepper, tomato, onion and olive

faves a la catalana	broad beans sautéed in olive oil and garlic with mushrooms and ham
flam	crème caramel
formatge	cheese
fricandó	veal and wild mushroom fricassee
fritada de peix	various fried fish
gambes	prawns
gelat	ice cream
graellada de peix	various grilled fish
llagosta	lobster
llenguado	sole
llet	milk
llom	loin of pork
lluç	hake
macedònia	fresh fruit salad
maduixes	strawberries
mandonguilles	meatballs
mel i mató	curd cheese and honey
meló	melon
menú del dia	set meal at reduced prices that restaurants offer for lunch on weekdays
mongetes	beans
musclos	mussels
navalles	razor clams
niu	chunky stew of swordfish, cod tripe and wild fowl
pà amb tomàquet	thick country bread, often toasted, smeared with fresh tomato and daubed with olive oil and salt
pà	bread
pastanagues	carrots
pebre	pepper
pebres	peppers
peix espasa	swordfish
pera	pear
pernil dolç	cooked ham
pernil Serrat	cured ham
pèsols	peas
pica-pica	a selection of different dishes for sharing, often seafood
pinxo	marinated pork kebab
pinya	pineapple
plàtan	banana
pollastre	chicken

poma	apple
pop	octopus
préssec	peach
raïm	grape
rap	monkfish
roger	red mullet
romesco	almond, tomato and garlic sauce
rovellons	wild mushrooms
sal	salt
salpicó de mariscos	cold shellfish salad with onions and peppers
salxitxó	salami-type sausage
sard	sea bream
sarsuela	fish and shellfish stew
seitons	fresh anchovies
sindria	watermelon
sípia	cuttlefish
sofregit	basic tomato, olive oil and onion sauce
sopar	evening meal

suc	juice
suquet	fish casserole
tallat	small white coffee
taronja	orange
tarta	cake
te	tea
tomàquets	tomatoes
tonyina	tuna
torrades	toasted country bread, often served as *pà amb tomàquet*
truita (espanyola /francesa)	omelette (potato/ plain)
truita	trout
vi negre/blanc /rosat	red/white/rosé wine
xai	lamb
xamfaina	onion, tomato, pepper and aubergine stew
xampinyons	mushrooms
xoriç	spicy sausage

Glossary

ajuntament town hall
aparcament parking
aplec a *sardana* meeting (see below)
badia bay
cala cove
Ca'n "the house of", similar to the French *chez*
claustre cloister
cova cave
cuina volcànica typical cuisine from Olot, based around a combination of any eleven of core ingredients, from such ordinary items as potatoes and beans to more exotic boar and truffles.
entrada entrance, admission ticket
església church
estanc tobacconist that sells stamps
far lighthouse
festa festival
Indianos Catalans who made their fortune in the Americas in the nineteenth and twentieth centuries before returning home, also known as Americanos.
jardí garden

mar i muntanya literally "sea and mountain": surf 'n' turf type of cuisine, blending seafood and fish with produce from the land
mercat market
mirador belvedere
Modernisme Modernista style – a purely Catalan art and architecture movement of the late nineteenth and early twentieth centuries, featuring classical and vegetal forms characterized by fluidity and imaginative juxtapositions of materials and symbols.
monéstir monastery
parróquia parish church
passeig boulevard, or an evening stroll
platja beach
pont bridge
pou well
puig hill
riu river
sender footpath
serra mountain range
sortida exit
xiringuito beach bar

Index & small print

A Rough Guide to Rough Guides

Costa Brava DIRECTIONS is published by Rough Guides. The first *Rough Guide to Greece*, published in 1982, was a student scheme that became a publishing phenomenon. The immediate success of the book – with numerous reprints and a Thomas Cook prize short-listing – spawned a series that rapidly covered dozens of destinations. Rough Guides had a ready market among low-budget backpackers, but soon also acquired a much broader and older readership that relished Rough Guides' wit and inquisitiveness as much as their enthusiastic, critical approach. Everyone wants value for money, but not at any price. Rough Guides soon began supplementing the "rougher" information about hostels and low-budget listings with the kind of detail on restaurants and quality hotels that independent-minded visitors on any budget might expect, whether on business in New York or trekking in Thailand. These days the guides offer recommendations from shoestring to luxury and cover a large number of destinations around the globe, including almost every country in the Americas and Europe, more than half of Africa and most of Asia and Australasia. Rough Guides now publish:

- Travel guides to more than 200 worldwide destinations
- Dictionary phrasebooks to 22 major languages
- Maps printed on rip-proof and waterproof Polyart™ paper
- Music guides running the gamut from Opera to Elvis
- Reference books on topics as diverse as the Weather and Shakespeare
- World Music CDs in association with World Music Network

Publishing information

This first edition published April 2005 by
Rough Guides Ltd, 80 Strand, London WC2R 0RL.
345 Hudson St, 4th Floor, New York, NY 10014,
USA.

Distributed by the Penguin Group
Penguin Books Ltd, 80 Strand, London WC2R 0RL
Penguin Group (USA), 375 Hudson Street, NY
10014, USA
Penguin Group (Australia), 487 Maroondah
Highway, PO Box 257, Ringwood, Victoria 3134,
Australia
Penguin Group (Canada), 10 Alcorn Avenue,
Toronto, Ontario, Canada M4V 1E4
Penguin Group (NZ), 182–190 Wairau Road, Auck-
land 10, New Zealand
Typeset in Bembo and Helvetica to an original
design by Henry Iles.
Printed and bound in China

208pp includes index

A catalogue record for this book is available from
the British Library

ISBN 1-84353-439-8

The publishers and authors have done their best
to ensure the accuracy and currency of all the
information in **Costa Brava DIRECTIONS**, however,
they can accept no responsibility for any loss,
injury, or inconvenience sustained by any traveller
as a result of information or advice contained in
the guide.

1   3   5   7   9   8   6   4   2

Help us update

We've gone to a lot of effort to ensure that the first edition of **Costa Brava DIRECTIONS** is accurate and up-to-date. However, things change – places get "discovered," opening hours are notoriously fickle, restaurants and rooms raise prices or lower standards. If you feel we've got it wrong or left something out, we'd like to know, and if you can remember the address, the price, the phone number, so much the better.

We'll credit all contributions, and send a copy of the next edition (or any other DIRECTIONS guide or Rough Guide if you prefer) for the best letters. Everyone who writes to us and isn't already a subscriber will receive a copy of our full-color thrice-yearly newsletter. Please mark letters: "Costa Brava DIRECTIONS Update" and send to: Rough Guides, 80 Strand, London WC2R 0RL, or Rough Guides, 4th Floor, 345 Hudson St, New York, NY 10014. Or send an email to mail@roughguides.com
Have your questions answered and tell others about your trip at www.roughguides.atinfopop.com

Rough Guide credits

Text editor: Ruth Blackmore
Layout: Umesh Aggarwal, Diana Jarvis,
Ajay Verma
Photography: Ian Aitken
Cartography: Ed Wright & Katie Lloyd-Jones

Picture editor: Sharon Martins
Proofreader: Jan Wiltshire
Production: Julia Bovis
Design: Henry Iles

The author

Chris Lloyd hopped on a bus from Cardiff to Catalonia in the early 1980s and stayed for the next twenty-odd years, apart from brief spells in Madrid, the Basque Country and a mill in Devon. He works as a freelance translator and, with his wife Liz, now lives in Wales, travelling frequently to Catalonia.

Acknowledgments

My thanks once again to everyone who helped with information and advice on the former Mini-Guide to Costa Brava. Extra thanks this time around to Concepció Bascompte (again!), Silvia Beleña and everyone at the tremendously helpful and informative tourist offices throughout the region, and to Will Pearson, Núria at the splendidly tranquil Hostal Miralluna and Franc at the superb La Gavina restaurant. Most of all, I'd like to thank Liz for everything.

Reader's letters

Thanks to readers who wrote in with comments on the Mini Rough Guide to Costa Brava:
Roma Amabile with Carol and Hannah, Sue Dale, Christopher Ettridge, Richard Fearn, Sarah Gardner, Emma Hawkins, Joy Heaton, Clare Ransom, Richard Robson-Smith, Terje Svendsen, Olive Williams.

Photo credits

All images © Rough Guides except the following:

p.1 Duck-crossing sign © Liz Lloyd
p.2 Calella de Palafrugell © Powerstock
p.4 Sa Riera cove © Powerstock
p.4 Belfry, Torrella © Liz Lloyd
p.4 Blanes © Powerstock
p.6 Changing booths, S'Agaró
p.7 Girona, pharmacy in old town © Alamy, Dalí Teatre-Museu © Robert Harding
p.8 Dona Marinera statue, La Selva ©, Cove at Sant Feliu, Baix Empordà © Alamy, Kite, Aiguamolls National Park © Corbis
p.14 Swimming pool, Casa-Museu Dalí © Gala-Salvador Dalí Foundation
p.19 Medieval festival in Castello d'Empuries © Corbis
p.21 La Sala del Cel, Girona © La Sala del Cel, Gelpi, Calella de Palafrugell © Liz Lloyd
p. 22 Festival Internacional de Músiques de Torroella de Montgrí © PTCBG
p.23 Peralada Festival (Woody Allen) © Corbis, Havaneres in Palafrugell © Turisme Palafrugell

p.24 Easter celebrations in Girona © Imagestate, skeleton dancers in Verges © Alamy
p. 25 Lateen sailing boats in Cadaqués bay © Powerstock, flower festival, La Pabordia © Josep Maria Oliveras,
p. 29 El Golfet, Calella © Alamy
p. 37 Hot-air balloon in Parc Natural de la Garrotxa © Vol de Coloms, Casal dels Volcans © Museu desl Volcans
p.39 Tinto Reserva © Castillo Peralada
p.41 Porto Cristo, Port de la Selva © Restaurant Porto Cristo
p.44 Skydivers over Empuriabrava © Skydive Empuriabrava
p.45 Empordà Golf Club © Alamy, aerial view of Costa Brava © Powerstock
p. 47 La Gavina, S'Agaro © Corbis, El Bullí, Roses © Corbis

Index

Map entries are marked in colour

A

accommodation 189
Aiguablava 115
Aiguafreda 115
Alt Empordà 6, 7

B

Baix Empordà 6, 8
ballooning 37, 69, 191
Banyoles 64–65
Banyoles 64
banks 194
bars (by area)
    Begur 119
    Blanes 79
    Cadaqués 169
    Figueres 161
    Girona 63
    Golf de Roses 154
    L'Escala and Empúries 146
    La Garrotxa 75
    Lloret de Mar 83
    Palafrugell 112
    Palamós and Sant Antoni de
        Calonge 104
    Port de la Selva 174
    Sant Feliu de Guíxols and
        Platja d'Aro 97
    Serra de l'Albera 183
    Torroella de Montgrí and
        L'Estartit 138
    Tossa de Mar 87
bars
    900 House Bar 97
    Aleshores 63
    Anchor 79
    Assac Bar 97
    Bel Air 104
    Beograd 154
    Bruixes 75
    Café de la Habana 169
    Café de l'Havana 183
    Café dell'Arte 146
    Café de Nit 161
    Café Espanya 174
    Café Royal 63
    Cal Sereno 175
    Can Bernat 138
    Cap de Creus 21
    El Castellet 104
    La Cava del Port 146
    El Celler de la Selva 174
    Classic 119
    Cocodrilo 75
    C-roack 119
    Crokis 146

El Federal 161
La Frontera 169
Gelpi 21, 112
Gran Café Latino 83
Habana Café 112
L'Hostal 21, 169
Hula Hula 83
Jo-Jo's 146
Kinggat 104
Mackintosh 175
Mar i Cel 87
Mariscal 138
Marítim 79
Mocambo 146
N'Gruna 138
Nummulit 63
Particular 63
La Plata 20, 104
Port de Nit 183
La Sal 119
Sant Jordi 79
La Serradora 161
Si Té 7 169
Si Us Plau 154
Stones 83
Sunset Jazz Club 63
Tahití 87
La Taverna del Pirata 183
La Terra 63
Tropical 169
L'Últim 119
Via 63
Begur 113–119
Begur 114
Besalú 18, 66–67
Besalú 66
Blanes 25, 76–79
    Cala Sant Francesc 78
    fireworks competition 25, 78
    Jardí Botànic Mar i Murtra
        31, 78
    S'Abanell 78
Blanes 76–77
boats 189
buses 188
Butterfly Park 42, 152

C

Cabana Arqueta 17
Cadaqués 15, 162–165
Cadaqués 163
cafés (by area)
    Cadaqués 167
    Girona 61
cafés
    L'Antiga 61
    Boia 167
    Casino 167

    El Cercle 61
    La Llibreria 61
    Maritim 168
    Tapa't 61
Cala Belladona 94
Cala Boadella 29, 81
Cala Canadell 149
Cala de l'Infern 166
Cala d'en Carles 86
Cala del Forn 101
Cala del Pi 94
Cala Canyelles 82
Cala Cativa 170
Cala dels Escalencs 94
Cala Estreta 100
Cala Figuera 86
Cala Fornells 170
Cala Futadera 86
Cala Giverola 86
Cala Jóncols 149
Cala Jugadora 166
Cala Llevador 86
Cala Montgó 140
Cala Montjoi 149
Cala Moreta 116
Cala Morisca 82
Cala Murtra 101
Cala Pedrosa 110
Cala Rostella 28, 149
Cala Rovira 94
Cala S'Alguer 100
Cala Sa Conca 35
Cala Sa Cova 94
Cala Tamariua 170
Calella 105–107
Calella and Llafranc
    108–109
Calonge 101
Camí de Ronda 11, 34–35,
    93, 100, 106, 113, 143,
    148, 166, 170, 179, 190
Camí de les Dunes 34, 143
campsites (by area)
    La Garrotxa 74
    Golf de Roses 153
    Serra de l'Albera 182
    Lloret de Mar 82
    Tossa de Mar 87
campsites
    Canyelles 82
    Lava 74
    Nautic Almatà 153
    Pola 87
    Santa Elena-Ciutat 82
    Vell Empordà 182
Cap de Creus 33, 35, 166
Cap de Norfeu 148–149
Cap Ras 28, 179–180
Casal dels Volcans 37, 71

Casa-Museu Dalí 14, 165–166
Castell de Begur 113
Castell del Montgrí 33, 134
Castell Gala-Dalí 15, 129
Castell Sant Salvador 19, 173
Castell d'Aro 94
Castellfollit de la Roca 73
Castelló d'Empúries 19, 27, 151–152
Catalan language 197
Central Baix Empordà 126–131
Central Baix Empordà 127
Centre de Reproducció de Tortugues de l'Albera 42, 177
clubs (by area)
    Girona 63
    Sant Feliu de Guíxols and Platja d'Aro 97
    Begur 119
    Torroella de Montgrí and L'Estartit 138
    L'Escala and Empúries 146
    Golf de Roses 154
    Serra de l'Albera 183
    Lloret de Mar 83
clubs
    Atico 97
    Bumper's 83
    Can Marc 119
    Club & Loft 97
    Maddox 97
    Maxim's 138
    Ona 154
    Palm Beach 97
    Passarel.la 154
    Platea 63
    Rachdingue 183
    La Sala del Cel 21, 63
    Up 6 146
    Zoom 83
Colera 180
consulates 194
Cova dels Capellans 118
Cova d'en Daina 17, 102
Coves de Serinyà 16, 65
Creu d'en Cobertella 148
cycling 190

D

Dalí Trangle, the 7, 10, 14–15
directory 194
diving 45, 135, 140, 191
driving 187–180

E

El Golfet 29, 107

emergencies 194
Empuriabrava 152–153
Empúries 11, 17, 141–144
Espolla 176
Estany de Banyoles 64
exchange 194

F

ferries 187
festivals 19, 24–25, 192–194
    calendar 193
    Festes de Primavera 105
    Festival dels Trobadors 152
Figueres 155–161
    bars 161
    Castell de Sant Ferran 158–159
    hotels 159
    Museu de Joguets 158
    Museu de l'Empordà 157–158
    Rambla and Barri Vell, the 155
    restaurants 160
    Teatre-Museu Dalí 156–157
Figueres 157
Figueres and around 156
flights 187
food festivals 193
Fornells 115

G

Garriguella 177
Girona 7, 10, 12–13, 51–63
    accommodation 59–61
    Banys Arabs 57
    bars 63
    cafés 61
    Cathedral, the 55
    Centre Bonastruc ça Porta 54
    City Walls, the 56
    clubs 63
    El Call 53
    Església de Sant Feliu 57
    hostels 60
    hotels 59
    Jewish history 53
    Mercadal 58
    Museu Arqueològic 58
    Museu Capitular 56
    Museu d'Art 27, 56
    Museu d'Història de la Ciutat 55
    Museu del Cinema 27, 59
    Rambla Llibertat 51
    restaurants 61
    shops 61
    turisme rural 60
Girona 52
glossary 200

golf 45, 191
Golf de Roses 147–154
Golf de Roses 148

H

havaneres 23, 107, 192
health 194
horse riding 192
hostels (by area)
    Banyoles and Besalú 68
    Girona 60
    L'Escala and Empúries 145
    La Garrotxa 74
hostels
    Alberg d'Empúries 145
    Alberg de Joventut, Girona 60
    Alberg de Joventut, Olot 74
    Alberg de l'Estany 68
hotels (by area)
    Banyoles and Besalú 67
    Begur 116
    Blanes 78
    Cadaqués 166
    Central Baix Empordà 130
    Figueres 159
    Girona 59
    Golf de Roses 153
    L'Escala and Empúries 144
    La Garrotxa 73
    Lloret de Mar 82
    Palafrugell 110
    Palamós and Sant Antoni de Calonge 102
    Pals, Peratallada and Ullastret 124
    Port de la Selva 173
    Sant Feliu de Guíxols and Platja d'Aro 95
    Serra de l'Albera 181
    Torroella de Montgrí and L'Estartit 137
    Tossa de Mar 86
hotels
    Aiguablava 116
    Aiguaclara 117
    Albons 144
    Los Angeles 160
    Arcs de Monells 130
    Bell Repòs 95
    Beverly Park 78
    Borrell 73
    Briaxis 153
    Cala Jóncols 153
    Cal Sastre 73
    Can Ceret 153
    Can Mencíó 73
    Carlemany 59
    Casa Felip 174
    Casamar 110
    Castell d'Empordà 47, 130
    El Cau del Papibou 124
    Ciutat de Girona 59
    Costa Brava 95
    Diana 86

Duran 159
Empordà 160
El Far 111
La Figuera 102
Fonda La Paz 67
Fonda Mitjà 137
Fornells Park 59
Garbí 145
La Gavina 47, 90, 95
Golf Peralada 160
Grimar 181
Guitart Rosa 82
Habitacions Marià 67
Històric 60
Hospederia El Convent 117
Hostal Bellmirall 59
Hostal Coll 59
Hostal Cristina 166
Hostal Doll 79
Hostal El Cisne
Hostal Juventus 181
Hostal La Riera 125
Hostal La Tina 174
Hostal Miralluna 124
Hostal Plaja 111
Hostal Santa Cristina 82
Hostal Sa Rascassa 117
Hostal Vehí 167
Hostalet 1701 130
L'Hostalet de Tossa 87
Hotel de la Moneda 153
Les Illes 137
Els Jardins de la Martana 67
Llané Petit 167
Maria Teresa 102
Marina 103
Mas Ferran 60
La Masia 181
Mas Pau 160
Mas Tapiolas 95
Mediterrani 111
Miramar 181
Misty 167
Nieves Mar 145
Palau Lo Mirador 46, 137
Parador d'Aiguablava 46, 116
El Pati 124
Peninsular 60
Pensió Adarnius 130
Pensió Can Fabrellas 102
Pensió Cap d'Or 86
Pensió Racó del Mar 137
Pensió Reina Isabel 82
Pensió Sol y Sombra 173
Pensió Vila 73
Pensió Viladomat 60
Plaça (St Feliu de Guíxols) 96
La Plaça (Central Baix
    Empordà) 130
Playa Sol 167
Port-Bo 111
Port-Lligat 167
Porto Cristo 173
Rambla 160
Ramblamar 153
Riomar 145
Riu 73
Rocamar 167

Rosa 117
Rosa dels Vents 103
Sant Antoni 79
Sant Ferriol 68
Sant Joan 103
Sant Pol 96
Sant Roc 111
Santa Anna 137
Sa Punta 125
Sa Riera 117
Sa Tuna 117
Tamariu 111
Trias 103
Ultonia 60
Vila del Mar 82

J

Jardí Botànic Cap Roig
    31, 107
Jardí Botànic Mar i Murtra
    31, 78
Jardins de Santa Clotilde
    30, 80
jet-skiing 191

K

kayaking 191

L

La Bisbal 126–128
La Fageda d'en Jordà 69
La Fosca 100
La Garrotxa 8
language 197
La Selva 6, 8
L'Escala 34, 139–140
L'Escala 142
**L'Escala and Empúries
    area 140**
Les Illes Medes 33, 135–137
L'Estartit 133–137
L'Estartit 136
Llafranc 29, 35, 107–108
Llançà 178–180
Llançà 179
Lloret de Mar 80–83
    bars 83
    Cala Boadella 29, 81
    Cala Canyelles 82
    Cala Morisca 82
    campsites 82
    Centre Cultural Verdaguer
        27, 80
    clubs 83
    Ermita de Santa Cristina 81
    hotels 82

Jardins de Santa Clotilde
    30, 80
Platja de Lloret and Fenals 81
restaurants 83
Lloret de Mar 81

M

maps 188
Monells 128
Montgó 140
motorbikes 188
Museu de l'Aquarel.la
    Martínez Lozano 179
Museu del Joguet 43
Museu de Pintura Palau
    Solterra 133
Museu Terracota, La Bisbal
    26, 126
music festivals 22
    Festival de Peralada 23
    Festival Internacional de
        Músiques, Torroella de
        Montgrí 22, 133
    Festival Internacional de la
        Porta Ferrada, Sant Feliu
        de Guíxols 89
    havaneres festival, Calella
        23, 107
    jazz festival, Calella 22

O

Olot 31, 69
Olot 72

P

Palafrugell 11, 105–112
Palafrugell area 106
Palamós 98–100
    bars 104
    Cala Estreta 100
    Cala S'Alguer 100
    La Fosca 100
    hotels 102
    Museu de la Pesca 98
    Platja de Castell 100
    restaurants 103
Palamós 99
Pals 120–121
**Pals, Peratallada and
    Ullastret area 121**
parasailing 191
Parc Natural de l'Albera 32
Parc Natural de la Garrotxa
    31, 35–37, 69–75
**Parc Natural de la
    Garrotxa 70**

Parc Natural dels Aigüamolls
de l'Empordà 32, 149–150
Peralada 159
Peratallada 18, 122–123
Peratallada 123
Platgeta de l'Ermita 101
Platja d'Aro 92–94
Platja d'Aro 92
Platja de Can Cristus 94, 101
Platja de Castell 100
Platja d'en Pas 170
Platja de Pals 29, 35, 123
Platja Salatar 148
Platja de Sant Lluis 166
Platja de Sant Pol 89
Platja del Senyor Ramon 86
Platja Garbet 179
Platja Grifeu 179
Platja Vallpresona 86
Poblat Ibèric d'Ullastret
16, 123
Poblat Ibèric de Castell 17
Portbou 180–181
Port de la Selva 170–173
Port de la Selva 171
Portlligat 166
post 194
public holidays 192
Púbol 129
Punta de S'Arenella 171

R

restaurants (by area)
Banyoles and Besalú 68
Begur 118
Blanes 79
Cadaqués 168
Central Baix Empordà 131
Figueres 160
Girona 61
Golf de Roses 154
L'Escala and Empúries 145
La Garrotxa 75
Lloret de Mar 83
Palafrugell 112
Palamós and Sant Antoni de
Calonge 103
Pals, Peratallada and
Ullastret 125
Port de la Selva 174
Sant Feliu de Guíxols and
Platja d'Aro 96
Serra de l'Albera 182
Torroella de Montgrí and
L'Estartit 138
Tossa de Mar 87
restaurants
restaurants ideas 40–41
L'Activa 79
Aiguaclara 118
Els Arquets 138
Art in Café 182
La Avenida 154

Bahía 96
El Barroco 168
La Bella Lola 112
El Bistrot 41, 61
Boira 62
Bona Vista 125
Bonay 125
El Bullí 47, 154
Ca l'Elvira 174
Ca l'Herminda 174
Cal Ros 62
Can Batlle 182
Cancliment i Sa Cuina 118
Candelària 125
Can Narra 182
Can Punyetes 160
Can Simon 87
Can Tarrades 83
Can Tito 168
Can Tomas 182
La Cantonada 131
Can Torrades 118
Cap de Creus 168
Casa Anita 41, 168
Casa Marieta 62
Es Castell 118
Cau del Pescador 96
Cava Nit 79
Celeste 168
El Celler de Can Roca 62
La Churraskita 160
Cipresaia 62
La Creperie Bretonne 62
El Cul de la Lleona 62
Curia Reial 68
Damajuana 79
La Deu 75
La Dolce Vita 145
El Dorado Mar 96
Duran 160
Flor de Lis 154
Els Fogons de Can Llaudes 68
Fonda La Paz 68
La Fusta 103
Garbet 182
Les Gavarres 103
La Gavina 112
La Gaviota 138
Gourmet 138
L'Hostalet d'en Lons 161
Hotel Canet 154
Llevant 112
Llevantina 174
La Lluna 87
La Lonja 83
Maria de Cadaqués 40, 103
Marisqueria El Port 79
Mar i Vent 118
Mar y Sol 154
La Masia 68
Mas Molí 161
Mas Pastor 131
El Molí de L'Escala 145
Monells 131
Pa i Raïm 112
La Païssa d'en Cardina 125
Papibou 125
El Pati 125

La Penyora 62
Els Pescadors 146
La Pizza 97
Pizzeria Cesar 168
Pizzeta 118
La Plaça 131
La Polenta 62
Pol Nord 62
Pont Vell 68
Porto Cristo 41, 174
El Racó 104
Ramon 75
Refugi dels Pescadors 104
La Riera 131
Robert 138
Sa Rascassa 119
Sa Tuna 119
La Sirena 169
Tango 112
La Taverna de la Sal 146
La Taverna del Mar 97
La Terra 75
El Tragamar 112
El Trull 83
Vehí 169
La Vela 183
Villa Elena 97
Xerinola 112
La Xicra 112
Zanpanzar 63
Zorba 83
Riells 140–141
Romanyà de la Selva 103
Roses 147–148
Roses 149
Ruta del Carrilet 190

S

S'Agaró 89
sailing 191
Sant Antoni de Calonge
100–101
Sant Feliu de Guíxols 88–89
Sant Feliu de Guíxols 90–91
Sant Martí d'Empúries 144
Sant Pere de Rodes 19,
172–173
Sant Pere Pescador 150–151
Sant Quirze de Colera 19,
177–178
Santa Margarida 148
Santa Pau 71
Sardana 192
Sarfa bus company 188
Sa Riera 35, 116
Sa Tuna 115
Selva de Mar 171–172
Serra de l'Albera 32, 34,
176–178
shopping 38–39
shops (by area)
Central Baix Empordà 131
Girona 61

INDEX

INDEX

L'Escala and Empúries 145
Palafrugell 111
Sant Feliu de Guíxols and
    Platja d'Aro 96
shops
    Ambrosia 38, 61
    Anxoves 145
    Cacao Sampaka 61
    Pastisseria Fauré 38, 61
    "El Rissec" Valls i Llenas 131
    Rogenca 131
    La Serra 111
    Llibreria Ulysus 61
    Valls 96
skydiving 44, 152, 191
sightseeing flights 45, 191
snorkelling 191
sports and outdoor pursuits
    191

T

Tamariu 35, 108–110
Teatre-Museu Dalí 15
telephones 194
time 194
tipping 194
Torroella de Montgrí 132–133
Torroella de Montgrí and
    L'Estartit area 134–135
Tossa de Mar 84–87

bars and clubs 87
beaches 86
campsites 87
hotels 86
Museu Municipal 85
restaurants 87
Vila Nova 84
Vila Vella 84
Tossa de Mar 85
tourist information 187
tourist offices 188
trains 187
turisme rural (by area)
    Banyoles and Besalú 68
    Central Baix Empordà 130
    Girona 60
    La Garrotxa 74
    Pals, Peratallada and Ullas-
    tret 125
    Serra de l'Albera 182
turisme rural
    Cal Pastor 182
    Can Garriga 182
    Can Maholà 68
    Can Pere Ni 125
    Can Pinyarol 60
    Mas de la Roda 61
    Mas El Carrer 74
    Mas Masaller 130
    Mas Saló 61
    Mas Salvanera 68
    Mas Violella 74
    Prat de la Plaça 74

U

Ullastret 123
ultralight 191

V

Verges 24, 137
Vilabertran 159
volcanoes 36, 69–73

W

walking 33, 190
    a short walk in the Serra de
        l'Albera 177
    a volcano walk 74
    a walk to the Castell del
        Montgrí 134
water parks 43
waterskiing 191
watersports 44, 191
windsurfing 191